SHIFTING BOUNDARIES OF THE FIRM

SHIFTING BOUNDARIES OF THE FIRM

Japanese Company–Japanese Labour

Mari Sako

OXFORD
UNIVERSITY PRESS

OXFORD
UNIVERSITY PRESS

Great Clarendon Street, Oxford ox2 6DP

Oxford University Press is a department of the University of Oxford.
It furthers the University's objective of excellence in research, scholarship,
and education by publishing worldwide in

Oxford New York

Auckland Cape Town Dar es Salaam Hong Kong Karachi
Kuala Lumpur Madrid Melbourne Mexico City Nairobi
New Delhi Shanghai Taipei Toronto

With offices in

Argentina Austria Brazil Chile Czech Republic France Greece
Guatemala Hungary Italy Japan Poland Portugal Singapore
South Korea Switzerland Thailand Turkey Ukraine Vietnam

British Library Cataloguing in Publication Data
Data available

Library of Congress Cataloging in Publication Data
Data available

Typeset by SPI Publisher Services, Pondicherry, India
Printed in Great Britain on acid-free paper by
Biddles Ltd, King's Lynn, Norfolk

ISBN 0-19-926816-9   978-0-19-926816-0

1 3 5 7 9 10 8 6 4 2

For Ron

Contents

Acknowledgements

The present study may be traced back to 1991, when I co-authored with Ronald Dore and Takeshi Inagami a report, *Japan's Annual Economic Assessment*, for a London-based lobby group, Campaign for Work. Britain joined the Exchange Rate Mechanism (ERM), and was in search of a way of making sure that the country's inflation rate did not go above the European average. Campaign for Work asked us whether there was anything that Britain could learn from the Shunto annual wage bargaining round in Japan, as a superior alternative to a formal incomes policy.

In the course of analysing the intricate nature of employer and union coordination during Shunto, I became intrigued by why and how such coordination developed and stabilized in post-war Japan. I therefore decided to dig deeper, interviewing union leaders and company managers, with funding from London School of Economics's (LSE) Centre for Economic Performance during 1994–6. In this research project, two things struck me as novel and under-reported. One was the binding nature of coordination between employers, both within and across industrial sectors. The other was that enterprise unions coordinated not just through their industry federations, but also through a federation of unions organized along the lines of the business group. These federations are generically known as *roren*. I then became fascinated by the question of what is the boundary of the firm for enterprise unions.

With funding from the UK Economic and Social Research Council (Award Number H524 27 5004 97) and the Japan Foundation Fellowship in 1997/98, I began a study of the historical evolution and the contemporary function of *roren* union networks in two industrial sectors, automobiles and electrical machinery. It was in 1997 and early 1998, during my stay at Tokyo University's Institute of Social Science, that the survey reported in this book was conducted with funding from the Japan Productivity Centre for Socio-Economic Development and the Japanese Ministry of Education and Science. I gratefully acknowledge these funding sources. Also, I thank Hiroki Sato in particular for generous and warm support in various ways during this period.

Subsequently, I continued to interview union leaders and company managers throughout a period of recession and fundamental regulatory changes in Japan. After my move from LSE to Oxford, during a sabbatical term in 2003, I spent a couple of enjoyable months at Research Institute of Economy, Trade, and Industry (RIETI) in Tokyo. There, I was able to complete my fieldwork and to extend the work with Gregory Jackson to examine trends at NTT and Deutsche Telekom. I thank RIETI and the then director, Masahiko Aoki, for providing a congenial research environment during this part of the research.

Many individuals helped shape and sharpen my thoughts, and I would like to acknowledge the following in particular: Colin Crouch, Panayotis Dessyllas, Ronald Dore, Andy Gordon, Howard Gospel, Sue Helper, Takeshi Inagami, Gregory Jackson, Bill Lazonick, Ricky Locke, Keisuke Nakamura, Hiroki Sato, Masahiro Shimotani, and Hideo Totsuka. I also thank many union leaders and company managers who gave generously of their time to fill in my questionnaire survey, and to be interviewed. Around a dozen interviews took place during 1997 and 2003 with union leaders and managers for each of the case study business groups (Matsushita, Toyota, and Nissan), eighteen interviews with management and unions at NTT Group, and another dozen or so meetings at Toyota, Nissan, and Honda to discuss supplier development. Others in the union movement, with whom I met many times and whose contribution went well beyond an interview, are Ikuo Ajima (then at IMF-JC, now JILAF), Hiroshi Gankoji (at Chubu Sanseiken), Fujikazu Suzuki (at Rengo Soken), and their colleagues at their respective organizations. Of the industries that I studied, the MIT International Motor Vehicle Program (IMVP) provided an invaluable source of knowledge about the automobile industry. I would like to thank the IMVP for financial support over the past decade, and all the researchers in this network for their indomitable friendship and mutual learning.

Also worthy of thanks are the participants of various seminars and conferences at which I presented an aspect of the research reported in this book, including the ones at the Institute of Social Science, University of Tokyo, in 1998; International Industrial Relations Association Congress in Tokyo in 2000; the European University Institute, Florence, in 1999; the Institute for Work & Employment Research at MIT Sloan School of Management in 2003; the Society for the Advancement of Socio-Economics in 2003; and the Industrial Relations Research Unit at Warwick Business School in 2004.

Acknowledgements

Chapter 6 of this book is largely based on an earlier publication, Mari Sako (2004) 'Supplier Development at Honda, Nissan and Toyota: Comparative Case Studies of Organizational Capability Enhancement', *Industrial and Corporate Change* (13/2, 281–308). Permission has been granted by the Oxford University Press to reproduce this material.

This book had been in the production pipeline for a long time. I am grateful to the OUP editors, Matthew Derbishire and David Musson, for their continued encouragement, support, and patience. I also thank Christine Seal at Saïd Business School for expert assistance in the preparation of the manuscript.

My family deserves acknowledgement, particularly my mother and sister for minding my daughter, Maya, whilst I was out doing the fieldwork in Japan for this study. Maya has grown to appreciate what is involved in being an author, though unfortunately, in her view, not of interesting books like Harry Potter. My husband, Suma Chakrabarti, has, as ever, given me unspoken support, as we juggled to fit all our travels, and as our study room went through varying degrees of untidiness that spilled over from desktop onto the floor.

Lastly, this book is dedicated to Ronald Dore, teacher, mentor, and friend for the past two decades. My port of call has been his explicitly comparative work as exemplified in his classic, *British Factory–Japanese Factory*. My book does not do full justice to the comparativist cause, as it is exclusively about Japan. But I have tried always not to forget 'what is universal and what is uniquely Japanese', and to show the sort of sharp sensitivity he displays in portraying what makes people tick in everyday life. I also focused my mind on variations within Japan, a theme that I believe is more important today than ever in understanding whether or not the 'Japanese miracle' institutions are indeed undergoing deep transformation.

List of Figures

List of Tables

Introduction

In major global industries, mergers, acquisitions, and strategic alliances are consolidating industry structure. At the same time, corporate strategies involving outsourcing and spin-offs are creating smaller, decentralized operational units within and across the boundary of the firm. The resulting fragmentation of organizations is associated with pressure on long-term employment relationships and the rise of market-mediated work that is contingent on the short-term needs of the organization. Corporate restructuring is a major driver in this transformation of labour markets and inevitably engenders concerns about employment security. Throughout the history of the modern corporation, management and labour have addressed these issues in a variety of ways.

Fashionable talk about 'virtual corporations' underplays the enduring importance of organizational boundaries and the institutional infrastructure that conditions how well market-mediated employment relations may function. For both management and labour, boundaries define what is internal and what is external, and these boundaries are often contested. On the one hand, corporate restructuring is seen as a source of instability in employment, and employees rely less and less on the firm to provide training and security of income. On the other hand, there still remains the core workforce, albeit ever diminishing in size, that enjoys relatively secure jobs. How the boundary between the core and the periphery is drawn affects not only labour market outcomes such as pay inequality but also business performance by structuring company incentives to invest in capabilities.

This book takes a unique perspective in understanding the link between corporate restructuring and labour markets, by focusing on the strategy and structure of management and labour organizations. The book takes a historical and contemporary look at how corporate management and union leaders in Japan chose their organizational boundaries so as to implement their respective strategies in growth, restructuring, and employment. The starting point for the book is therefore Chandlerian: How does strategy determine structure, and what are the complex ways in which structure and strategy interconnect? Here, *strategy* may be defined as the planning and carrying out of the growth of organizations, and *structure* is understood to mean the organizational form devised to administer activities and resources (Chandler 1962: 13). Where the current study departs from the usual analysis in business strategy and history is the equal regard given to the strategy and structure of labour organizations. The enterprise union as the predominant form of unions in Japan makes it all the more pertinent to examine the contested terrain when boundary decisions by management and labour do not necessarily coincide.

The situation in which Japanese enterprise unions find themselves crystallizes the issue at hand, as they have no choice but to reconsider their own organizational structure every time a corporation restructures. There has been a wealth of research on corporate structure and corporate groups from a managerial perspective in Japan. It is therefore all the more surprising that there has not been any systematic study of what the enterprise should mean for enterprise unions. Is it the core part of a multi-establishment enterprise, excluding all subsidiaries and affiliates? Or, does the union structure encompass the whole corporate grouping? The answer depends on specific cases, and this book's task is to identify reasons for the variation in existing boundaries. The study shows that unions typically have a choice in extending or contracting their boundaries, and that their boundary decisions affect subsequent choices of corporate structure by management.

Recent legal changes in Japan make it a particularly opportune time to examine how unions are reacting to, and working upon, corporate restructuring. Japan was largely a success story until the late 1980s. Thereafter, the prolonged recession has led not only to contraction in output and employment, but has also exposed fundamental weaknesses in the key institutions that had contributed to Japan's success. This means that in the past, external pressures such as intensified international competition elicited Japan-specific responses mediated by the existing institutions (Dore 1986). But in the twenty-first century, these responses also involve transforming the institutions themselves.

The numerous legal changes in the relevant areas of company law and labour law are the harbinger of further institutional changes to come. The major ones are as follows: First, pure holding companies, banned immediately after the Second World War, were made legal again in 1997. This triggered a debate, which remains unresolved, on whether or not a corresponding labour law reform was necessary, in particular to oblige holding company-level management to engage in works council-like consultation with employee representatives at operating companies (Rengo 2000).

Second, legislation on spin-outs (*kaisha bunkatsuho*) in 2000 gives the parent company the right to transfer a line of business to a separate company whilst obliging the employees who had worked for that business to move to the new corporate entity. Here, enterprise unions have to consider whether or not to assist with the unionization of the new company. This may be a difficult decision, particularly if the new firm is in a different industrial sector from the parent company's home ground. Then in 2004, the Labour Standards Law was revised to reassert employers' right to dismiss based on 'objectively reasonable' grounds (Nakakubo 2004). Also in 2004, the dispatching of workers by labour placement agencies, hitherto prohibited in manufacturing settings, became legal (Mizushima 2004).

Despite the empirical focus on Japan in this book, there are some generalizable parallels to be found in the international and national economies of advanced industrial countries. For example, a long-standing literature on international trade unionism concentrates on the threat multinational companies (MNCs) pose for nationally based trade unions due to (*a*) MNCs' capital mobility across national boundaries; (*b*) MNCs' broad financial base due to their size and diversified businesses; and (*c*) lack of transparency in where decisions are made (subsidiaries might claim that decisions are made at the headquarters (HQ), while parent firms may maintain that they are decentralized) (Lea 1971: 149). Given these problems, how can trade unions stop continually chasing the structure of transnational corporations?

In major advanced national economies, Katz (1993) noted the decentralization of collective bargaining as a universal trend in sectors with intense market competition, and as a manifestation of unions' wish to bring their decision-making levels to correspond with those of management. As corporations decentralized with the creation of strategic business units or profit centres, unions tried to strengthen their organizations at those levels. At the same time, if strategic decisions over new investments or closures were seen to be made at the HQ level, then unions would want more effective articulation of worker representation at the central and decentralized levels.

In Germany, works councils have existed not only at the workplace level (Betriebsrat, BR) but also at the enterprise level (Gesamtbetriebsrat, GBR) and where appropriate at the corporate group level (Konzernbetriebsrat, KBR). The 2001 reform of the Works Constitution Act allows company management and works councils to adjust employment representation structures to introduce works councils for specific product or business units, works councils for subsidiaries of an establishment, or joint works councils for several establishments. This reform is meant to empower social partners to bring the structure of employee representation in line with modern forms of company organization as they restructure through mergers and acquisitions (M & A) and spin-outs. But ultimately, the choice of the organizational boundary for works councils is left to labour and management. This availability of choice in boundaries brings the German situation close to the one in Japan, where the Trade Union Law has been neutral as to whether unions are enterprise-based, industry-based, or geographically based. The organizational boundary is a choice variable for both management and labour in Japan as elsewhere.

The following questions served to guide the scope of this study: What is the impact of corporate strategy and structure on unions' structure? In particular, how does the boundary of the firm chosen by the enterprise union change as companies restructure? In what ways has union strategy constrained or facilitated management's choice over corporate structure? What is the impact of the above interactions on the nature of internal labour markets, the extent of harmonization of terms and conditions of employment, the extent of information flow and know-how diffusion, and the speed and degree of corporate restructuring?

A unique contribution of this book is in bringing together two separate arenas of academic study, one on business strategy and the other on industrial relations. More specifically, this study examines the extent to which the strategy and structure approach can be applied to enterprise unions in Japan and to unions more generally. The notion of strategic choice for unions is not new. Kochan et al. (1984: 35) sought to further our 'understanding of the consequences of the strategic choice of all the key actors in industrial relations'. Their contribution lay in recognizing 'the active role played by management in shaping industrial relations as opposed to the traditional view, which sees management as reactive, responding to union pressure' (Kochan et al. 1984: 20). But the converse is necessary to redress the balance in the study on industrial relations in Japan, where the traditional view is that of unions largely responding to managerial initiatives. The present study takes a view that unions, as much as management, have had strategic discretion in Japan.

Ultimately, this study shows that organizational boundaries emerge as a result of political contestation between management and labour in specific situations. Thus, unless strategic choice and contestation are taken into account, more conventional theories—based on product markets (Commons 1909), labour markets (Ulman 1955), or historical legacy

4

concerning technology and skills (Clegg 1976)—are generally not capable of explaining why organizational boundaries differ in the same industry in a specific country.

Outline of the Book

Chapter 1 reviews the existing literature on modern corporations and unions in Japan. It is shown that the prevailing paradigm is insufficient to account for firm and union boundaries. In particular, the existing analysis of corporate structure presupposes networks with a multidivisional core firm surrounded by group companies, but there is no adequate explanation of what determines the boundary between internal divisions and subsidiary companies. Moreover, the industrial relations literature takes the boundary of the enterprise union as given. This assumption of a fixed boundary constitutes both a theoretical and an empirical deficiency that requires rectification.

The chapter then posits an analytical framework, called the Strategy–Structure–Institutions (SSI) framework. This addresses the deficiencies noted earlier. In this framework, corporations and unions choose their respective preferred organizational boundaries. When there is a consensus over the boundaries, the actual boundary coincides with the desired choice. But when they are contested, relative power is important in leading to a specific imposed or bargained boundary. After developing a typology of enterprise unions based on this framework, the chapter discusses product market, labour market, and technology characteristics that explain why union strategy and structure may differ in different industrial sectors. The chapter concludes by noting that unions (and firms) differ even within the same sector due to strategic choice and the accumulation of distinct capabilities over time.

Chapter 2 gives a history of unions in Japan. It describes a broad trend in the transformation of the structure of companies and unions since the end of the Second World War to the present day. Four periods are identified: the first decade after 1945 when many unions sprung up at the factory level; the second period into the 1950s and 1960s when corporate consolidation led to the unification of factory unions into enterprise unions; the third period in the 1970s and 1980s when the diffusion of corporate groupings led to the formation of *roren*, i.e. union federations organized along the lines of corporate group; and the last period since the 1990s recession when corporate spin-outs and rationalization are challenging unions to redraw their boundaries. In each period, the chapter discusses which types of corporate boundary, hierarchical boundary, or workforce boundary become topical and contentious.

Chapters 3 and 4 are company-based case studies. Chapter 3 analyses the evolution of corporate and labour strategy and structure at Matsushita Group. A Chandlerian analysis is applied to interpret how Matsushita's corporate strategy led to an early adopter of a multidivisional form and hive-offs to create a corporate group. The Matsushita Union was established as an enterprise-wide union from the start. It responded to corporate growth by extending its boundary to include not only all the internal divisions but also hived-off companies and subsidiaries. The resulting extension of the internal labour market has given much flexibility in securing stable employment, as uniform working terms and conditions facilitate the movement of workers between divisions and hived-off companies. But there has been a gradual introduction of diversity in working conditions within the company and the corporate group since the 1990s.

Chapter 4 is about management and labour at Toyota Group. It discusses Toyota's business diversification from textile machinery to automobiles and more recently into other areas such as telecommunication. However, compared with Matsushita, Toyota has remained focused on automobile production, with a functional organizational structure. Toyota unions were originally factory unions that became unified as an enterprise union in 1951. But unlike at Matsushita, corporate hive-offs led to the establishment of separate enterprise unions, rather than the extension of the focal union's boundary. The chapter also traces parallel developments of consolidation and fragmentation at major suppliers, Toyoda Automatic Loom Works and Aisin.

Chapter 5 draws on a questionnaire survey of enterprise unions affiliated to *roren* federations. The survey data are analysed to identify the key structural and functional differences between two sectors—automobiles and electrical machinery. The chapter classifies *roren* into those based primarily on capital affiliation and those based on trading links. Capital affiliation is more important in drawing the boundary of electrical machinery *roren*, while trading links with parts suppliers are generally more important for *roren* in the automobile industry. Reasons for this contrast are provided, as are the consequences of these structural differences for the role of the *roren* in pay bargaining, employment adjustment, and worker participation.

Chapters 6 and 7 turn to intrasectoral differences, an important aspect of the SSI framework. With apology to Richard Nelson (1991), whose article in *Strategic Management Journal* was entitled 'why do firms differ, and how does it matter?', these chapters investigate why companies and unions differ within the same industry and how it matters. Chapter 6 analyses why firms in the same line of business differ and why the differences matter, by studying supplier development activities in the automobile sector. The national institutions of corporate governance in Japan make it easier for all Japanese automobile companies to engage in know-how exchange beyond legally distinct units of financial control. Despite this identical institutional environment, Toyota has emerged as distinct in its strategy and internal structure for engaging in capability enhancement activities.

Chapter 7 turns to intrasectoral differences in union strategy and structure. Specifically, contrasts are drawn between Nissan Roren and Toyota Roren. Compared with Toyota Roren, Nissan Roren formulated a clearer strategy of organizing smaller suppliers in an earlier period (in the late 1950s). Consequently, Nissan Roren had been much more centralized with respect to union finance, personnel, and collective bargaining, until the 1990s pressure to decentralize and diversify.

Finally Chapter 8 examines the impact of union and management structure and strategy on specific labour outcomes. In particular, Shunto wage and bonus settlements are analysed for specific *roren* federations at Toyota, Nissan, and Matsushita. There is systematic evidence that the dispersion in settlements has increased since the late 1990s in all cases. The chapter also examines how increasingly diverse working conditions came to be introduced, with specific reference to Matsushita Group and NTT Group. In both cases, there is a clear trade-off between retaining lifetime employment (but with greater pay variations) and retaining income security (but with greater job losses).

The book concludes with three points. First, the SSI framework is used to summarize the key themes and empirical findings of the book. Second, the framework is applied to illustrate its utility in internationally comparative studies. Third, the chapter speculates on the future of Japanese firms and unions, and more specifically how much diversity they could tolerate. The framework predicts a relatively high degree of variety as it highlights the importance of the interaction of strategy and structure on both sides of industry to accommodate considerable variations within a sector.

1

Strategy, Structure, and Institutions of Management and Labour

Why have some corporations, as they grow, created new internal divisions and others fully owned subsidiaries? And why have some enterprise unions organized employees in those divisions and subsidiaries, whilst others have excluded them? There is no body of literature that offers a reasoned explanation of how and why these specific organizational boundaries are drawn. In the case of corporations, theories do not account for the distinction between internal divisions and fully owned subsidiaries, a distinction at the heart of understanding the emergence of corporate groups. In the case of enterprise unions, union boundaries are treated as given, and are rarely subjected to systematic analysis of why and how such boundaries change. Ultimately, these structural characteristics are interesting because of our central concern: what do corporations and unions really do in Japan, and how do their objectives influence their organizing principle?

This chapter begins by reviewing the existing literature on modern corporations and unions in Japan. The prevailing paradigms are not well equipped to account for changes in enterprise and union boundaries over time. Section 1.1 shows that the typology of a *keiretsu* corporate network, with a multidivisional core firm surrounded by group companies, leaves unexplained what determines the boundary between internal divisions and subsidiary companies. Section 1.2 shows that the existing literature on Japanese unions takes the boundary of the enterprise union as given. This constitutes a theoretical deficiency that requires rectification.

One way of making these boundary decisions explicit is proposed in Section 1.3, which posits an analytical framework called the SSI framework.

This constitutes the backbone of this book. In this framework, corporations and unions choose their respective preferred organizational boundaries, based on their strategy. When there is consensus over the boundaries, the actual boundary coincides with the desired choice. But when the preferred boundaries differ, the more powerful party imposes, or bargains for, its boundary. Boundaries, therefore, are likely to be contested when labour strategy affects corporate boundaries, and corporate strategy affects union boundaries. Section 1.4 applies this general framework to the case of enterprise unions in Japan. The chapter concludes by noting that whilst product markets, labour markets, and technology offer general explanations of why organizational forms differ by industrial sector, the SSI framework is necessary to explain why companies and unions may differ within the same sector.

1.1. The Prevailing Paradigm: Modern Corporations in Japan

In Japan, modern corporations had their origin in the second half of the nineteenth century, when large enterprises were created in textiles, shipbuilding, iron and steel, and other heavy industries. They were established either by private initiative or by the government, which later sold their undertakings to private business concerns. Large enterprises at this time were noted for their rational bureaucratic administrative structure which was a legacy of government undertakings, leading to a relatively early development of a professional managerial cadre (Morikawa 1997). At the same time, these late-nineteenth-century firms provided education and training, extensive welfare benefits, and an ideology of firm-as-family to stabilize their workforce (Hazama 1997).

A key focus of academic study on corporate strategy and structure has been corporate groups. In contrast to the Chandlerian focus on the growth of the multidivisional corporation, Japanese scholars concentrated more on the seamless way in which multidivisionalization led to the formation of corporate groups in Japan. Thus, much has been written about the Zaibatsu in the pre-1945 period, a family-owned corporate group with a holding company, controlling a conglomerate consisting of operating companies in all key sectors of the economy, including a bank, a trading company, a textile concern, a shipyard, an iron and steel mill, and so on. With the dissolution of the Zaibatsu and the banning of holding companies in the late 1940s, operating companies were forced to become free-floating, independent from group affiliation.

9

However, only a decade or so later, they reconstituted themselves into horizontal *keiretsu* corporate groups (Gerlach 1989). The reconstitution took place either around the old Zaibatsu lines, such as for Mitsui, Mitsubishi, and Sumitomo, or around a 'main bank', as in the case of Sanwa, Fuji, and Daiichi Kangyo Bank. Each corporate group developed a complex web of cross-shareholding and interlocking directorship amongst the operating companies. At the height of success of the Japanese economy in the 1980s, these features became simultaneously a source of admiration on account of their superior corporate performance and of criticism for their exclusionary business practices that prevented foreign firms' access to Japanese markets.

Distinct from these horizontal *keiretsu* are the vertical *keiretsu*, corporate groupings that are based on purchasing–supply relationships, as typified by the Toyota Group. Here, the boundary of the grouping is defined not so much by ownership as by stable long-term trading relationships. Transaction cost economics (TCE) gave credence to an efficiency-based explanation of such vertical *keiretsu*, as an alternative to the Marxist perspective of control and exploitation that remained a dominant analytical paradigm in Japanese academic circles. Relational contracting, as an organizational form intermediate between market and hierarchy, facilitates the adoption of low-inventory flexible production systems such as lean production (Womack et al. 1990).

The bursting of the financial bubble in the early 1990s led to some bankruptcies and M & A particularly amongst financial institutions in their attempts to recover from the burden of non-performing loans. Many M & A have crossed the corporate group boundaries. Most notably, Mizuho Bank was formed through a merger of Fuji Bank, Daiichi Kangyo Bank, and the Industrial Development Bank of Japan. Consequently, Mizuho Bank became in effect a main bank for 70 per cent of all quoted companies and the largest creditor for 30 per cent of them (Shimotani 2001: 12). Beyond such specific signs of the largest six corporate groups breaking down in Japan, a formal network analysis of horizontal and vertical corporate groups demonstrates that the multilateral corporate networks are withering away, albeit very slowly, giving way to more focused relationships based on competitive strategy (Lincoln and Gerlach 2004).

Alongside the study of corporate groups, some scholars have studied the internal structure of Japanese corporations more directly (e.g. Kagono et al. 1985; Shiba and Shimotani 1997). The multidivisionalization of corporations, together with hive-offs, is a mode of managing corporate growth without overburdening the task of top management at headquarters. In Japan, the multidivisional form (M-form) therefore spread particularly in the high growth period of the 1960s. Suzuki found that of the largest 100 manufacturing firms, those that adopted the multidivisional structure increased from twenty-nine in 1960 to fifty-five by 1970 (Suzuki 1991: 101). The M-form was more prevalent in firms that supplied producer goods than those that supplied consumer goods, except in a few cases such as household electrical companies (Suzuki 1991: 102). Nevertheless, compared with US firms, many more Japanese firms retained the unitary, centralized, and functional structure (i.e. U-form) up to the early 1980s.[1]

More recently, in the 1990s, Japanese companies accelerated their pace of diversification, this time to overcome stagnant sales by entering new markets. But by the late 1990s, there was evidence of a bifurcation between sectors (such as textiles, food, steel, metals) that continue to diversify and sectors (such as chemicals and drugs) that are refocusing on niches (Ministry of Finance 2003). In international comparisons, Japanese companies were characterized by a relatively high degree of focus in the main line of business, with diversification taking the form of related diversification, and rarely unrelated or conglomerate diversification (Odagiri 1994). However, after the 1990s, Japanese companies became more diversified, converging towards US companies that were moving in the opposite direction, refocusing on their 'core competence' (Itoh 2003).

But multidivisional corporations in Japan continue to retain distinctive characteristics, rooted in Japan's corporate governance and employment systems. Specifically, the degree of divisionalization has been incomplete, in the sense that internal product divisions do not have much autonomy, especially in the functions of personnel, control, and finance (Kagono et al. 1985: 40). One implication is that divisions do not have the authority to make investment decisions without the close involvement of corporate headquarters (Kagono 1993). The centralization of the finance function enables Japanese firms to ride out short-term financial adversity for the sake of long-term investment, not just in physical but also in human assets.

In the 1990s, a new Japanese–English term—*kanpanii-sei* (internal company system)—was coined in an attempt to push for greater independence of divisions. Behind this term was a normative stance that each divisional head should become more autonomous in managing the whole process from product planning to production and sales. Sony is credited with first introducing such a system in 1994. Nevertheless, a 2003 survey of companies quoted on the First Section of the Tokyo Stock Exchange

11

(excluding utilities and financial institutions) shows that the 'internal company' (i.e. the internal division thus renamed by the surveyed companies themselves) has low *de facto* autonomy, not dissimilar to divisions, particularly in financial matters (Ministry of Finance 2003: 80). The same survey also shows that the extent of autonomy over various matters (e.g. business planning, operations, structural reform, sales and purchasing, and finance) is quite similar for the three organizational forms identified in the survey (i.e. internal division, 'internal company', and 100 per cent subsidiary). The only marked difference lay in personnel matters, with subsidiaries having much greater autonomy than the other two types in devising their own human resource system. Moreover, 74 per cent of the respondents cited the reduction in labour costs as a key reason for establishing subsidiaries. Thus, the distinction between internal divisions and external subsidiaries is clearest in personnel management.

Japanese corporations are noted for hiving off internal divisions into subsidiaries, which had been the origin of corporate groups from the early twentieth century (Suzuki 1991; Shimotani 1997). Corporate hive-offs to create subsidiaries may take place at three distinct levels: at the level of the corporate headquarters for totally new businesses, at the level of the product division, and at the level of the factory. Typically, there are multiple ripples from the centre (corporate headquarters), consisting of divisions and other establishments (such as factories), subsidiaries and affiliates, and suppliers and dealers with trading (but no shareholding) links. Corporate restructuring since the 1990s is taking the form of both (*a*) internal restructuring to bring about a strong strategic centre with more decentralized autonomous divisions and operating companies; and (*b*) intergroup M & A, blurring the boundary of each horizontal *keiretsu*.

The above account of the modern corporation in Japan is adequate as a description, but poses one theoretical challenge. In particular, two prominent theories of the firm, namely transaction cost economics (Klein, Crawford, and Alchian 1978; Williamson 1985) and the property rights approach (Hart 1995), define the firm by its unified ownership of non-human assets. In these frameworks, a wholly owned subsidiary cannot be distinguished from an in-house division, as both are owned by the same entity. In fact, Sakamoto and Shimotani (1987), in analysing Japanese corporate groups, but mainly with the Matsushita Group in mind, interpret the group primarily as an internal organization, and regard internal product divisions and subsidiaries as functional equivalents. Nevertheless, if a firm is regarded as a legal entity, an in-house division is inside and a subsidiary is outside this entity. So why make this distinction? Also, how can one explain the phenomenon of an incompletely divisionalized structure and the prevalence of corporate groups in Japan? These are critical questions that are often mentioned but in fact are skirted around.

One reason for the inability to fully answer the above questions is that the prevailing theories of the firm rely solely on the ownership of non-human assets. In fact, Holmstrom and Roberts (1998), in revisiting theories on the boundaries of the firm, recommend giving greater attention to human assets, and note that the legal boundary of the firm affects the structuring of employee incentives. In particular, in Japan, the internal labour market within the firm may be segmented from the internal labour market for the corporate group. A clear case is in manufacturing, where the norm of company-wide bargaining of uniform pay and conditions typically prevails. Then, hiving off internal factories to be subsidiary companies enables the core firm to pay lower wages to workers at these factories. Less obvious at first sight is the case of internal product divisions. On the one hand, giving autonomy to divisions creates more senior posts for managers, motivating them to experience risk and build up their managerial skills. On the other hand, the internal promotion system for general managerial careers in large Japanese firms, with managers moving from division to division, requires a low degree of autonomy in these divisions. As long as there is a presumption that employees may move from division to division, the firm must keep a uniform administrative entity for managing workers in such an internal job posting system.

To summarize, the firm has different boundaries depending on whether it is regarded primarily as a legal entity, an entity of autonomous financial control, an administrative entity, or as a pool of learned skills, physical assets, and liquid capital (Chandler 1992: 483). The preoccupation in Japan with corporate groups as networks on the one hand and M-form corporations with internal divisions on the other has distracted our attention from analysing the relationship between the two. Moreover, the distinction in the boundaries of the Japanese firm and the corporate group cannot be explained fully if we rely on the disfinition of the firm by the unified ownership of non-human assets alone. Instead, the firm is a bundle of assets (both human and non-human) that make commitments to firm-specific investment, in which incentives (of managers and workers) are structured by the way boundaries are drawn (Blair 1999). The boundary of the firm as a pool of specific investments may well be bigger than the boundary of the firm as a legal entity. Indeed, the legal boundaries of the firm may be less important than *de facto* business groups that extend control across a group of legally independent firms (Granovetter 1995).

1.2. The Prevailing Paradigm: Unions in Japan

Enterprise unionism is well known as one of the pillars of industrial relations in Japan. An enterprise union draws its entire membership from one enterprise. At higher levels, these unions are organized into industry-level federations, such as Denki Rengo (Japanese Electrical Electronic & Information Union (JEIU)) or Jidosha Soren (Confederation of Japan Automobile Workers' Unions (JAW)), which in turn affiliate to national-level confederations, the largest of which is Rengo (Japanese Trade Union Confederation). National-level confederations affiliate to political parties and participate in policymaking. This characterization of the Japanese trade union structure in terms of an articulated three-level hierarchy tends to focus on the political role of unions at the national level and on whether enterprise unions are bone fide or not. Discussion on these two topics has diverted our attention from examining what unions really do in Japan, and how their objectives influence their organizing principle around the firm and the corporate group. The prevailing paradigm, by taking the boundary of enterprise unions as fixed and given, fails to analyse how and why enterprise unions change their organization structure over time.

Since an enterprise union is the basic unit of trade unionism in Japan, much writing has addressed the issue of whether this form of union deserves to be called a union at all. One dominant perspective that dismisses enterprise unions as house unions would argue that real unions must be judged by their independence from management. Here, the overriding criterion for judging union independence from management is the existence of a union organization that extends beyond the boundary of a firm, normally encompassing an industry or an occupation or a craft. More radical anti-capitalist writers also assert that such extension of union organization should not be along the lines of the logic of capital, but must counter such logic (Tokunaga 1983; Kawanishi 1992). Consequently, the extension of the enterprise union to incorporate workers from affiliated and supplier companies would be dismissed as a natural extension of the logic of house unionism.

There had also been a notion that an evolution from a craft to an industrial union is somehow normal, and enterprise unions were an aberration from this norm. For Galenson (1976), an enterprise union is a primitive form of worker organization still in the process of becoming a proper union dealing with multiple employers, which had serious drawbacks arising from its submissiveness to management control. Three decades on, not many industrial relations scholars subscribe to the convergence thesis of Kerr et al. (1960), with which Galenson evidently identified. There is even revisionist thinking that company unions in pre-Wagner Act United States were a positive force in employee relations, benefiting workers and the broader society (Kaufman 2000). Okazaki (2002) essentially reinforces the same viewpoint, by demonstrating quantitatively that Sanpo organizations during the Second World War had a 'voice' effect of reducing labour disputes and enhancing productivity. Thus, it is not so hard to push the case that vulnerability to managerial interference does not reduce all enterprise unions to 'house unions' dominated by management. In particular, there are active enterprise unions, whose leaders are entrusted with confidential information by management and can express strong collective voice vis-à-vis management; there are also passive unions with weak collective voice and little access to confidential management information (Inagami 1995). Thus, enterprise unions' access to corporate management is seen as both a strength and a weakness, and some enterprise unions play out this balancing game better than others.

Nevertheless, in the above discussion and elsewhere, the enterprise union tends to be accepted as given or as some sort of a historical legacy. Enterprise unionism has been a poor cousin to the other two pillars of the Japanese industrial relations system, namely lifetime employment and seniority-plus-merit (*nenko*) pay, receiving far less attention to reasons for its emergence, persistence, and transformation. Moreover, explanations about why enterprise unions persist are better established than the reasons why they emerged or why they might transform themselves over time.

The story of why enterprise unions in Japan emerged is told with a combination of three explanatory factors, namely late development, cultural predisposition, and management policy towards lifetime employment. First, Japan experienced a compressed process of industrialization, with no time for industrial workers to develop craft or occupational identity. The resulting absence of craft and industrial unions created a vacuum that was filled by enterprise unions. 'Industrial workers in Japan from the Meiji era onwards had no trade-based organizing tradition to inform their decisions. In such a context, the most logical base for organizing and for action was the familiar workplace, the site of a person's most significant group of peers outside the family' (Gordon 1998: 128).

Second, management in large enterprises adopted policies that encouraged the development of internal labour markets since the late nineteenth century. Lifetime employment, with in-company training, reward based largely on seniority, and company-provided welfare, led to the formation of some friendly societies and blue-collar unions, with the enterprise as the boundary of their organization (Shirai 1983: 124; Hazama 1997). In the post-war period, 'the diffusion of the *nenko* wage and permanent employment strengthened the functional reasons for the emergence of enterprise unionism' (Cole 1971: 277).

Third, facilitated in part by the lifetime employment system, Japanese workers have had the disposition to identify themselves with the enterprise as a community (Dore 1987; Sako 1997*a*). The sense of social identity goes beyond the notion of common interests, and may be best characterized as 'enterprise consciousness'. A competing collective identity of people with similar skills did not develop in Japan because they were far less mobile in the external labour market. 'Given the strength of enterprise consciousness and the absence of a market-based wage system, it was inevitable that when powerful unions developed they have been enterprise unions' (Dore 1973: 400).

The sense of inevitability is heightened by the view that workers had no choice, that there was something innate about their wanting an enterprise-based union: 'For Japanese workers, the enterprise union was the only, and most natural, form of organization because their basic common interest as industrial workers had been formulated within an industrial enterprise' (Dunlop and Galenson (1978) as quoted by Shimada 1983: 258).

Clearly, there were attempts, some successful, at creating general and industrial unions in Japan during the interwar years and after the Second World War (Large 1979). Moreover, worker identification with the enterprise is a necessary, but not a sufficient, condition for fully understanding how unions came to change their organizational boundary. There are some anomalies that cannot be explained with the existing framework that relies on a combination of worker identity and internal labour markets. To point out the deficiencies of the prevailing paradigm, broad-brushed trends are identified below, to account for the redrawing of corporate and union boundaries in post-war Japan.

(1) *Establishment of Factory Unions.* The first period immediately after the Second World War saw the rapid establishment of unions as they were legalized for the first time in Japanese history. These were not so much enterprise unions as factory or establishment unions, and one might concur with the notion of a 'spontaneous' identification of workers with their own workplace. The late 1940s were, however, a period of enormous turmoil. Many workers either voluntarily left their workplaces or lived in

constant fear of losing their job, in anticipation of the dissolution of Zaibatsu conglomerates. At this time, communists attempted to mobilize workers through worker control of the means of production (Gordon 1985). The deflationary macroeconomic policies and the Red Purge in 1950 led to wholesale dismissals and the defeat of communist leadership. Thus, it was precisely at the point when employers were not able to deliver on lifetime employment that factory unions were established. This suggests that internal labour markets were far from being a precondition for enterprise unionism; rather, enterprise- and factory-based unions had a hand in establishing (and re-establishing) stable employment as a reality as well as a norm.

(2) *Consolidation into Enterprise Unions*. The second period, in the 1950s and 1960s, is marked by Korean War-initiated boom and the sustained growth in the size of modern corporations. Firms were most concerned about consolidating their ever-expanding operations into a coherent entity. Subsequently, some establishment-based unions became consolidated into enterprise unions. But the specific timing of each consolidation differed from union to union, and the reasons for the differences cannot be fully attributed to any changes in worker identity or internal labour markets alone. In fact, Matsushita Union encompassed the whole corporation with several establishments from the start in 1945, whereas Toyota's plant unions consolidated into an enterprise union in 1951. In the iron and steel industry, mill or works unions remained loosely associated as an enterprise federation (*kigyoren*) well into the 1990s, despite a tendency towards management centralization in their attempt to standardize the work systems among different mills.

(3) *Formation of* Roren. The third period, with slower economic growth from the mid-1970s, is marked by the consolidation of corporate groups, including vertical production *keiretsu*. Enterprise unions were newly created in smaller companies including affiliates and suppliers. At the same time, union networks organized along the lines of corporate groups, known generically as *roren*, were formed. With slower growth, the corporate community has been extended as core employees were sent on temporary or permanent transfers from their originating enterprises to affiliates and suppliers (Nakamura et al. 1988; Kawakita et al. 1997; Inagami 2003). The transferred employees remain on the payroll of their originating enterprise and tend to retain the membership of the enterprise union at the originating firm. Thus, the extension of the internal labour market beyond the boundary of the focal (or core) firm accounts in part for the rationale behind extending the organizational boundary of the

enterprise union as well. But the internal labour market does not explain the separate existence of the focal enterprise union, i.e. the union at the focal firm, and the *roren* organization.

(4) *Divisionalization and Diversity within Unions.* In the fourth period of prolonged recession since the early 1990s, Japanese corporations have been diversifying and restructuring. Notably, large firms have adopted a corporate form that in effect separates out strategic management at the headquarters (or holding company) level and operations at constituent business units, be they internal divisions or hived-off companies. Corporate management has introduced the notion of a different human resource system for each division or affiliated company, leading to greater diversity of employment contracts for a single corporation. Unions are responding either by retaining uniformity of conditions within the core union and externalizing diversity to the *roren* network, or by introducing diversity within the core by decentralizing internal structure. Thus, a key characteristic of enterprise unionism, namely the relative homogeneity of the quality of labour within the firm, is being challenged severely.

In summary, the prevailing paradigm applied to Japanese unions has recognized the political role of unions at the national level, and attributed little scope for action, political or otherwise, to enterprise unions. But as we shall see in this book, enterprise unions are not of uniform characteristics, with some being more active and others more submissive to management. There has also been a significant shift in the centre of gravity within the enterprise-based union organizations, away from factories towards the enterprise. Moreover, the timing of these shifts has been different between unions even in the same industry. These variations and shifts cannot be explained solely by resorting to an implicit framework in which unions merely mirror managerial organizations, albeit with a time lag.

1.3. The Strategy–Structure–Institutions Framework

This section presents a framework for explaining the transformation of enterprises and unions over time. It was shown in Sections 1.1 and 1.2 that the prevailing paradigms are not well equipped to account for changes in enterprise and union boundaries over time. In particular, existing theories (e.g. TCE, property rights) fail to account for the distinction between internal divisions and subsidiary companies, a distinction crucial to understanding the formation of corporate groups. Moreover, enterprise unions have extended their boundaries, from factories to corporate groups. But the traditional explanations, based on worker identity and internal labour markets, do not provide an adequate account of the shifting boundaries of enterprise unions.

The analytical framework developed in this section relies on the notion of strategic choice in the context of structural and institutional constraints and opportunities, in order to allow us to explicitly examine these boundary decisions by firms and unions. The framework combines insights from literatures on company strategy (Chandler 1962) and institutional analysis of national business systems (Whitley 1999; Hall and Soskice 2001).

We set out to show the following. First, corporate strategy affects corporate structure, along the lines demonstrated by Alfred Chandler. Second, Chandler's strategy–structure framework is extended and applied to organizations of collective labour representation, including unions. Third, the interaction between corporate strategy and labour strategy explains the contested nature of organizational boundaries. The framework focuses on strategic conflicts in relation to asymmetries in structure between corporate organizations and labour organizations, which then lead to contestation and bargaining. Here power differentials play an important role in whether each side can push the realized structure closer to the one intended by its strategy. Fourth and last, the framework suggests the importance of institutional factors in shaping how strategy, structure, and power interact. Institutional constraints and opportunities shape the strategies available to both firms and labour unions in ways that differ across national business systems. Conversely, bringing strategy and power back into institutional analysis also gives insight into how institutional structures change. We now look at each of these four elements in turn.

1.3.1 Corporate Strategy and Structure

Chandler (1962: 13) defined strategy as the planning and carrying out of the growth of organizations, and structure as the organizational form devised to administer activities and resources. One element of strategic decision concerns the scope of the business portfolio. Business portfolios differ in terms of the horizontal scope of the products and markets being served (e.g. diversified or focused on related products), as well as the vertical scope of activities that the firm does in-house (makes) or does not do (buys). Corporate structure concerns how formal authority within the firm itself is distributed. In particular, corporate structure is distinguished into several basic types based on the extent to which responsibilities are distributed according to basic business functions (e.g. production, marketing, finance, human resources) or the types of products, regions, or customers.

In the Chandlerian view, strategy determines structure. Single-product firms should be organized along functional lines, multiproduct firms around different product divisions, and more complex firms along matrix lines. As companies constantly reassess their commitment to business in specific product markets, they decide whether or not to enter new markets and withdraw from existing ones. The resulting business strategies of product diversification have led single-product firms to adopt either a multidivisional structure (M-form) or a holding company structure (H-form).

More recent processual and evolutionary perspectives on strategy see strategy and structure more as two sides of the same coin (Mintzberg 1983; Kagono et al. 1985; Whittington 2001). Thus, *strategy* is not 'the planning and carrying out of the growth of organizations' (Chandler 1962: 13) but 'a set of broad commitments made by the firm that define and rationalize its objectives and how it intends to pursue them' (Nelson 1991: 67). *Structure* is not 'the organizational form devised to administer activities and resources' (Chandler 1962: 13), but 'how a firm is organized and governed, and how decisions actually are made and carried out' (Nelson 1991: 67).[2] Here existing structures condition capacities of the firm to pursue future strategies, and may also entrench managerial interests that shape the process of strategy formulation (Gospel 1999). In this sense, what an organization can do well may take something of a life of its own (Nelson 1991). The current framework adopts this evolutionary perspective where matching strategy and structure involves ongoing mutual adaptation. One implication is that firms with different organizational capabilities may adopt different strategies even if they are in the same line of business facing identical market conditions.

Chandler's strategy and structure framework has been used extensively to understand the historical evolution of work organization and labour–management relations in a comparative perspective.[3] Here, we focus on the impact of corporate strategy and structure on human resource systems, namely a set of human resource policies and practices to manage employees, including the work organization, the reward system, training, and job security.[4] The strategy literature implies that as corporations diversify, firms may strategically seek to introduce different human resource systems for divisions or operating companies. This will be true to the extent that divisions or operating companies in varied product markets require different technology and employee skills to manage their business. Conversely, evolutionary approaches might see human resources as an opportunity or constraint on diversification. As firms adopt M-form or similar corporate structures, human resource management functions may become more decentralized as part of operational management, thus facilitating greater diversity of human resource practices within the boundary of the firm. This suggests a proposition, that as corporations diversify, they adopt either M-form or H-form structures, and that they adopt more diversified human resource systems within the corporate group in order to cater for different employment needs and skill patterns in different lines of business.

1.3.2 Labour Strategy and Structure

The strategy and structure framework can be extended to apply to labour representative organizations such as unions. Whereas a key element of corporate strategy is the range of products and services to be marketed, a parallel aspect of labour strategy concerns the scope of employees whose interests the organization protects and promotes. Labour unions draw their boundaries with regard to such factors as the growth of product markets (Commons 1909), the development of national labour markets (Ulman 1955), historical legacy of technology and skills (Clegg 1976), social identity (Herrigel 1993), and embeddedness in the ideas and beliefs in the wider society (Dunlop 1948; Jacoby 2005). These criteria may result in a variety of specific forms of union organizations, such as craft, industrial, enterprise, and conglomerate unions. Internally, the organizational structure of unions may also be seen in terms of the distribution of administrative authority between functions and different levels of the vertical hierarchy (Undy et al. 1981, 1996). The resulting organizational structure may be centralized or decentralized, with the centre of gravity in the vertical articulation of organizational units being high or low in the organizational hierarchy.

The 'strategy determines structure' logic appears again here. Strategies for employee representation are formulated with a view to promoting the interests of workers with a specific identity, and such strategy determines the desirable structure of employee organizations. As interest associations such as unions become more encompassing in their scope and strategic purpose, their internal structure is likely to become more differentiated and complex (Schmitter and Streeck 1999). This implies that unions may also decentralize some authority to less encompassing bargaining units, parallel to the case of the M-form. At the same time, the pre-existing union structure has a momentum in giving rise to certain types of strategy. For instance, craft unions may defend their members' interest through demarcation even when those craft skills in question become obsolete. Streeck (1993) points to this two-way causation in linking identity, interest, organizational structure, and institutions. These considerations may also apply to other non-union forms of collective employee representation, such as works councils and labour–management consultation committees.

Unions must thus balance cross-pressures for greater diversity or solidarity. Our framework examines such pressures in terms of what Schmitter and Streeck (1999) call the 'logic of membership' and the 'logic of influence'. Interest associations such as unions must structure themselves to offer incentives to secure their membership, but also secure sufficient external influence to extract strategic resources. To the extent that organizations strategically respond to the logic of membership, human resource outcomes are likely to be characterized by high fragmentation across employee groups with diverse needs. The logic of influence pushes organizations in the opposite direction because aggregating interests across a larger boundary may increase resources available to achieve goals vis-à-vis employers or public authorities, although at the cost of responsiveness to particularistic interests of their members. Complex layered structures may also exist where bargaining is decentralized but subject to various degrees of coordination across organizational boundaries (e.g. through a federation of unions).

But generally, as membership becomes more diverse, unions will adopt a more decentralized structure and shift strategy from the promotion of uniform working conditions for all members towards acquiescing to a degree of diversity in conditions. In summary, strategies of encompassing interest representation lead labour organizations to adopt structures with greater functional differentiation, and to delegate authority across more layers in the organizational hierarchy. Encompassing organizations with more decentralized structures will promote more diversified human resource systems within the corporate group, other things being equal.

1.3.3 Interaction between Corporate Strategy and Labour Strategy

Corporate strategy and labour strategy interact over time. For example, labour strategy leads to the choice of a certain union structure (arrow C in Figure 1.1). In turn, management takes into account the way unions are

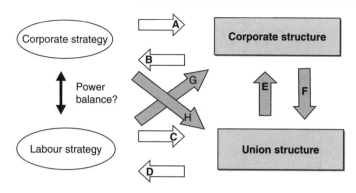

Figure 1.1 Strategy–Structure–Institutions (SSI) framework

structured when deciding on corporate structure (arrow E in Figure 1.1). For example, one reason why British companies adopted the M-form structure was supposedly to institute division-level bargaining to undermine plant-level trade union power (Marginson 1985; Armstrong et al. 1998). Labour strategy may also influence corporate structure more directly, for instance by being consulted on the creation of new subsidiaries or plans for hiving off internal divisions (Arrow G in Figure 1.1). Conversely, corporate strategy has effects on union structure. Changes in corporate structure, for instance a merger, may motivate labour organizations to change their own structure (arrow F). And corporate strategy may attempt to influence union structure directly, for example, by fragmenting it to weaken union power (arrow H).

A key insight from this discussion is that conflicting strategies or structural mismatches lead to contention over organizational structures as a form of social boundary (see Lamont and Molnar 2002; Tilly 2004). Moreover, whenever boundaries are contested, strategy is a matter of choice relative to the other actor's action. This implies that boundaries are relational in the sense that they can be defined only by identifying what is in *and* what is out (Carlile 2002).

Figure 1.2 shows that each side may be equally centralized and favour uniform human resource practices, or decentralized and prefer more diverse human resource practices. But their strategies do not necessarily coincide. Whenever the corporate boundaries within which a uniform human resource system is to apply are contested between company management and labour organizations (as in quadrant II or IV in Figure 1.2), power play between the two sides may lead to a negotiated boundary or a

		Corporate structure	
		Decentralized	Centralized
Labour structure	Decentralized	Consensus on diversified HR systems I	Contested: management prefers uniform, labour prefers diverse, HR systems II
	Centralized	Contested: management prefers diverse, labour prefers uniform, HR systems IV	Consensus on homogeneous HR system III

Figure 1.2 **Human resource outcomes resulting from structural conditions**

boundary one party imposes on the other. Bargaining power that firms or labour organizations can command to realize their strategy may reside in taking political action (e.g. political activities in electoral, regulatory, and legislative arenas) as much as in the structural characteristics of their organizations.

This line of argument suggests that whenever the structures of the human resource system pursued by corporate strategy and labour strategy do not coincide, the boundaries of organizational structures are likely to be contested. The resulting structures and human resource systems are those preferred by the party that can mobilize greater power resource in the implicit bargaining process.

1.3.4 Institutions Influence Strategy and Structure

Yet it would be misleading to view the dynamics of strategy, structure, and contention only as a general set of universal contingencies. A large literature now shows the importance of how organizations are embedded within the broader social and political context. Here, strategy and structure are shaped by the broader institutional context of the national business system such as systems of industrial relations, finance, corporate governance and inter-firm relationships. For example, highly market-oriented corporate governance systems facilitate corporate strategies requiring rapid shifts in investment and R & D than bank-oriented systems. Likewise, labour strategies are shaped by factors such as the legal framework for collective bargaining and representation, or the involvement of the state and employers' associations.

The nature of institutions as a collective phenomenon keeps them outside the control of any single firm, and thus strategic decision-makers generally take them as exogenous 'social facts'. While institutions may exist at sectoral, regional, or transnational levels, this literature has stressed the importance of institutions at the national level as giving rise to differences in organizational strategy and structure across countries. For example, Germany and Japan are often seen as being similar 'coordinated' business systems (Hall and Soskice 2001), despite important differences between them in the nature of non-market coordination (Yamamura and Streeck 2003).

Institutions affect organizations by legitimating particular patterns of authority (Biggart 1991). In addition, institutions coordinate transactions and influence the degree of investments in relationship-specific economic assets (Hall and Soskice 2001). Thus, Hall and Soskice argue that 'there are important respects in which strategy follows structure.... Our point is that (institutional) structure conditions (corporate) strategy, not that it fully determines it' (Hall and Soskice 2001: 15). Adding this insight to the framework suggests that institutions themselves may shape patterns of conflict over organizational boundaries, and that the outcome of such power play may, in turn, shape the trajectory of institutional change. In short, differences in institutional patterns across national business systems will give rise to differences in strategies and structures of organizations across countries. Institutions affect *structure* by providing legitimacy to different structures of authority. Institutions also affect *strategy* through the level of resources strategically available to organizations.

This framework, based on the notions of strategy, structure, and institutions, will be referred to as the SSI framework in the rest of this book. It introduces the following modifications to existing approaches: First, it departs from Chandler (1962) by not focusing solely on the corporate side of the story, but by giving equal weight to labour and corporate strategies. Second, by adopting an evolutionary perspective on strategy and structure, the framework allows for firms (or unions) with different organizational capabilities to adopt different strategies even if they are in the same line of business facing identical market conditions. Third, the interaction between labour and corporate strategies highlights the often-contested nature of organizational and institutional boundaries. Fourth, this insight modifies the Varieties of Capitalism view of institutions primarily as strategic opportunities. Consequently, institutions are seen to emerge as the outcome of strategic interaction and contestation over institutional constraints.

1.4. Applying the SSI Framework to Enterprise Unions and Their Networks

Enterprise unions in Japan have made commitments to pursue their generic goal of protecting members' employment security and raising their general standard of living. This strategy, however, is consistent with a variety of structures within the broad parameters of unions being enterprise-based. For instance, some enterprise unions may believe that participation in management's strategic decision-making and early access to confidential managerial information through both formal and informal channels are essential to pursue their goals effectively. The stronger this belief and the more they aspire to exercise collective voice over business plans, to influence the accompanying decisions concerning new investments, the movement of product lines between factories, and the closure or creation of divisions, the greater the unions' incentive to match the centre of gravity in their organization to reflect that in the managerial organization. For instance, factory-level unions may find that management makes much of the crucial strategic decisions above their heads at the corporate headquarters level. If this is the case, the union has an incentive to organize at this higher corporate-wide level in order to participate in such decision-making. In effect, the desirable boundary of the enterprise union is the whole corporation, not individual factories.

In order to operationalize the notion of the boundary of enterprise unions, three dimensions are chosen for analysis in subsequent chapters, namely the *corporate boundary*, the *hierarchical boundary*, and the *workforce boundary*. First, as explained earlier, unions must define their boundary against corporate structure. Whenever a corporation changes its structure, for example by creating a new subsidiary, the enterprise union must decide whether to incorporate the subsidiary within the bounds of the existing union or facilitate the creation of a new union. Second, enterprise unions must decide up to what ranks of employees in the corporate hierarchy are eligible for union membership. This hierarchical boundary is an issue given the continuum in workers' internal promotion system, where first-line supervisors and managers are regarded as senior employees rather than those on the other side of the bargaining table. Third, enterprise unions, just like other unions, look to homogeneity of conditions within their boundary. As firms employ workers with various contractual arrangements, unions must draw a line between the core membership and those who are deemed to be outside the target membership group. Typically, contingent workers fall outside the workforce boundary, but the boundary line is by no means fixed and may change over time.

Next, in order to examine how unions and their federations are governed, three elements are identified to constitute a typology of enterprise unions. They are, namely, the level at which bargaining and consultation take place, the ways in which financial and personnel resources are allocated to run the union organization, and the level at which strikes can be called. Taken together, they give a good indication of the degree of centralization or decentralization in union governance.[5]

The first element is the structure of collective bargaining and joint consultation. Following conventional analysis, the level of collective bargaining, either at the establishment level, enterprise level, or corporate group level, points to where the centre of gravity lies in union activity. It is also worthwhile to identify the level of joint consultation separately, although it may be the same as the collective bargaining level in some cases.

The second element in the typology is the ways in which financial and personnel resources are allocated within the union organization. First, as Iwasaki (1994) notes, enterprise unions with multiple branches have one of two ways of collecting dues. One is for the union headquarters to collect subscription directly from members, and distribute some of the revenue to branches for branch-level activities. A less centralized mode is for branches to collect their own dues and a proportion of branch revenues to be handed over to the union headquarters. Second, the degree of centralization can be gauged through the extent to which full-time union officials are based at the union headquarters, as opposed to their originating workplaces.

The third element in the typology is the level at which strikes can be called. Some enterprise unions reserve the right to call a strike by headquarters only, whilst other unions give branches the right also. The merit of applying this typology is that regardless of the label given in practice, enterprise union and its network structures may be gauged by a combination of whether or not a unit of union organization has the right to conclude a collective agreement, to collect union dues, and to call a strike.

The three dimensions of the boundary of enterprise unions operationalize the external structure of unions, whilst the typology of enterprise unions facilitates the analysis of the internal structure of unions. The subsequent empirical chapters use both to analyse the external and internal governance of enterprise unions.

1.5. Summary: Why Do Unions Differ, and How Does It Matter?

With apology to Nelson (1991), whose *Strategic Management Journal* article was titled 'Why do firms differ, and how does it matter?', this chapter developed a framework to explain why unions, as much as firms, differ and how it matters. The SSI framework elaborated in this chapter gives at least two reasons why unions and firms may differ. The first reason depends on the notion of organizational capability. Such capability evolves in a unique way due to past interaction between strategy and structure, be it for the firm or the union. As a result, firms in the same sector may differ in their strategy and structure. As do unions in the same sector. A second reason is due to the interaction between corporate strategy and labour strategy. If strategies clash in their preferred structural outcomes, the result may deviate from the preferred option.

Thus, even for a given market or technological condition, firms and unions may pursue widely different strategies. The interaction between firms and unions also adds to the diversity of outcomes in enterprise and union structures. In short, markets and technologies matter for explaining inter-sectoral differences. The evolution of capability and strategic interaction matters for within-industry differences. This section summarizes the mechanisms by which specific market or technological conditions are said to influence the structure and strategy of unions.

1.5.1 Product Markets Matter

John Commons singled out the importance of product market as a determinant of trade union structure. He argued that the basic unit of economic analysis should be twofold. First, there should be a focus, not so much on individuals, but on institutions, defined as any kind of collective action in control of individual action. Second, economics should not so much focus on commodities and goods, but on transactions, defined as the arrangements through which commodities are exchanged (Commons 1934). This institutional economics foundation led him to analyse how the size of market, its geographical boundaries, and intensity of competition influence transactional arrangements. Such arrangements shape the structure of organization of the firm. In turn, different organizational structures influence the pattern of labour movement.

In his study of American shoemakers, Commons illustrated how economic conditions, found in the development of new markets rather than changes in production technology as such, determine the forms of organization: 'widening out of the markets with their lower levels of competition and quality, but without any changes in the instruments of production, destroys the primitive identity of master and journeyman cordwainers and split their community of interest into the modern alignment of employers' association and trade union' (Commons 1909: 50). Thus, as product markets expanded from a locality to the nation (and eventually overseas), master craftsmen who made only 'bespoke' products for custom order gave way to merchant masters and capitalists, who employed journeymen to undertake both shop work and order work. In parallel, craft guilds gave way to a division between an employers' association and a trade union by the mid nineteenth century in the United States.

1.5.2 Labour Markets Matter

The development of national markets for products is a necessary, but not a sufficient, condition for national unions to develop (Ulman 1955). Ulman is most well known for pointing out that the geographic mobility of labour leading to the development of national labour markets is a sufficient condition for national unions to emerge. With labour mobility, inter-regional competition in labour markets was inevitable, and powerful locals could not flourish in the absence of relatively powerful national union organizations (Ulman 1955: 175).

Ulman combines product markets and labour markets to explain the presence or absence of national unions. To provide a counterfactual to Commons' case, Ulman argues that national product markets may not exist, but a national union may emerge as long as there is mobility in the national labour market. This was the case with the Typographical Union in its early days, when journeymen travelled a long way, creating national labour markets, whilst product markets (for newspapers) remained local. Moreover, a national product market may exist but no national union emerges where powerful large firms undermine unions' bargaining power and organizability. Thus, 'Commons and his associates emphasize the intensifying effects of competition in discussing the widening of market areas, but they say little about the growing size of the business unit and the multiple plant firm or "combination"' (Ulman 1955: 45). Even Ulman, writing nearly half a century after Commons, did not develop this theme, indicating a wide gulf at the time between labour studies on the one hand and the study of the rise of modern corporations on the other.

Another way in which product markets and labour markets may be combined to explain trade union structure is by referring to the Marshall–Hicks conditions. Put simply, unions interested in maintaining a union mark-up on wages can do so by paying attention to the conditions that underlie an inelastic demand for labour. According to the Marshall–Hicks conditions, the derived demand for labour is inelastic if (*a*) substitution of inputs in production is difficult, (*b*) the supply of other inputs is inelastic, (*c*) the demand for the final product is inelastic, and (*d*) the labour share in total cost is small. So a union can choose its organizational (or jurisdictional) boundary so as to make the demand for its members as inelastic as possible, for instance, by restricting the supply of labour through a closed shop or a long-term apprenticeship (Ulman 1955: ch. 11). In a more modern setting, unions choosing restrictive boundaries are more likely to succeed, therefore, if they are in industries that are capital-intensive, and whose products face relatively inelastic demand. As we shall see in following chapters, these conditions apply more to automobiles than to consumer electronic products.

1.5.3 Technology and Skills Matter

A conventional typology of union organization—craft, occupational, and industrial—is largely based on the type of technology and skills required in a particular trade or sector. But rarely is there a simple objective mapping of technology on the one hand to union type on the other. Reasons are multiple. One reason is that there is a vintage effect. 'The structure of many unions reflects the state of technology and industrial organization at the time of their birth and growth; the new skills of the industrial revolution led to craft and promotion unions; mass production favoured industrial and general unions; white-collar employees have multiplied, and their unions have grown with the large-scale organizations of the present century' (Clegg 1976: 39). Ultimately, the layers of sediment are laid down, which have inertia built in.

Another reason is union expediency. Turner (1962) pointed out that the common categories of craft, occupational, industrial and general unions often fail to yield a sharp jurisdictional definition of membership coverage in practice. This is because many unions are apparently reluctant, 'when it comes to the point, to sacrifice a potential membership for the sake of a pre-announced structural principle. Organizational theories have, in practice, often served for little more than to justify the immediate recruiting ambitions of particular unions. So such theories have proven proportionately adjustable to subsequent expediency and opportunity' (Turner 1962: 241).

Turner developed a morphology of trade unions into closed and open forms by studying the specific cases of spinners and weavers in the English cotton industry. 'Open' unions impose no restrictions on entry. They are content to recruit all workers in those occupations when the employers engage them. These unions are inevitably expansionist because their bargaining power depends not on the monopsonistic power of restricted labour supply, but on strength of numbers (equivalent to Schmitter and Streeck's (1999) 'logic of influence' noted earlier). By contrast, 'closed' unions base themselves on their capacity to control the supply of labour to particular occupations and maintain an exclusive claim to employment within more narrow occupations. They are necessarily restrictive because their interest lies in limiting the intake of labour into the jobs that they control.

In reality, many unions tend to be of mixed type, or in transition from moving from one type to another, as open and closed unions interact. For instance, when closed unions encounter open unions in the same arena, the former may have an incentive to merge to counter their relatively small size. Alternatively, open unions may develop sectional interests within them, which may be dealt with by developing a closed section within the union. Thus, Turner sees trade union structures to be in a continuing process of change, even in the absence of any technical, economic, or institutional change, due to the dialectic between the opposing trends towards exclusiveness and expansion. 'Logically, trade unionism's natural course of structural evolution would appear to lie, first, through the emergence and splitting-off of new occupational or sectional identities from the membership of the great mass unions, and next through regrouping—by way of merger or federation—of the new sectionalisms into alliances for bargaining or other purposes of mutual interest' (Turner 1962: 267). In the present-day setting, corporate diversification has led to mergers and takeovers amongst unions. Streeck and Visser (1997), in their Dutch–German comparisons, note that conglomerate unions face a challenge in their management of internal diversity, 'where they seem to be subject to a dialectic of centralization and decentralization' (Streeck and Visser 1997: 325).

1.5.4 But Ultimately, Unions Differ...

To conclude, this section outlined pre-existing frameworks for understanding trade unions' external structure, namely Commons' product
market-based explanation, Ulman's labour market-based explanation,
and Clegg's explanation based on technology and skills. These factors
explain why the structure and strategy of unions may differ in different
industrial sectors. But as Turner's open versus closed union typology and
Schmitter and Streeck's 'logic of membership' versus 'logic of influence'
illustrate, unions typically must reconcile competing principles when
drawing their boundaries. Moreover, as the rest of this book demonstrates,
because of strategic choice and different capabilities developed over time,
unions (and firms) differ even when facing the same market or technological conditions.

Notes

1. Kagono et al. (1985) conducted a questionnaire survey of Fortune 1000 US
   companies and Japanese companies listed on the Tokyo Stock Exchange in
   1980. They found that whereas 94.4 per cent of US firms adopted a multidivisional structure, only 59.8 per cent of Japanese firms had this structure.
2. Chandler (1992) himself came to endorse a more evolutionary view.
3. Notable are works by business historians, such as Gospel (1992), Lazonick
   (1990), and O'Sullivan (2000a).
4. The system of collective employee representation is excluded from what we
   mean by human resource systems, as it is considered to be part of labour
   structures in the next subsection.
5. This typology takes two out of the three dimensions identified by Benson and
   Gospel (2005). Their third dimension, namely the focus of identification of union
   members, is left out in the current exercise as it is often assumed that such focus
   for Japanese workers is the business enterprise. The social construction of union
   boundaries due to social identity is nevertheless important (Herrigel 1993).

2

From Factory to Enterprise, from Enterprise to Business Group

This chapter gives a stylized history. It explains how and why union boundaries and the centre of gravity in union activities shifted from the factory to the corporate group in post-war Japan. These shifts occurred as a result of corporate restructuring, the transformation of human resource practices, and unions' own strategy. Union strategy towards worker participation is particularly important for understanding different boundary choices. The aim of the chapter is to explain how union boundaries changed over time, which is a different focus from a more conventional one centred around explaining the taken-for-granted nature of enterprise union structure. The chapter examines changes in union boundary with respect to the three dimensions identified in Chapter 1, namely *corporate boundary* (the boundary in relation to corporate structure), *hierarchical boundary* (the boundary in the organizational hierarchy), and *workforce boundary* (the boundary between core and periphery workers). The historical account is necessarily broad-brushed, and does not give much regard to sectoral variations or to peculiarities of individual companies or unions. Specific paths taken by companies and sectors will be dealt with in subsequent chapters.

The impact of national politics will be discussed only where relevant. In particular, the early rise of the Communists and their fall during the Red Purge in 1950 left a legacy in Japan's union politics, producing different resolutions at different enterprises and corporate groups. In some cases, the mass sacking of Communist union leadership led to a complete break from the past, with the formation of a cooperative second union. In other cases, there remained a degree of continuity in union leadership. These scenarios produced divergent strategies of enterprise unions, particularly with respect to worker participation. Moreover, the national union movement was, from the start, a battleground between 'national centres' that supported competing political parties. This rivalry has had a structural impact on lower levels, notably by creating rival industry federations in the same sector. This, in turn, created disputes within enterprise unions concerning the federation to which they should affiliate. Rivalry in national politics also led to different motivations for forming *roren*, a federation of enterprise unions within a corporate group. In some cases, *roren* was formed with a view to affiliating to an industry federation (as was the case in the automotive industry). In other cases, *roren* was promoted as a way of overcoming the divisive influence of politically afflicted industry federations (as was the case in electrical machinery).

The post-war period in Japan is divided into four phases in order to structure the narrative in this chapter. The first decade immediately after 1945 saw the rapid establishment of factory-based unions as trade unions were legalized for the first time in Japanese history. The second period, in the 1950s and 1960s, is marked by rapid economic growth, when firms were most concerned with consolidating their ever-expanding operations into a coherent entity. Establishment-based unions followed suit to consolidate at the enterprise level. During the third period, starting with slower growth from the mid-1970s to the 1980s, the wider adoption of the multidivisionalization of companies and vertical *keiretsu* led to the diffusion of enterprise unions to smaller companies including suppliers. It is during this period that *roren*—union networks organized along the lines of corporate groups—emerged as an organizational form. In the fourth period, since the 1990s recession, corporations have been restructuring through diversification and by giving greater autonomy to internal divisions, challenging unions to reconsider their own boundaries. Unions are responding either by decentralizing the internal structure of the enterprise union or by using *roren* networks. These four stages of development represent a broad sweep, and variations exist in the speed with which a specific union has travelled along this path.

The Basic Survey of Trade Unions in Japan, conducted annually since 1958, gives an overview of how union structure has changed over the past half-century. The survey distinguishes between single-branch unions (SBUs) and multiple-branch unions (MBUs), and counts the number of branches per MBU. SBUs and MBUs are both bounded normally by a corporation rather than a corporate group, so the survey figures capture trends in enterprise unions, but not in *roren* (the federation of enterprise unions organized around a corporate group). Although branches do not coincide perfectly with the corporate structure of establishments or factories, they give a good indication of the growth of union size through the multidivisionalization of unions. During 1958 and 2002, the number of MBUs increased more than the number of SBUs, nearly threefold compared with one and a half times. In 2002, there were 2,529 MBUs with an average of 15 branches per MBU, and 27,648 SBUs.

Figure 2.1 shows that basic union organizational units, be they SBUs or branches of MBUs, continued to grow until the mid-1980s. Thereafter, the numbers started to decline, coinciding with the timing of the decline in total union membership, from a peak of 12.4 million members in 1985. In the early years, in the 1950s, there were more SBUs than branches organized as MBUs, but the latter overtook the former as early as in 1962 (see Figure 2.1). The early 1960s saw particularly fast growth in MBUs compared with SBUs, a pattern repeated in the early 1970s and the mid-1980s (see Figure 2.2 for rates of change).[1] The historical account below provides some insight into why these formation peaks occurred at these particular times.

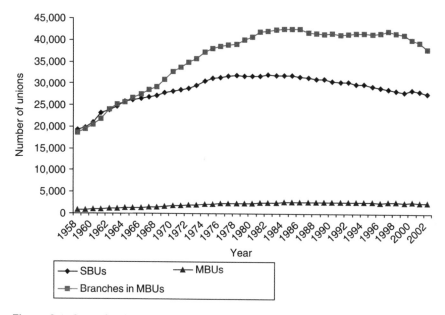

Figure 2.1 Growth of unions in Japan

Note: SBU = single-branch unions; MBU = multiple-branch unions.
Source: MHLW (various years, *a*), *Basic Survey of Trade Unions in Japan*.

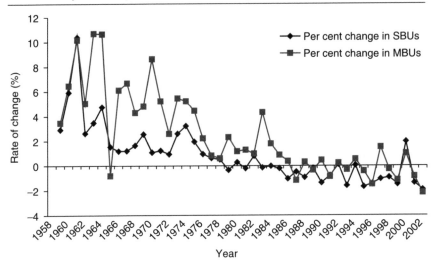

Figure 2.2 Growth rates of unions in Japan

Note: SBU = single-branch unions; MBU = multiple-branch unions.
Source: MHLW (various years, *a*), *Basic Survey of Trade Unions in Japan*.

2.1. Establishment of Factory Unions (1945–50)

Immediately after the Second World War, unions were established rapidly as they were legalized for the first time in Japanese history. These were not so much enterprise unions as factory or establishment unions. Workers and union leaders at the time chose this boundary initially for a number of reasons, but a combination of historical legacy and pragmatic constraints due to corporate restructuring led to this immediate choice.

Before 1945, political repression and large employers' industrial paternalism prevented the Japanese labour unions from developing an active mass movement. Lifetime employment and company-provided welfare made skilled workers more loyal to the company than to any national labour federations. Consequently, the labour movement found itself squeezed out of the large modern enterprises where employer-sponsored friendly societies were the norm, and operated mainly in the small-firm sector (Large 1979). After 1938, workers' enterprise consciousness was further institutionalized by the wartime patriotic labour organization, Sanpo, which mobilized workers factory by factory (Gordon 1985: ch. 8). When the war ended, some factory managers attempted to convert the activities under Sanpo into those of a cooperative union, but their attempt remained largely abortive. Many factory-based Sanpo branches renamed themselves as unions, rejecting the docility and patriotism associated with the Sanpo label.

Apart from these legacies, however, there was a pragmatic reason why workers felt most able to build organizations first in factories or establishments, rather than at higher levels of the corporate hierarchy. This is less to do with the oft-cited 'spontaneous' identification of workers with the firm, and more due to the instability of management and drastic revisions in corporate structure. The account here therefore focuses on the impact of corporate restructuring in the 1945–50 period on union structure.

The second half of the 1940s was a period of enormous turmoil. The Allied Occupation Force initially saw labour unions as a force for democratization, buttressing them with three labour laws during 1945–7. But the immediate concern of workers and war returnees was to obtain basic food and clothing. As the government pursued expansionary fiscal policy to resuscitate the moribund economy, hyperinflation—with the retail price of rice quintupling in 1946 and rising another six times in 1947—led to the development of black markets. Workers with jobs considered themselves lucky, but they could not rely on wages alone to feed their families. Some grew vegetables—potatoes, pumpkins, corn—on derelict factory grounds. Others made pots and pans using factory equipment and sold them in exchange for food in the countryside. Not surprisingly, a 'living wage' was a key demand of workers.

At the same time, large corporations came under attack, as previous monopoly was considered anti-democratic. The Holding Company Liquidation Committee specified ten corporate groups as Zaibatsu to be dissolved and identified numerous other companies as 'restricted companies' (Okazaki 2001). Zaibatsu families were stripped of their stocks and shares, and older incumbent managers were dismissed to give way to younger managers less tainted by the war experience (Morikawa 1997). 'Restricted companies' were required to submit their restructuring plans for government approval. The Anti-Monopoly Law in 1947 banned the pure holding company (i.e. a holding company without any operations within its internal structure), contributing to the Allied Force's efforts to reduce the monopolistic concentration of Japanese industry. Soon thereafter, in December 1948, the so-called Dodge Line, a draconian plan to deal with inflation by contractionary macropolicies, led to further corporate restructuring and factory closures. Consequently, throughout the second half of the 1940s, some workers did not bother to go to work after they found that their employers were not able to pay wages. Many lived in constant fear of losing their job, as redundancies became a common occurrence. Thus, no stable internal labour markets existed at the time factory unions sprung up.

The uncertainty over the future of individual establishments in large corporations made it sensible for unions to treat each establishment as the basic building block. The case of Mitsubishi Heavy Industries (MHI) gives an insight into the impossibility of defining a stable enterprise union boundary if the corporate boundary is not settled. In December 1946, MHI was identified as a holding company, and all its shares were turned over to the Holding Company Liquidation Committee (Shiba 1997: 176). Plans were also under way for the company's disintegration. However, during a rather prolonged period (1946–8), the exact ways in which MHI was to be split up was not decided, as General Headquarters (GHQ) kept on not responding to, or rejecting, proposals made by the MHI managers. The proposals ranged from breaking up MHI into three companies (in shipbuilding, machinery, and rolling stock), to the extreme of making each of the twenty-three factories into a separate company. No wonder a union at MHI had to be based at each shipyard or factory. It was not until January 1950 that the former MHI was finally divided into three new companies along geographical lines. (They were eventually reunited into a new Mitsubishi Heavy Industries Co. Ltd. in June 1964.)

At other major companies that proliferated multiple establishments before and during the war, workers also organized first by factory, shipyard, or steel mill. Toshiba is a typical case. After an abortive attempt by management to build on the remains of the Sanpo organization, workers at the largest Toshiba factory at Horikawacho founded an all-employee factory union in November 1945 (Gordon 1985: 340). Other Toshiba factory workers followed suit. In autumn 1946, Toshiba unions went on a fifty-five-day strike, demanding no lay-offs, a livelihood wage, and the democratic reconstruction of industry. By March 1948, there were unions at forty-five factories and establishments (Hasegawa 1984: 260).

To enable coordination over wage bargaining between factories, Toshiba workers formed federations of factory unions, starting with three regional federations in 1946. These regional federations were then consolidated into a company-wide federation, Toshiba Roren, in 1948 (Toshiba Union 1981: 20).[2] Interestingly, the first collective agreement was signed in 1946 between each regional federation and Toshiba Corporation. But each factory union retained the formal right to demand its own wages and the right to call a strike. Nevertheless, factory unions joined forces to coordinate a 'joint struggle' through Toshiba Roren. To every demand by Toshiba Roren to negotiate at the company-wide level, Toshiba headquarters management responded by imposing a 'divide and rule' policy. In effect, the company insisted on signing a separate agreement with each factory on the pretext that factories had autonomy over their budget (Hasegawa 1984: 299). This management stance was underpinned by the banks that insisted on factory-based accounting and the closure of smaller loss-making factories as conditions for a much-needed loan of 600 million yen. By 1949, twenty-eight out of the forty-four Toshiba factories were forced to close despite worker protest, and about a quarter of the 22,207 employees, including Communists, were fired. In the process, management was able to play on the fear of losing a job to split the union. Non-Communist factory unions were newly established in competition with the existing unions and eventually absorbed the latter. With these factory unions on a new footing, they formed a new federation, Toshiba Roren, in 1951.

The 1945–50 period was marked by initial bursts of union activity followed shortly by management backlash. This up-and-down cycle in a matter of five years is evident in the signing of collective agreements and the formalization of worker participation in management. Initial success by organized labour to gain a fair claim to shared management authority took the form of production control by workers, as in the case at NKK and Yomiuri Newspaper. While a minority of radical Communist unions pushed for worker control of production, the majority were more interested in the broader notion of the democratization of management. This meant the establishment of management discussion councils (*keiei kyogikai*) that bound management to consult and gain consent of the union in virtually all matters related to personnel policy and wages, as well as production plans. Two-thirds of all collective agreements in mid-1946 had management discussion councils (Gordon 1985: 345–6). By mid-1947, 86 per cent of unions had a collective agreement at the establishment level, and nearly all of them had provision for a management discussion council (Okochi 1956: ch. 9). In accordance with their respective ideologies, the Socialist Sodomei was keener to guide affiliated unions to intervene in management from the inside, whilst the Communist Sanbetsu was more inclined to fight against management from the outside (Okochi 1956: 243–4).[3] Despite these differences, these councils formally gave considerable co-decision authority to establishment unions.

But events soon took a different course. First, the Allied Occupation Force abandoned its pro-union stance, when the union movement became more evidently imbued with Communist and Socialist ideologies, culminating in the banning of the national general strike in February 1947 and the subsequent Red Purge. Second, the Dodge Line policies made job protection an impossible dream, and management at various companies started to pick the timing and targets of dismissals, reneging on earlier promises of no lay-offs. Third, as part of a new management determination to take on unions in 1949–50, company management in many cases proposed revisions of collective agreements, involving the emasculation of the management discussion councils to become a weaker advisory or consultative body. Large-scale job cuts at shipyards, steel mills, and factories were going on in the midst of such proposals to reassert management's right to manage. In fact, management generally abandoned the previous agreements when they expired. Some unions, such as at Mitsubishi shipyard in Nagasaki, capitulated immediately, but others held out, leading to the so-called no agreement era (*mukyoyaku jidai*). In May 1950, only half (44.9 per cent) of union members and 37 per cent of unions were covered by collective agreements (Ohara 1952). This era lasted for a few years in most cases, but much longer in other cases such as at Matsushita until 1956 (see Chapter 3) and Toyota until 1973 (see Chapter 4). Communist-led Sanbetsu had made industry-wide collective agreements a matter of priority in 1946, and made minor achievements in electric power, printing, and some machine industries. But even those were disappearing by 1950 with the destruction of Sanbetsu due to the Red Purge.

Apart from corporate boundaries, a major concern of workers in early post-war unions at the factory level was whether or not blue- and white-collar workers should be in the same union. One key objective of all unions at the time was the abolition of the status system (*mibunsei no teppai*). In the pre-war period and during the Second World War, wide differentials existed in social status between staff (*shokuin*) and workers (*koin*), reflected both in a feudalistic atmosphere and in concrete working conditions. At the time of founding, most unions debated whether or not the objective of abolishing status discrimination could best be achieved by forming a single all-employee union. Workers at Toshiba organized such an all-employee union for those below the position of department chief (*bucho*) from the beginning (Gordon 1985: 342). The situation was similar at Matsushita and Toyota, as we shall see in Chapters 3 and 4. Status differential was so large, however, that in some cases blue-collar workers felt unable to cooperate with their supervisors. For example, Hitachi unions started as separate blue- and white-collar unions.

At Hitachi Co. Ltd., twenty-two factories and offices formed unions between December 1945 and March 1946 (Hitachi Factory Union 1964: 93). In all cases, a white-collar union was formed separately from a blue-collar union. From the start, however, the blue-collar union at the largest factory, Hitachi Factory Workers Union, felt the need to coordinate both between the blue- and the white-collar unions and across factories.[4] But, in response to its first demand to double wages for all Hitachi workers, factory management responded that 'deciding wages at one factory on its own would be inconvenient for various reasons, including the movement of personnel between factories, so we would need to consider the matter for Hitachi Co. Ltd. as a whole' (Hitachi Factory Union 1964: 89). This incident triggered the formation of the company-wide federation of factory unions—Hitachi Sorengo—in February 1946 (Hitachi Factory Union 1964: 97). Hitachi Sorengo, thereafter, was instrumental in encouraging the merger of blue- and white-collar unions, which happened at the Hitachi Factory in May 1946.

According to a survey conducted by Tokyo University's Institute of Social Science in 1947, 81 per cent of unions were mixed (in the sense of including both blue- and white-collar workers), whilst 14 per cent were blue-collar unions and 5 per cent white-collar unions (Okochi 1956: 92). Excluding white-collar unions from the analysis, nearly a third of the remaining unions organized section chiefs (*kacho*), whilst one in two unions included subsection chiefs (*kakaricho*) (Okochi 1956: 11; Chapter 3, this volume). In many cases, these lower middle-level managers provided the vital skills in early union activities, such as preparing negotiation documents based on management information. But with the revision of the Trade Union Law in 1949, a union that included as members 'those representing the interest of employer' was deemed not to be a proper union.

Subsequently, the hierarchical boundary between union members and management at factory and enterprise unions was a matter explicitly stated in collective agreements. These agreements were necessary because the expectation of internal promotion led workers to regard managers as senior employees rather than representatives of employer interest, offering no obvious cut-off point between union and non-union members in the internal hierarchy (Ujihara 1989: 158). Generally, most unions considered that the broader the definition of workers, the stronger the worker voice. But managers also had an incentive to adopt a broad definition of non-union member managers, so as to keep as many as possible on the management side of the negotiating table and to keep as many as possible working during disputes. But as compared to 1945–9, the hierarchical boundary was subsequently lowered to exclude section chiefs (*kacho*) to conform to the law. Moreover, the de-unionization of foremen was sometimes subject to negotiation, as was the case at Yawata Steel where management demanded it as a quid pro quo for agreeing to the introduction of shop floor production committees in 1963 (Suzuki 2000: 88).

In summary, the immediate post-war period saw the growth of factory unions precisely at the point when employers were not able to deliver on lifetime employment. Factory unions sprung up, also, precisely at the time when corporate restructuring due to Zaibatsu dissolution and the Dodge Line made the future of enterprise boundaries uncertain. Although unions felt the need to coordinate their demands at the corporate level when they demanded employment security and a living wage, such coordination remained quite loose. Nevertheless, this organizational characteristic enabled the union movement to increase its membership from a mere 380,000 workers (3.2 per cent of the labour force) in 1945, to 4.9 million (41.5 per cent union density) in 1946, reaching a peak at 6.6 million (55.8 per cent union density) in 1949 (Shirai 1983: 140).

2.2. Consolidation into Enterprise Unions: 1950s and 1960s

The second period, in the 1950s and 1960s, is marked by an economic boom resulting from the Korean War and the growth of the size of modern corporations. The multidivisional structure spread in Japanese firms particularly in the 1960s, as they considered ways to consolidate their ever-expanding operations into a coherent entity. Of the largest 100 manufacturing firms, those that adopted the multidivisional structure increased from 29 in 1960 to 55 by 1970 (Suzuki 1991: 101). Some factory unions already had a company-wide federation, but such a federation was consolidated into a unified enterprise union in order to centralize control and coordination. The specific timing of such consolidation, however, differed from union to union. This section looks at corporate strategy and union strategy as major reasons for the consolidation.

A key proposition in this section is that the more centralized corporate management decision-making is and the greater the union's intent to participate in corporate strategy formulation, the more incentive establishment unions have to consolidate into an enterprise union. At one extreme, as we shall see in Chapter 3, Matsushita Electric Union encompassed the whole multi-establishment corporation from the start in 1946. Given the concentration of managerial power in the owner-manager, Konosuke Matsushita, the union leaders deemed it wise to match the centre of gravity of union activity with that for management at the corporate headquarters. Even after a period of disagreement between management and labour in the early 1950s, Matsushita Union was able to reintroduce a relatively strong form of management council, unlike at other companies. Subsequently, the union has put much more emphasis than other unions in developing its capability to gather information and to make suggestions towards management policy. Participation in management strategy (*keiei sanka*) in this proactive mode is a hallmark of Matsushita Union (Ujihara 1989: 178).

However, the Matsushita case is an exception rather than the norm. Various obstacles undermined unions' attempts to consolidate into enterprise unions, not all of which were management's making. As we saw in the previous section, Toshiba factory unions wanted to bargain and conclude a collective agreement at the corporation level. But management gained an upper hand by insisting on bargaining with individual factories, on the pretext of financial autonomy of each factory. Although Toshiba Roren existed as a company-wide federation of factory unions since 1951, the consolidation of this *roren* into a unified Toshiba enterprise union was not achieved until 1970 (Toshiba Union 1981: 251).

A key obstacle to unification was an ingrained history of autonomous factory unions that belonged to a number of federations with widely different political conviction. Initially, Toshiba's factory unions affiliated to the Communist-controlled Sanbetsu until its demise in 1950. Thereafter, with the internal split within Toshiba unions, different unions affiliated to different national bodies. Factory unions at Horikawacho, Osaka, and Yanagicho belonged to Zenkinzoku, the metal union federation that supported Sohyo. Factory unions at Tsurumi and Fuchu affiliated to the heavy electrical union federation, Judenki Roren (Toshiba Union 1981: 55). When the latter got together with the light electrical union federation to form Denki Roren (the main industry federation for the electrical machinery sector) in 1953, the metal union federation was excluded from this merger due to its support for Sohyo. At this time, unions were organized either at the factory or at the enterprise level, when they affiliated to Denki Roren. Thereafter, Toshiba Roren made numerous attempts to unify it into a single enterprise union, by setting up committees to harmonize the union rules, the system of full-time officials, and the union subscription rates for all factory unions (Toshiba Union 1981: 67–70). Nevertheless, factory-level union leaders, whilst agreeing on the general principle of eventual unification, resisted implementing these centre-directed measures, outwardly reasoning that the union organization was too immature to cope with such restructuring and inwardly fearing the loss of local autonomy.

A similar story can be told of Hitachi unions. Factory-based accounting autonomy also played a part in Hitachi factory unions retaining their right to bargain and to call a strike. But a more lasting obstacle to unifying the company-wide federation into an enterprise union was of the unions' own making. This concerned ideological disagreements over affiliation to higher-level union organizations, Sanbetsu or Sodomei. For example, the union at Hitachi Factory affiliated to Zen Nihon Kiki, regarded as a 'long arm' of the Communist Sanbetsu, in January 1947 (Hitachi Factory Union 1964: 204). By the 1950s, other Hitachi factory unions affiliated to Sohyo, whilst others remained politically neutral.

Apart from political disagreement, rivalry between industrial sectors also played a part in Hitachi Sorengo's inability to bring about unification. In particular, Hitachi unions in the steel sector were suspicious that a unified enterprise union would be centred on the interest of electrical machinery (particularly after the affiliation of many factory unions to Denki Roren in the early 1950s). Splits in opinion over which sectoral needs should predominate made it impossible for Hitachi Sorengo to push for a unified enterprise union, as the move required agreement from all constituent factory unions. As at Toshiba, it took until 1970 for Hitachi Sorengo to become a unitary enterprise union (Dore 1973: 181; Inagami and Whittaker 2005: 127).

In the steel industry, workers organized first by mills, as at Hitachi or Toshiba. But the fact that there were two competing national centres from the start—Sanbetsu and Sodomei—created a cacophony of unstable structures. The first attempt at forming an industrial union, Zentetsuro, was short-lived when its affiliation to Sanbetsu in 1946 led the Kawasaki union (with a tradition of pre-war Sodomei activity) to object and quit the industrial union. This political split at the national level led mill-based unions belonging to the same corporation to affiliate to different national centres. When Tekko Roren (the industry-level union federation for steel) was finally established in 1951, in the aftermath of the destruction of Sanbetsu, affiliation was by individual mill-based unions. Even at this stage, Tekko Roren had the ambition to become an industrial union, but given the reality of Japanese unions at the time, they resolved to work towards this end whilst respecting each union's autonomy (Tekko Roren 1981: 27). At the same time, mill-based unions remained loosely associated as an enterprise federation (*kigyoren*) for the large major steel makers such as Yawata, Fuji, Kawasaki, and Kobe Steel. Despite a trend towards corporate centralization of personnel management in order to formalize the work systems among different mills, enterprise federations of mill-based unions persisted well into the 1990s.

There was a general tendency for enterprise federations of factory unions to become more centralized, as corporations centralized their decisions in strategic and personnel matters (Ujihara 1989: 156–7). One reason for such managerial centralization derived from corporate strategy of growth. In the 1960s, many companies were diversifying and creating new divisions and factories. These new establishments required management and technical support, involving the movement of managerial staff between establishments. At the same time, rapid technological changes, for instance in the steel industry and in telecommunications, led to the creation of surplus workers, requiring companies to move workers from areas of excess labour supply to those of excess demand. The need for interfactory labour mobility led to a consensus between management and labour to harmonize the personnel system across factories so as to ease the movement without loss of pay and other benefits. Such consensus led to the signing of an enterprise-level collective agreement, for example at NTT Public Corporation, in order to formalize the rules of inter-establishment transfers (*haichi tenkan*) (JIL 1996).

Whereas the blue- versus white-collar distinction was an important workforce boundary between 1945 and 1950, the period of the 1950s and 1960s saw a contest in drawing the union boundary between regular employees (*honko* in factory settings) and temporary workers (*rinjiko*). The use of temporary workers reached a peak around 1960, accounting for 8 per cent of all workers in manufacturing, and much higher in some cases (Gordon 1985: 401). Unions at this time were very much for regular employees only. Some unions, for example at Toyota, acquiesced to management hiring seasonal workers (*kikanko*) and temporary workers (*rinjiko*), but had no intention of organizing them. Other unions came to negotiate over the number of temporaries that could be upgraded to regular status. For example, at Toshiba, one-third of the workforce (around 51,000) were temporaries in 1961, and the union took a lead in negotiating their pay and transfer to a regular worker status (Toshiba Union 1981: 148). In total, around one-fourth of temporary workers in Japan were promoted to regular status each year during 1960–2, and around one-third in 1963–4 (Gordon 1985: 404).

To summarize, the centralization of management decision-making was the primary reason why unions had an incentive to redefine their boundary around the enterprise, rather than at establishments. The greater the union's intent to participate in strategic management decision-making, the closer the matching of union organization to management organization. The 1960s was also a time of labour market fluidity, when workers moved between establishments and factories, and new technology led to uneven distribution of areas of excess labour demand and supply. In order to facilitate such internal transfers, management centralized personnel decisions and attempted to create a standardized human resource management system for the whole corporation. This establishment of corporate-wide systems also contributed to the consolidation of factory unions into an enterprise union. Nevertheless, some factory unions remained reluctant to give up their autonomy, particularly when they belonged to different industrial sectors and had different political leanings.

2.3. Extension of Union Boundaries and the Formation of Roren: 1970s–80s

As we noted in Section 2.2, the multidivisional form spread rapidly in the Japanese industrial economy in the 1960s. At the same time, corporate groups developed, both through hiving off internal divisions and through acquisition of supplier companies. Meanwhile, enterprise unions were created in smaller companies including affiliates and suppliers. Figure 2.3 shows how concentrated union organizing activity has been in the large-firm sector throughout the period under study. But if we focus our attention to the 1960s only, union density declined from 69 per cent in 1960 to 63 per cent in 1969 in enterprises employing 500 or more workers, but increased from 4.8 per cent to 6.4 per cent in enterprises employing less than 100 workers. It was also in the 1960s that the union at the parent company began to formalize its link to unions at affiliates and suppliers by establishing

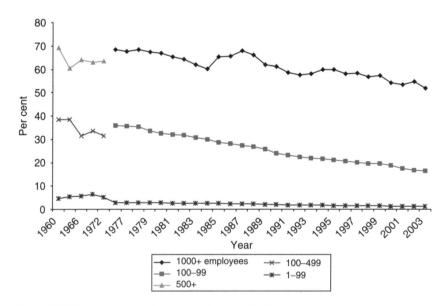

Figure 2.3 Union density by enterprise size in Japan

Source: MHLW (various years, *a*), *Basic Survey of Trade Unions in Japan*.

federations, known as *roren*. In this study, the parent company is referred to as a 'focal firm', and the union at the parent company as a 'focal union'.

According to an authoritative survey of unions, three-quarters of enterprise unions were in firms that belonged to a corporate group. Of these, 60 per cent belonged to a *roren*. Around 40 per cent of these federations were formed before the 1973 first oil shock (Inagami 1995: 11).[5] It is evident, therefore, that the formation of some *roren* was triggered by the slower economic growth after the 1973 oil shock, when large industrial firms consolidated their corporate groups and their vertical production *keiretsu*. But the origin of some other *roren* federations predates the slower growth. This is not difficult to explain once we recognize explicitly that the formation of *roren* was encouraged just as much by the focal union's objective to stabilize group-wide labour–management relations as the corporate group expanded (in the 1960s), as to protect the conditions of workers who were transferred from the focal firm to group firms in order to cope with slower growth (after 1973).

An account of the formation of such *roren* networks of enterprise unions along the lines of corporate groupings is often not developed fully in the existing literature, a gap that this book intends to fill. The boundary of an enterprise union may be extended, either because the corporate structure is revised through a hive-off or because, whilst the corporate structure remains unchanged, some employees are transferred from the core firm to affiliate or supplier companies. In the former case, the same group of workers that had been in an internal division are now working for a separate—ex-divisional—company. In the latter case, again, the union has an incentive to retain membership of the same employees, even if they work not within the enterprise but within the corporate group. Separate from either of these cases is the unionization of workers who had always worked for affiliate and supplier companies. The focal union's incentive to form a *roren* federation to coordinate the activities of these group company-based enterprise unions is different from its incentive to continue organizing the same employees when their place of work shifts to group companies.

For managers and employees, lifetime employment—an implicit guarantee of employment and income until retirement—was never confined to a particular workplace. As we saw for the earlier period, they were required to be flexible enough to move from establishment to establishment within a corporation. It was a natural extension to require employees also to move from the parent company to affiliates and suppliers within the corporate group. The practice of *shukko* (personnel transfer from the parent to affiliate or supplier company) began in the late 1950s in large companies, but it was put to different use for different types of employees thereafter (Inagami 2003: ch. 1). Initially, in the 1960s, managers were dispatched to hived-off divisions and other subsidiaries, in order to give managerial guidance to group companies. This practice of *shukko* for executive managers dates back to before the Second World War, when some group companies relied on their parent firm to recruit salaried employees and allocate them amongst their subsidiaries (Suzuki 1991: 72).

When rapid growth was halted by the oil shocks in the 1970s, companies resorted to *shukko* for ordinary employees. Slower growth and recession created promotion blockages for white-collar employees, and executive managerial positions at group companies became part of the jobs to which parent company employees could be promoted. Moreover, as manufacturing volumes declined for some product lines, surplus blue-collar workers were transferred to affiliates and suppliers. In these cases, older workers—3–5years before the mandatory retirement age—were targeted, as they were the most expensive in the seniority-based payment system. These workers were transferred on *shukko* with the 'domicile' remaining with the dispatching parent company, before they were transferred permanently on *tenseki*, when the 'domicile' was moved to the receiving company.

It is important to remember that there have always been significant inter-industry differences in the practice of *shukko* and *tenseki*. As Inagami (2003: 55) points out, in retail banks, virtually everyone, except a small number of non-managerial workers (such as drivers), was on temporary transfer (*shukko*) to subsidiaries by their late forties unless they made it beyond the branch manager level to top management. By contrast, in department stores, more or less all employees stayed on at the core firm until the retirement age of 60. The practice of manufacturing firms lie in between these two extremes. At Nippon Steel Corporation (Shin-nittetsu), for example, there were 1,700 employees on temporary transfer in 1975, and 2,400 in 1980, constituting only 2.1 per cent and 3.4 per cent of the total workforce, respectively. Then, the 1985 Plaza Accord induced a serious recession in steel in Japan, pushing the number of employees on *shukko* to 6,100 (10 per cent of the workforce). By 1990, the number tripled to 15,000, and throughout the 1990s, nearly 30 per cent of the total employees were on *shukko*, despite the fact that many dropped out of the Shin-nittetsu payroll by being subjected to permanent transfer (*tenseki*). The core workforce directly employed by Nippon Steel Corporation dropped from 440,000 in 1995 to 260,000 in 2001 (Inagami 2003).

As the internal labour market was extended from within a corporation to a corporate group, the enterprise union also extended its boundary. The most obvious mode was to retain the membership of employees on temporary transfer, particularly as they had the option to return to the parent company by remaining on the payroll of the originating company. Thus, the spinning out of an internal division, consisting solely of transferred employees, was an occasion for the enterprise union to continue covering them as members in the same union. Unions' key concern was to ensure that the income of their members was maintained. Thus, it was typical practice to negotiate a top-up for the members' salary if there was a shortfall as a result of a transfer to subsidiaries and affiliates (Dore 1986; Inagami 2003).

Enterprise unions responded to the extension of the internal labour market beyond the boundary of the core firm, by formulating a policy to continue the membership of employees on *shukko*. In so far as unions could negotiate and deliver on lifetime employment and an income guarantee, they were happy to retain the same employees who had been in the union as members. This bargaining stance also helped preserve an important principle for the enterprise union, namely the homogeneous treatment of members within an enterprise union.

There is one sense in which the movement of workers within an extended internal labour market of a corporate group is necessary and sufficient.to motivate a focal union to form a *roren* federation of enterprise unions. Just as factory unions wanted to regularize rules for movement of workers between factories in the earlier period (1950s and 1960s), so enterprise unions had an incentive to regularize rules for *shukko* and *tenseki* transfers within a corporate group. This motivation is reflected, in part, in the aforementioned survey that indicates that regular group-wide labour–management consultation and a group-wide collective agreement were important activities for 45 per cent and 18 per cent of *roren* federations in the survey, respectively (Inagami 1995: 11–12).

But the same survey also shows that the joint training of union officials and *roren*-wide coordination of pay bargaining were important activities for three-quarters of the *roren* federations in the survey. This suggests that whilst it is not possible to gauge from the survey why *roren* federations were initially formed, once they were, the *raison d'être* of these federations went well beyond the protection of conditions for employees and ex-employees of the focal firm. With the stabilization of relationships between the core firm and its group companies, some focal unions helped unionize these smaller companies, providing know-how in how to run a union.

Such acts were not necessarily altruistic. Hitachi's focal union, for example, found that as Hitachi's *keiretsu* group grew in size, it was asked to intervene in group-wide labour problems, whenever a second union cropped up suddenly at a supplier, or when subsidiary management announced lay-offs without consultation. Thus, with an intent to police and stabilize industrial relations at group companies, Hitachi's focal union formed a loose gathering of enterprise unions at affiliated companies as early as in 1961. It grew into a formal Zen Hitachi Roren federation with forty-eight unions in 1974 (Zen Hitachi Roren 1981: 14, 16, 50).

Other objectives of the focal union in developing *roren* federations were to exploit economies of scale in providing *roren*-wide union welfare plans and in standardizing pay and conditions through *roren*-wide coordination of collective bargaining. Thus, whilst a focal enterprise union could cope with continuing to organize ex-employees when internal divisions were hived off, a *roren* federation became necessary in order to police industrial relations for the corporate group that included acquired firms and suppliers with independent ownership but close trading linkages.

Whist internal labour markets were extended beyond the boundary of a single firm, they applied only to regular workers to the exclusion of non-regular workers. Union membership tended to follow this demarcation also. But the union status of so-called part-timers (*paato*)—defined as persons working less than thirty-five hours per week—became contentious during this period. In 1985, there were 4.7 million part-timers, constituting 11 per cent of total employees in Japan. Apart from their shorter working week, part-timers, many of them women, came to have longer average job tenure in the 1980s than in the 1970s (Wakisaka 1997). However, in manufacturing, they tended to be excluded from unions' purview. By contrast, in the retailing, wholesale, and food and beverage sectors, they came to be treated as quasi-members of the firm as community. Some unions, notably UI Zensen, became active in organizing part-time workers. In response, some employers came to pursue a strategy to minimize differences in employment rights between regular and part-time workers (Oh 2004). By 2002, just over 70 per cent of all establishments in Japan had part-time workers. Of those, 14 per cent included these workers as union members. As expected, the incidence of part-timers as union members was much higher in the service sectors than in manufacturing (MHLW various years, *a*).

To summarize, as corporate groups developed by hiving off internal divisions, enterprise unions considered extending their boundary or forming federations of enterprise unions within the corporate group. At the same time, as trading relationships with acquired and independent firms stabilized, the focal union had an incentive to help organize workers at these operations. The key activities of *roren*, involving coordination over pay bargaining, the training of union officials, and the provision of *roren*-wide welfare plans, indicate a mix of union motives.

2.4. Divisionalization of Unions and Internal Diversity since the 1990s

In the fourth period of prolonged recession since the early 1990s, Japanese corporations generally did not grow, but restructured through diversification, strategic alliances, and M & A. In this climate, large firms found themselves attracted to a corporate form that in effect separated out strategic management at the headquarters from operational management at constituent business units, be they internal divisions or hived-off companies. The legalization of the pure holding company as a corporate form in 1999 also encouraged this mode of thinking about a managerial focus that tolerated greater operational diversity within an enterprise. A corollary of this is the notion of a different human resource system for each division or affiliated company, leading to greater diversity of employment contracts for a single corporation. Changes taking place at Matsushita Electric, described in Chapters 3 and 8, is a good case in point.

Unions are responding either by decentralizing their internal structure or by externalizing diversity to the *roren* network to retain a manageable degree of uniformity within the core union. Thus, a precondition of enterprise unionism, namely the relative homogeneity of the quality of labour within its boundary, is being pushed to its limit. Greater details of exactly how specific unions are wrestling with these pressures will be given in the ensuing chapters.

One indication of diversity in working conditions within corporate groups is the gradual erosion at the margin of the underlying human resource policy principles. The principles were that (*a*) the focal firm would top-up pay for employees on *shukko* to maintain the pre-transfer salary level and (*b*) the company has the obligation to secure a place of employment, normally within the corporate group. With respect to the first principle, only 40 per cent of employees on *shukko* had an income guarantee by the late 1990s (Inagami 2003: 47). Increasingly, in the 1990s, permanent transfers (*tenseki*) at younger age (50 rather than 55, 45 rather than 50) became more common than temporary transfers (*shukko*). This reinforces the idea that pre-transfer income guarantee is necessary only whilst the transfer is temporary, but not necessary once a permanent transfer takes place. At the same time, early retirement schemes have become more prevalent, undermining the notion of 'lifetime employment' even within the corporate group. A good example of this is the case of the NTT Group, elaborated in Chapter 8. Moreover, as the management of corporate groups is decentralizing, the focal firm is increasingly not in a position to impose unwanted employees on affiliates and supplier companies (Inagami 2003: ch. 2).

In response, some unions are beginning to no longer attempt to retain employees on *shukko* as union members. According to the 2001 official survey of industrial relations, 47 per cent of unions responded that there were union members on *shukko* (MHLW 2001: Tables 14–19). Of these unions, 85 per cent still had a policy to continue the membership of employees on *shukko*, but the rest did not insist on this or had a policy to exclude them from membership. The survey also indicates that around two-thirds of all unions with *shukko* employees had a say on the policy of transfers, either through labour–management consultation or through collective bargaining, but the rest did not.

Another source of diversity is the increased use of non-regular workers, who constitute a much more significant presence in the 2000s than in the 1980s. In 1982, the proportion of non-standard workers (*hiseiki jugyoin*) (including part-time, temporary, and dispatched workers) was 8 per cent of the male employee workforce and 31 per cent of the female employee workforce (Japan Productivity Centre 1994: 102). By 2003, these proportions rose to 15 per cent for men and 46 per cent for women (JILPT 2004: 35).

In particular, the rate of increase of dispatched workers (workers dispatched by labour placement agencies) has been spectacular, as the total number doubled in the 1990s, from 510,000 in 1990 to just over 1 million in 1999, and to 1.75 million by 2001 (JILPT 2004: 18). Until 2004, the Labour Dispatching Law (*haken ho*) had prohibited the use of agency labour in production areas. This led some on-site contractors (*kounai ukeoi*)—who must provide (or are leased) machinery and equipment as well as labour—to grow into areas where employers would have preferred hiring agency labour. These areas were concentrated in electronic assembly in the late 1980s and in auto component manufacturing and car assembly in the 1990s. Workers tend to be young men and women, who typically undertake tasks in assembly, inspection, packaging, and transportation. In a sample of 105 manufacturing establishments surveyed by Sato et al. (2003), 18 per cent had over 60 per cent of their workforce provided by inside contractors, and a further 20 per cent had between 41 per cent and 60 per cent of their workforce as contingent workers of this sort. At the same time, the 2003 revision of the Labour Standards Law, extending the maximum length of fixed-term contracts from one year to three years, is likely to increase the use of temporary workers. As membership based on regular employees declines and workers on non-standard forms of contract increase, enterprise unions may need to seriously reconsider the workforce boundary they have drawn between regular and non-regular workers (Whittaker 1998: 292).

To summarize, the period since the 1990s is marked by decentralization of enterprise unions and *roren*, and the introduction of considerable diversity in the treatment of union members within each unit of organization. The gradual erosion of management commitment to income guarantees and lifetime employment has introduced a significant degree of diversity into the existing regular workforce. At the same time, inside contractors and temporary workers remain outside the union boundary.

2.5. Summary

This chapter demonstrated that since the Second World War, the centre of gravity of Japanese unions shifted from factory to enterprise and from enterprise to corporate groups. Table 2.1 summarizes these shifts in union boundaries with respect to the corporate boundary, and also positions the other two types of union boundaries (namely hierarchical and workforce) against specific management and union concerns. In particular, hierarchical boundary—up to what rank of workers should be organized as union members—was contentious in the first period (1945–50), but was largely settled thereafter. By contrast, the workforce boundary— what types of workers should be organized—remained contentious and shifted from period to period, with attention paid to seasonal workers in the 1960s, employees on transfer and part-timers in the 1970s and 1980s, and agency labour and inside contractors since the 1990s.

The shifts in the union boundary in relation to corporate structure took place over time as a result of corporate restructuring, the transformation of human resource practices, and unions' own strategy. In the immediate post-war period, the dissolution of the Zaibatsu holding companies made corporate boundaries and employment contracts highly unstable. This situation made organizing unions at the factory or establishment level, rather than at the enterprise level, both attractive and feasible. Soon, however, as corporate growth picked up in the 1950s and 1960s, the need to move workers between factories led management to centralize the personnel system across factories and led factory unions to unite into enterprise unions to regulate the corporate-wide internal labour market. The internal labour market was extended beyond the parent firm to the corporate group in the 1970s and 1980s, giving an incentive for unions to extend their boundary also. More recently, unions have acquiesced to the

Table 2.1 Shifting concerns in three types of union boundaries during 1945–2000

Period	Corporate boundary	Hierarchical boundary	Workforce boundary	Management concerns	Union concerns
I 1945–50	Establishment	Up to section chief (*kacho*) initially, up to subsection chief (*kakaricho*) thereafter	Separate unions for blue- and white-collar?	Zaibatsu dissolution and corporate restructuring	Abolition of discrimination by status; democratization of management
II 1950s–1960s	Enterprise	—	Regular core employees vs seasonal/temporary workers	Corporate growth; centralization of personnel system within enterprise	Control over the mobility of members between factories (*haichi tenkan*)
III 1970s–1980s	Enterprise and corporate groups	—	Employees on transfer to group companies (*shukko, tenseki*) Part-timers	Consolidation of corporate groups and vertical *keiretsu*	Harmonization of conditions for workers within a corporate group
IV 1990s–	Internal divisions and subsidiaries	—	Exclude agency labour (*haken*) and on-site contractors (*ukeoi*)	Groupwide consolidated management, strong HQ strategy, and relatively autonomous divisions & subsidiaries	Acquiescing to diversity of conditions within a union

introduction of greater diversity in employment conditions within the corporate group and, in some cases, within the firm.

In all this, it is possible to be explicit about unions' own strategy. We noted that those unions that are keener to participate in managerial decision-making have been quicker to organize at the enterprise level than those that had a more limited objective. At the same time, political rivalry at the national and sectoral levels constituted a considerable obstacle to unifying factory unions into enterprise unions.

As we shall see in the rest of the book, unions' organizational boundaries may shift due to initiatives from different quarters. They may change primarily due to unions responding to a managerial initiative in corporate restructuring. For example, Matsushita Union extended its boundary in reaction to corporate hive-off of internal divisions (see Chapter 3). By contrast, Toyota Union decided not to extend its boundary but set up a separate enterprise union when Toyota Kyushu Ltd. was established (see Chapter 4). In other cases, however, boundary changes are entirely due to unions' own strategy, independent of any managerial action. A case in point is Nissan Union's decision to unify its parts supplier union organization (see Chapter 7). We will now turn to specific ways in which corporate strategy and labour strategy interacted, starting with the Matsushita Group.

Notes

1. In the mean time, union density continued to decline from a peak of 55.8 per cent (6.6 million members) in 1949 to 25.2 per cent in 1990 and 19.6 per cent in 2003 (MHLW various years, *a*).
2. Here, the term *roren* was used to refer to an enterprise-wide federation of factory unions. Not to be confused with the later, and more common, use of the term to refer to a network of enterprise unions.
3. Sanbetsu (Congress of Industrial Unions of Japan) (established 19 August 1946) was a national trade union centre composed primarily of radical public-sector unions. It was under the control of the Japan Communist Party. Sodomei (the Japan Federation of Trade Unions) (established 1 August 1946) consisted of moderate private-sector unions and became linked to the Japan Socialist Party.
4. Note that Hitachi is both the name of the company and the name of the largest factory in the company.
5. The survey was conducted in 1992, with responses from 1,050 unions with 500+ members in private-sector industries. The response rate was 43.5 per cent.

3

Strategy and Structure at Matsushita Group

This chapter and the next present detailed historical case studies of Matsushita and Toyota. Over the decades, these corporations, each with its strong corporate culture, have produced official company histories. The enterprise unions have been equally assiduous in recording their achievements. The aim, therefore, is not to add to the volume of writing that already exists. Rather, these chapters have a focused objective to bring new insights by analysing the *interaction* between company strategy and union strategy in the process of corporate restructuring. The SSI framework elaborated in Chapter 1 provides the organizing principles for presenting the narrative.

This chapter is on Matsushita Electric Industrial (MEI). Section 3.1 describes the main junctures at which Matsushita management considered structural changes, starting with the adoption of the multidivisional structure in 1933, up to the most recent restructuring plan that began in 2003. This is very much a story of the corporate headquarters avoiding administrative overload by steering between delegating and regaining control over an ever-changing portfolio of products. On the whole, Matsushita is a moderately diversified company, and has adopted a half-functional, half-divisional structure, consistent with the norm of incompletely autonomous divisions noted in Chapter 1. In fact, Matsushita is more centralized than most of its competitors like NEC, Hitachi, and Toshiba.

Section 3.2 then follows the logic behind changes in Matsushita unions' strategy and structure. The focal union has been remarkably successful in extending its boundary beyond the focal firm to include hived-off and affiliated companies. The union's strategy derives from its desire to mirror the centralized management structure and to participate in managerial decision-making. Lastly, Section 3.3 analyses the nature of the extended internal labour market that developed as a result of the ways in which the corporate head office and the focal union drew their boundaries. It is argued that until the mid-1990s, both management and the union had their own reasons for maintaining a uniform set of working conditions for this extended internal labour market, prescribed in a single collective agreement.

3.1. Strategy and Structure at Matsushita Electric Industrial

Matsushita Electric's company history (e.g. MEI 1968) presents a view of the company as a pioneer in adopting a multidivisional structure in 1933. Except during a short interlude when wartime exigency led to centralized control and the near destruction of sales channels, the company repeatedly enforced a divisional structure. But divisions were always incompletely autonomous, with management accounting, personnel management, and marketing being controlled by headquarters. Moreover, Matsushita established divisions along finely defined product lines. The resulting proliferation of divisions—hovering at well over 40 since the late 1960s[1]—was managed by adopting a three-tier structure, with divisions as basic units, divisional groups at the mezzanine level, and the corporate headquarters overseeing those groups.

Four periods are identified in this section: (*a*) the adoption of the M-form in 1933 and the immediate formation of a corporate group through hiving off a division; (*b*) post-1945 reconstruction from the wartime control structure, and the establishment of a half-functional, half-divisional structure in the 1950s; (*c*) the development of divisional groups and divisional companies up to the 1990s; and (*d*) the deeper corporate restructuring since 2001. The last subsection addresses the impact that these changes in MEI's internal structure have had on the development of the larger business group.

3.1.1 Pre-War Origin and Development

After working as an apprentice in a bicycle shop and as a wiring engineer at Osaka Dento (Osaka Electric Light Company) for six years, Konosuke Matsushita quit this secure job to start his own business. A fascination with electricity and a conviction about its future potential led him to take this step. He founded Matsushita Electric Works in 1918, and started producing rotary attachment plugs and double-cluster sockets. Two presses constituted the totality of his capital equipment, and his wife and brother-in-law the sole source of labour. Within fourteen years (by 1932), the company grew to a substantial size, employing 200 shop assistants and over 1,000 factory workers. Some 200 product types were made, categorized into four product groups, namely wiring equipment, heating equipment, lamps and batteries, and radios. Already, the company operated out of ten manufacturing locations, and had a nationwide network of five branch shops (MEI 1968: 93).

With such a diverse product range based on relatively new technology at the time, it is perhaps not surprising, with the benefit of Chandlerian hindsight, that Matsushita Electric was a pioneer in the multidivisional form of organization. 'In the period 1933–6, paralleling Pierre Du Pont's efforts to develop the divisionalized organization in the United States, Konosuke Matsushita and his controller Arataro Takahashi were evolving a similar concept in Japan' (Pascale and Athos 1981: 32).[2] In 1933, just as the construction of the new headquarters in Kadoma was about to be completed, Konosuke Matsushita decided to divide the company into three product divisions (*jigyobu*) (radios, lamps and batteries, and wiring and electric heaters) (MEI 1968: 111). Each division was made responsible not only for production but also for all the processes from product development to sales. This meant that all product development personnel, factories, and sales offices came under the jurisdiction of one of the divisions. The aim of divisionalization was twofold: to clarify the performance of each division so as to make its evaluation easier and to provide a training ground for general managers by giving them managerial autonomy (MEI 1968: 113). Soon after, in September 1935, the central office was formally given the functions of control, planning, development, and advertisement for the entire company (Shimotani 1998: 64).

In December 1935, Konosuke turned his operations into a limited company, Matsushita Electric Industries Co. Ltd. At the same time, he started creating a corporate group, the Matsushita Industrial Konzern, initially by hiving off internal product divisions into independent subsidiaries. The first six to be established were Matsushita Radio Company, Matsushita Dry Battery Company, Matsushita Electric Company, Matsushita Heater Company, Matsushita Metal Company, and Nippon Electric Company (Shimotani 1998: 62). During 1935–44, the Konzern grew considerably, creating thirty group companies, either by hive-offs or by acquisition, to facilitate overseas expansion (especially in the colonies of Korea, Taiwan, and Manchuria) and munitions supply.

With the hive-off system in place in 1935, MEI became a pure holding company. It managed mainly the personnel and financial aspects of its subsidiaries, and was slimmed down from employing 609 workers in November 1935 to 108 by May 1936 (Shimotani 1998: 66). Each hived-off company was to undertake its production and sales activities with a greater sense of self-responsibility than was the case when they had been internal divisions (MEI 1968: 138). However, countering this managerial autonomy at subsidiaries was a strong pull towards central strategic control. In particular, all subsidiaries at this time were 100 per cent owned by the holding company, and Konosuke Matsushita was the president in every hived-off company. Also, 1937 saw the formalization of a rule that headquarters approval was needed for all new investments by subsidiaries (Shimotani 1998: 67). In order to retain central control of accounting and finance, personnel in this function were appointed by the holding company and sent out to subsidiaries.

The outbreak of the Second World War led MEI to engage in the production of ships, aircraft components, and even airplanes. Wartime exigency had a hugely expansionary impact on MEI, which saw a near fivefold increase in the number of employees in eight years (1936–44) (MEI 1968: 168); by 1944, the MEI Group employed 30,000 at sixty-seven factories and thirteen branch offices (*shucchojo*). Such expansion went hand in hand with the need for group-wide coordination to deal with raw material and manpower shortages. In response, the company started to centralize by consolidating all the divisional sales and marketing operations at the headquarters level. Between 1942 and 1944, MEI dissolved its subsidiaries and integrated their operations under MEI's direct control. Then in 1944, a 'manufacturing works system' (*seizosho sei*) was introduced to control all factories centrally, in order to eliminate waste and overlap that resulted from the autonomous management of divisions. But the establishment of a central control structure coincided with diversification into unfamiliar territories, as the military ordered Matsushita to build new operations, notably in shipbuilding and aircraft manufacturing. By the end of the war, MEI was a munitions company with little need for a sales network (with 84 per cent of total output for military use) (Shimotani 1998: 107–15).

3.1.2 Post-War Reconstruction and Restructuring

Konosuke Matsushita was quick to announce MEI's company policy to switch production from munitions to consumers the day after the war ended. By the autumn of 1945, production resumed at some of the factories that were not directly involved in munitions production. However, the Matsushita family was soon certified as a Zaibatsu family, and in June 1946 the Gheadquarters ordered the entire assets of MEI frozen, including the shares held in its subsidiaries. Konosuke Matsushita and Arataro Takahashi (Konosuke's right-hand man and MEI's controller at the time) made numerous visits to GHQ in their attempt to convince the authorities that MEI was an entrepreneurial firm founded by a commoner and that its business had always been the production of necessities for peaceful home life. Their efforts paid off eventually when the Matsushita family was delisted from the Zaibatsu family register at the end of 1949.

Nevertheless, in December 1946, by virtue of being a holding company, MEI had to accept the GHQ's order to separate thirty-two of its subsidiaries into independent companies. Holding companies were made illegal in Japan with the adoption of the Anti-Monopoly Law in 1947, and the MEI holding company therefore had to be abandoned. It was not so easy to convert ex-munitions factories into non-military operations, and only ten out of the thirty-two subsidiaries, such as Matsushita Wiring Device Co. Ltd. (Matsushita Denko K.K.) and Matsushita Electric Trading Co. Ltd. (Matsushita Denki Boeki K.K.), were viable as independent firms (MEI 1968: 201). With this reorganization, MEI saw a labour force of 15,000 employees nearly halve to 8,000 within eighteen months.

The Dodge Plan in 1949 had a further contractionary impact on MEI, as consumer demand fell for the company's products. MEI responded by reducing production and by negotiating a redundancy package (involving 843 voluntary and 54 compulsory redundancies) with the union (MEI 1968: 207). Existing factories were turned into profit centres, whilst some factories were temporarily closed. In this rationalization process, MEI adopted a functional organization under Konosuke's direct control to weather difficult times, but quickly revived its divisional structure in 1950 to cope with an expanding product range (Shimotani 1998: 133–4). The three divisions created were the same as the ones introduced originally in 1933, and for the time being Konosuke was head of each so-called division. The headquarters function was slimmed down to focus on general administration, management of staff, and accounting and financial matters (MEI 1968: 209).

Subsequently, the company began to proliferate product divisions and spin-off companies, but only quite slowly in the 1950s. Heating equipment was separated from the second division to become the fourth division. Next, in between Konosuke's first visit to the United States and his visit to Europe in 1951, the lighting part of the first division was separated to create the fifth division. This was in preparation for importing electronics technology from abroad. Philips was chosen as a partner for a joint venture, called Matsushita Electronics, established in 1952 in order to produce light bulbs, fluorescent lamps, vacuum tubes, cathode ray tubes, transistors, and semiconductors (MEI 1968: 226). The product divisions were defined very narrowly, in many cases to capture just one product line, reflecting Matsushita's management principle known as detailed specialization (*senmon saibunka*). This principle was based on Konosuke's idea that anyone anywhere could become a world-class expert if given responsibility to specialize in a narrowly defined business area (MEI 1968: 185).

The Korean War boom brought an annual doubling of sales of electrical goods. At this time, however, MEI was not so diversified, as just two products—batteries and radios—jointly accounted for 66 per cent of Matsushita's total sales in 1951 (Shimotani 1998: 147). Once the war was over, demand fell and price cutting followed, leading to bankruptcies among some firms in the industry. In order to reduce internal costs and to improve efficiency in the deployment of funds, MEI decided in 1954 to introduce four functional departments (*honbusei*) in planning and control, technology (with a central R & D lab), sales, and operations. The ten so-called divisions came to be part of this Operations Department. The nature of product divisions therefore changed, became less a unit that followed through a product line from development to sales, and focused more around manufacturing. Hitherto, Konosuke as president was in direct control of many functions, but from then on four top executives other than the president took charge of each of the four functions.

It was in the context of this half-functional, half-divisional structure that Matsushita's Business Plan System (*jigyo keikaku seido*) emerged and was formalized in 1954 (Shimotani 1998: 137). Still in use today, this system requires each product division to submit an annual business plan within the parameters set out in the president's new year speech. After bilateral discussion between the divisional head and the headquarters planning and control department, the plan is approved with specific targets to be met in sales turnover, profitability, and other areas. Divisional performance is monitored throughout the year by accounting and personnel professionals who are all hired directly by the headquarters and are on temporary transfer to various divisions. Thus, in the 1950s, managerial autonomy granted to so-called product divisions was mainly in the area of manufacturing operations. Over time, some of the planning, design, and marketing functions were passed on to these divisions, but the finance and personnel functions remained centralized at headquarters throughout the history of Matsushita Electric.[3]

3.1.3 Divisional Groups and Divisional Companies: From the 1960s to the 1990s

The subsequent history of MEI is marked by related product diversification. The company not only produced batteries and radios, but also stood at the forefront in realizing the consumer boom in electrical appliances (especially the so-called three treasures of television sets, refrigerators, and washing machines) in the 1960s. Later, it started producing audio and electronic equipment such as video recorders, DVD players, mobile telephones, and digital cameras. In order to facilitate this growth strategy, the MEI head office followed a cyclical path of proliferating so-called divisions, resuming a tight rein on them by reintroducing a functional organization, before giving greater freedom to these divisions again. The repeated ebb and flow within a largely half-divisional, half-functional structure attest to the difficulty of balancing the benefit of central control against the cost of administrative overload.

Three key organizational instruments were used to manage an ever-increasing product portfolio (in the 1960s, MEI produced 47,000 different types of products). First, new divisions were created, typically by splitting off from existing divisions. For example, the fourth division was split into three separate divisions (hot plates, washing machines, and electric heaters) in 1956. By this mechanism, the number of divisions increased exponentially, from fifteen in 1956, to twenty-three in 1960 and forty-six in 1967 (MEI 1968: 323).[4] The peak was reached with sixty-five divisions in 1974 (see Table 3.1 for time trends).

Second, in order to manage an ever-increasing number of divisions, some divisions were bundled together into a divisional group (*jigyo honbu*). As soon as the three separate divisions were created out of the fourth division in 1956, they were bundled into a newly created Electrical Divisional Group (Shimotani 1998: 155). From 1963, the practice of bundling divisions into divisional groups was formalized. This three-tier structure—with MEI head office at the top, divisional groups in the middle, and individual divisions at the bottom tier—took root subsequently and was kept until 1997, when divisional companies (*shanai bunsha*) were created to take on the middle tier (more on this later). As shown in the last column of Table 3.1, the divisional groups also grew from just one in 1956 to seventeen in 1972, before they were abandoned and then reintroduced in the 1970s and 1980s.

Table 3.1 Structure of Matsushita Union and Company compared

Year	Union structure			Corporate structure	
	Union members	Number of branches (*shibu*)	Number of branch groups (*rengo shibu*)	Number of product divisions (*jigyobu*)	Number of divisional groups (*jigyo honbu*)
1946 January	7,056	28		—	—
1946 December	10,674	40		—	—
1947	6,498	27		—	—
1948	7,008	28		—	—
1949	6,127	24		—	—
1950	4,012	25		4	—
1951	3,511	23		5	—
1952	4,445	24		5	—
1953	5,544	25		7	—
1954	7,660	26		10	—
1955	8,284	31		10	—
1956	9,418	32		15	1
1957	11,166	33		15	1
1958	15,459	34		14	3
1959	15,350	34		20	4
1960	19,550	34		22	4
1961	23,660	37		25	4
1962	27,850	37		28	7
1963	31,600	38		33	8
1964	32,070	40		35	8
1965	34,180	44		36	8
1966	33,415	44		38	11
1967	34,465	44		46	12
1968	38,602	46		47	13
1969	42,604	46		51	14
1970	51,543	54		57	15
1971	59,574	57		59	16
1972	61,799	58		63	17
1973	62,309	61		63	0
1974	64,662	65		65	0
1975	64,746	66		62	3
1976	60,844	67		61	3
1977	60,600	69		57	3
1978	61,693	70		47	0
1979	62,262	71		48	0
1980	62,914	72		48	0
1981	68,574	72		49	0
1982	75,565	72		49	0
1983	78,823	74		50	0
1984	79,166	72		34	4
1985	83,026	67		35	4
1986	84,902	67		35	4
1987	85,245	67		36	4
1988	85,134	67		37	4
1989	82,541	65		39	4
1990	86,313	59	12	41	5
1991	88,059	59	12	42	5
1992	92,873	67	13	42	5

(*Continued*)

Table 3.1 (*Continued*)

Year	Union structure			Corporate structure	
	Union members	Number of branches (*shibu*)	Number of branch groups (*rengo shibu*)	Number of product divisions (*jigyobu*)	Number of divisional groups (*jigyo honbu*)
1993	94,892	67	13	49	5
1994	93,838	69	15	48	5
1995	92,739	69	15	56	5
1996	90,351	70	15	56	5
1997	87,963	70	15	46	8(4[a])
1998	85,248	71	14	45	4[a]
1999	84,260	71	14	43	7[a]
2000	83,485	68	13		
2001	80,496	68	13		
2002	73,988	65	15		

[a] From 1997, the number refers to in-house 'divisional companies' (*shanai bunsha*).

Sources: For the union figures, Matsushita Electric Union (1997, Data Volume: 13; update 1990–2002 from Matsushita Union). For company figures, MEI (2000), and *Yuka Shoken Hokokusho* (Reports to the Ministry of Finance).

Third, MEI spun off some key internal product divisions into affiliated hived-off companies (*bunsha*). There were six such companies, which are as follows.

(1) Matsushita Electronics, established in December 1952 as a 70:30 joint venture with Philips, by hiving off the fifth product division (which in itself was created in 1951 by spinning off from the then first product division).

(2) Matsushita Communication Industrial, established in January 1958 by spinning out the Communications Product Division.

(3) Matsushita Electronic Components, established in January 1976, by hiving off jointly ten product divisions and a number of other regional companies.

(4) Matsushita Industrial Equipment, established in January 1977, by hiving off jointly two product divisions and other operations including a research laboratory.

(5) Matsushita Housing, established in January 1977 by hiving off jointly five product divisions and a research laboratory (this company was absorbed back into MEI in 1995).

(6) Matsushita Battery, established in January 1979, by hiving off six product divisions and a number of other affiliated companies.

These six companies, together with the focal firm MEI, constituted the core of the Matsushita Group until the late 1990s.

There was corporate restructuring at least once every decade at Matsushita. In 1972, the divisional group system (*jigyo honbusei*), formalized less than a decade earlier, was scrapped. This was because the divisional group's strong command-and-control style was considered to be undermining managerial incentives at the level of individual divisions. But in reaction to the first oil shock, MEI had another attempt at consolidating at the mezzanine level, with the introduction of three general divisional groups (*sokatsu jigyo honbusei*). As the economy recovered, this system, however, was scrapped in 1978, when all the forty-seven divisions came under the direct purview of the MEI president (Shimotani 1998: 157–8). But no one person could oversee so many divisions at once. Consequently, in the late 1970s, with the abolition of the divisional group system, several divisions were bundled together and hived off as a subsidiary. But in turn, some of the hive-offs themselves, notably Matsushita Electronics and Matsushita Communications, also proliferated their own divisions and adopted divisional groups.

The 1980s saw the reintroduction of divisional groups. In 1984, a three-year management campaign, called ACTION 61, was launched with a view to 'achieving a transformation from a consumer electronics manufacturer to a full-line electronics manufacturer' and 'strengthening the management capability and profitability of existing business operations' (Shimotani 1987: 82–3). During this campaign, thirteen out of the thirty-four existing product divisions were classified into four divisional groups, namely for television sets, video equipment, audio equipment, and electrical goods. Divisional groups were reintroduced so as to enable managers to make more agile decisions in an age of fast technical change, diversified customer needs, and the internationalization of operations. By devolving some responsibilities to the divisional groups, the MEI head office slimmed down from 1,300 to 600 employees, and focused on group-wide strategic issues.

By the 1990s, the MEI headquarters functions were well established in marketing, overseas operations, personnel, public relations, law, corporate planning, finance, and R & D, whilst the product divisions took responsibility for product design, manufacturing, and sales. Nevertheless, the number of divisional groups kept on increasing, as MEI adopted a strategy to grow its business in information technology (IT) and prefabricated housing. The four divisional groups in the mid-1980s grew in 1991 to five (for television sets, audio and video equipment, IT equipment, consumer electrical goods, and air conditioners), and in 1997 to eight (consumer

AVC, system AVC, IT, AVC device, consumer electrical goods, air conditioners, housing, and motors).

In part to thwart this trend in the growth of divisional groups, April 1997 saw major restructuring, with the creation of four 'divisional companies' in AVC, electrical goods and housing, air conditioning, and motors. 'Divisional companies' is Matsushita's official label for *shanai bunsha*, although the Japanese phrase may be translated more literally as 'in-company hive-offs', which bring out the oxymoron inherent in the label. This is Matsushita's version of the so-called *kanpanii-sei* (internal company system), noted in Chapter 1 as a fashionable 1990s organizational reform to push for greater autonomy for internal product divisions.

This new system of 'divisional companies' was rather like divisional groups to the extent that it rationalized the number of divisions. Thus, thirty out of the forty-six existing divisions were bundled into four divisional companies in 1997, whilst the rest (sixteen divisions) remained stand-alone, reporting directly to the MEI head office. But the system also

Table 3.2 Core of Matsushita Group (as of March 1998)

Company name	Capital (in million yen)	Per cent owned by MEI	Date established
Focal Company			
Matsushita Electric Industrial	209,416	n.a.	
Divisional companies			
AVC Company	(not		April 1997
Home Appliance & Housing Electronics Company	disclosed)		April 1997
Air Conditioner Company			April 1997
Motor Company			April 1997
Hive-offs			
Matsushita Electronics[a]	41,000	100.0	December 1952
Matsushita Communication Industrial[b]	28,856	56.4	January 1958
Matsushita Electronic Components	23,012	99.0	January 1976
Matsushita Industrial Equipment	3,000	100.0	January 1977
Matsushita Battery Industrial	10,500	97.8	January 1979
Affiliates			
Matsushita Refrigeration Company	11,942	51.8	November 1972
Kyushu Matsushita Electric[b]	29,845	51.1	April 1951
Matsushita Seiko[b]	12,092	59.0	August 1962
Matsushita Denso System[b]	1,500	67.2	July 1970
Matsushita Kotobuki Electronics Industries[b]	7,907	57.7	November 1969

[a] Became three separate divisional companies, Semiconductor Company, Display Device Company, and Lighting Company, in April 1999.
[b] Made into 100% subsidiary in October 2002, in preparation for the January 2003 restructuring.

Source: Company reports and website.

provided an opportunity to redraw the focal firm's boundary through *de facto* vertical integration of technologies considered of great potential for future product development. In particular, three divisional companies (in semiconductor, display device, and lighting) were newly created by bringing the operations of Matsushita Electronics (the first hive-off created in 1952) in-house in April 1999.

Thus, in 1999, there were three ranks to the core of the Matsushita Group: the 'divisional companies' in-house, the hive-offs, and major affiliates (such as Matsushita Denso System Ltd. and Victor Company of Japan Ltd.). At this point, two questions were pending for Matsushita management. The first is what has changed materially by making a divisional group into a 'divisional company', which after all remains an internal unit of the focal firm. The answer lay in greater authority given to the divisional company head, compared with the group head. In the past, a divisional group head was no more than a coordinating boss, merely overseeing the process of individual divisions submitting and negotiating a business plan with the headquarter. But with the divisional company, it is that unit that is in charge of business planning, budgets, and accounts. The corporate headquarter also monitors the performance of divisional companies, not individual divisions within each.

The other question relates to the difference between hived-off companies (created earlier during the 1950s up to the 1970s) and 'divisional companies'. Officially, 'divisional companies' are to be treated as if they were separate companies, whilst they are also to benefit from technological exchange internal to the focal firm at the same time. But in reality, the ambiguity in the distinction between 'divisional companies' and hived-off companies presaged the next organizational restructuring to come.

3.1.4 Dismantling of the Divisional Structure?

Soon after MEI's president Yoichi Morishita gave way to Kunio Nakamura in June 2000, the latter announced a three-year medium-term business plan, called Creative 21 Plan. The burst of the dot.com boom, combined with intensified competition from the rest of Asia, led to Matsushita's failure to fulfil its projection on mobile phone and device sales. The plan was formulated in full knowledge of likely losses, which amounted to a consolidated operating loss of 211.8 billion yen in the 2001/2 financial year, the largest in Matsushita's history. Nakamura set out to create what he called a Schumpeterian dynamic of 'destruction' in the year 2001, leading to 'creation' from 2002 onwards. The 'destruction' phase involved not only 10,000 voluntary redundancies (Nikkei 2002: ch. 6), but also top

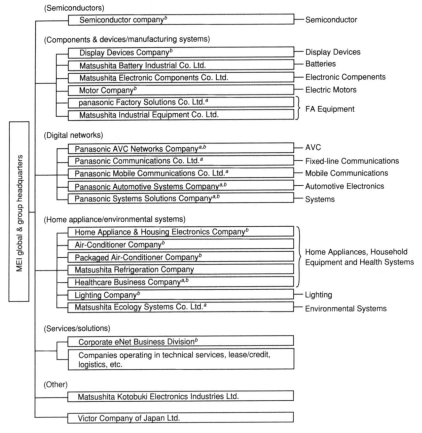

Figure 3.1 Matsushita's new organizational structure (effective 1 January, 2003)

Source: Press release 'Matsushita Announces Specifics of New Group Units' 30 October 2002, on website http:// *www.matsushita.co.jp* (accessed 2 December 2002)

management brainstorming fundamentally to rethink the role of the divisional structure.

The result was a strong reassertion of the functional (i.e. U-form) logic in organizing. In particular, domestic factories that belonged to a specific division were consolidated into a so-called Factory Centre that competed for business from various divisions. Moreover, the sales and marketing channels were centralized, away from product lines, into two main brands, namely Panasonic and National. Gone were the days when divisions were made to compete with each other internally for similar businesses. In the name of efficiency, the plan also set out to eliminate overlaps in business areas between divisions and subsidiaries.

Also, product classification was subjected to a fundamental review as a way of identifying a new corporate structure. References were made to the so-called Smile Curve with profitability being higher both upstream (in devices) and downstream (in system solutions) than in the middle (in appliances and equipment). The transformed corporate structure, adopted in January 2003, is one with five key business areas, in semiconductors, components and devices, digital networks, home appliance and environmental systems, and services and solutions (see Figure 3.1). The first four business areas are classified into fourteen 'domains', some of which are further broken down into strategic business units. In total, there are twenty-two separate units, of which twelve are internal divisional companies or divisions, whilst the others are subsidiaries or affiliates.

In order to arrive at this structure, five companies were made into 100 per cent subsidiaries of MEI in October 2002, in order to facilitate further rationalization through merging or splitting these companies. They were Matsushita Communication Industrial (56.4 per cent), Kyushu Matsushita Electric (51.1 per cent), Matsushita Seiko (59.0 per cent), Matsushita Kotobuki Electronics Industries (57.7 per cent), and Matsushita Denso System (67.2 per cent) (with the percentage held by MEI just prior to this subsidiarization shown in brackets). Subsequently, seven new companies were created in January 2003, three of which are in-house 'divisional companies'. For instance, the main part, but not the whole, of Matsushita Communication Industrial was turned into Panasonic Mobile Communications Co. Ltd. Also, Matsushita Denso System and Kyushu Matsushita Electric were merged to form a company called Panasonic Communications & Imaging Ltd. With these changes, several operating units changed their status between being in-house 'divisional companies', hived-off companies, and other affiliates.

As is familiar by now, organizational restructuring was again accompanied by the reform of the headquarters functions in April 2001. The reform separated out the corporate strategic function (in formulating strategy and monitoring group companies) from the provision of professional services (in human resource management and accounting). Some of the latter are to be outsourced (Nakamura 2002: 46). The head office is also charged with the effective use of group-wide resources in order to spearhead initiatives that require collaboration from different parts of the company. Digital camera was such an example, leading to the successful launch of the LUMIX model.

3.1.5 Affiliates, Sales Outlets, and Suppliers: Defining Broader Boundaries of Matsushita's Business Group

Before the 1997 restructuring, MEI, as the focal firm of Matsushita Group, had treated the five hived-off companies as the internal core of Matsushita Group, jointly employing around 40,000 regular full-time workers. Recruitment for these hive-offs has been managed centrally by MEI, which allocates workers to them. There are five further key affiliates that eventually became part of this core in the 2001 reform (see Table 3.2).

This subsection gives a brief account of the much broader definition of the Matsushita Group, which is frequently employed to refer to a corporate web of affiliates, sales outlets, and suppliers. The Matsushita Group incorporates 700 or so affiliates, with around a quarter of a million employees worldwide. The total number of affiliates grew steadily over time, from 70 in 1955, to 332 in 1965, 656 in 1975, and 671 in 1991, before declining somewhat to 646 in 1997 (Shimotani 1997: 8). The 1960s increase is in part due to the construction of regional manufacturing companies in order to secure labour from outside Osaka's metropolitan area. Most were newly created subsidiaries, whilst a minority were acquired from locally based firms. Matsushita Kotobuki Electronics Industries, for instance, was created on the island of Shikoku as a joint venture between a local entrepreneur and MEI in 1969. The introduction of the consolidated accounting system in the mid-1970s led companies, including Matsushita, to declare their subsidiaries more comprehensively, leading to an apparent acceleration in the total number (Shimotani 1997: 8).

There are two groups of players that do not show up in the above list of subsidiaries because they have no share ownership links with MEI, but nevertheless are considered part of the Matsushita corporate family. One is in wholesale and retail distribution, and the other is in production. Matsushita is renowned for its strong network of wholesale agents (*dairiten*) and retail shops (*renmeiten*). Wholesale agents tended to have exclusive dealings with Matsushita goods (sold under National or Panasonic brand names), and each had a list of retail shops that signed up to deal with that agent. Retail shops were given the status of 'National Shop' if their performance in the exclusive sales of Matsushita goods was considered satisfactory. Moreover, since the late 1950s, MEI started establishing wholesale companies (*hanbai gaisha*) with exclusive territories, owned typically by Matsushita and a wholesale agent jointly. Over time, independent wholesale agents (*dairiten*) were replaced by these affiliated wholesale companies. But the rise of supermarkets and discount shops, as early as the 1970s, threatened this *keiretsu* structure of exclusive dealings, as the proportion of consumer electrical goods sold through these alternative channels rose from 15 per cent in 1972 to 50 per cent by 1985 (Shimotani 1998: 203). In 1990, Matsushita consolidated the sixty wholesale companies into twenty-eight, and set up a nationwide network of sales support offices (known as Matsushita LEC (Life Electronics Corporation) for retail shops. The year 1994 also saw the establishment of a subsidiary, Matsushita Consumer Electronics, to consolidate the nationwide network of wholesaling to discount shops, into one company.

In manufacturing, there were 6,000 or so subcontractors who supplied materials or undertook assembly work for one of the core Matsushita companies (see Shimotani 1998: ch. 6). Of the 6,000, around 600 accounted for 80 per cent of total purchasing expenditure. MEI planned to reduce the total number of suppliers to 3,000 in 2002 and 2,000 in 2003, by making divisional companies (rather than divisions) responsible for selecting suppliers. Typically, their stocks and shares are not owned by Matsushita companies, but they are heavily dependent on Matsushita Group for business. Within the group, subcontractors have been referred to as co-prosperity companies (*kyoei gaisha*) since 1961. A supplier association, Kyoeikai, was established for just under 300 key subcontractors in 1970 with a view to improving their technological and managerial capabilities. As the criteria for membership—100 or more employees and 20 million yen or more in sales to Matsushita—indicate, nearly all these subcontractors are small and medium-sized enterprises. As assembly subcontracting shifted overseas, especially to China, Kyoeikai member companies declined dramatically, from 346 in 1984 to 161 in 2002.

Summary

Matsushita's strategy had long been to market a diverse range of household goods at affordable prices. The extension of this logic led to an ever-diversifying product portfolio involving not only consumer electronics, but also devices and system solutions. In order to implement this strategy, Matsushita adopted a multidivisional form of organization from the 1930s. But the head office never let go of controlling specific functions (notably finance and personnel), and reasserted its centralized control over other functions (e.g. sales, technology, and manufacturing) at regular intervals.

As product diversification progressed, the company avoided administrative overload by relying on three interrelated instruments of organizational reform. First, MEI created new product divisions by spinning out existing divisions. Second, divisional groups (and later 'divisional companies') were created as a mezzanine level, to oversee groups of divisions. Third, divisions (and later divisional groups) were hived off as affiliated companies, which became part of the Matsushita Group. Despite these decentralizing devices, MEI's head office has remained strong, and divisions' and hived-off companies' policies cannot be understood without reference to the head office's close watch over their business plans. The strength of MEI headquarters is manifested in the 2001 strategic review, which led to the tighter vertical integration of hived-off companies in key technologies such as electronic devices and telecommunications.

Whilst it is recognized that decentralization and centralization are not necessarily conflicting concepts in management, it is the constant rebalancing of the two that has led to Matsushita's organizational restructuring at frequent intervals. Konosuke Matsushita, the founder, advocated managers to be a master of simultaneously reinforcing strong divisional autonomy and horizontal coordination between divisions. He stated: 'I think that the essence of divisionalization is whether or not horizontal coordination is managed well or not' (Nikkei 2002: 19, quoting an internal corporate journal in 1973). Certainly in the first decade of the twentieth-first century, Matsushita Electric's head office is promoting more horizontal coordination of this type in technology and product development.

3.2. Strategy and Structure of Matsushita Unions

Having reviewed the corporate side of the story, this section provides the perspective of labour unions at Matsushita. The focal union at Matsushita was highly centralized to reflect a strong headquarters in strategy making on the management side. This structural mirroring did not avoid clashes between the union's strategy and managerial thinking, leading to a contest in drawing organizational boundaries. Three areas of labour–management contests are analysed in turn, namely (*a*) the nature of labour–management consultation; (*b*) the extent to which the focal union can extend its boundary to organize employees at affiliates; and (*c*) the multi-divisionalization and the eventual breakup of the focal union. We also trace the changing role of the focal union in Matsushita Roren, the federation of unions organized at Matsushita's affiliated companies. Since unions were not legal entities until 1945, our review starts from the period after the Second World War.

First, from an early stage, the union developed a desire to participate in the head office's managerial decision-making, whilst managers intended only to consult labour. Despite this difference, and even after a period without a collective agreement, the subsequent practice of worker participation has given workers an effective voice in strategic issues. Second, whenever product divisions were hived off as independent companies, the focal union argued successfully for the extension of the existing union boundary to incorporate these new companies. Clash occurred when the union attempted to extend this practice to other affiliates that were either newly created or acquired. But after years of negotiation, the union's view prevailed in the mid-1980s. Third, having organized twenty-eight separate companies into a single unified focal union, Matsushita Union developed a multidivisional structure, not only to mirror the corporate structure, but also to prevent its own internal administrative overload. Soon after the company announced corporate restructuring in 2003, the focal union took the opportunity to speed up the process of decentralization by breaking it up into fourteen separate unions federated under a *roren*.

3.2.1 Enterprise Union from the Start; Strong Desire to Participate in Management

The main strategic decisions that labour leaders at Matsushita had to make in 1945 were (*a*) the level of hierarchical ranks at which employees should become union members, and (*b*) at what level of company organization (factory or enterprise) the union should be organized. Both issues were subject to debate within the preparation committee to launch the Matsushita Union. With respect to the first issue, some leaders (e.g. Shigeo Yamamoto at Matsushita Shipbuilding) argued in favour of separate unions for blue- and white-collar workers, but a view of a single union for all employees up to section chiefs (*kacho*) won out. Section chiefs remained members until the 1949 revision to the Trade Union Law excluded them for representing the interest of management. As for the second issue, Matsushita Union consciously chose the enterprise level. As noted in Chapter 2, factory unions were quite common at other companies (notably Hitachi and Toshiba) at the time. But labour leaders at Matsushita felt that such fragmentation would be disadvantageous, given the concentration of decision-making power in the hands of the owner-manager, Konosuke

Matsushita. In effect, he owned all of the Matsushita factories and operations, and he controlled all decisions concerning their future. Combining this realization with the union leaders' desire to participate in managerial decision-making led to the conclusion that a single union should incorporate employees at all establishments and subsidiaries.

The move to organize workers started immediately after the war. Encouraged by the GHQ's democratization policy, over 400 unions blossomed in Japan by the end of 1945. At Matsushita also, labour leaders, some novices, and others with pre-war experience began to prepare for a union. In the meantime, after the dissolution of Sanpo, the wartime corporatist organization, Konosuke Matsushita wanted to revive the pre-war friendly society, Hoichikai (established by him in 1920), and entrusted Kenji Kondo (a section chief who was transferred to the head office) with this mission. The hope was to substitute the friendly society for a labour union. But Kondo was a believer in all employees developing an organization for themselves, and was not in favour of a friendly society imposed from the top. He tried to persuade Konosuke of the need for a labour union—Konosuke remained adamantly opposed—and soon abandoned the work for Hoichikai. He then joined forces with labour leaders, including Kenzui Asahi, a blue-collar leader who became the first president of the Matsushita Union.

Just as in other companies at the time, Matsushita Electric retained a feudalistic status distinction between workers (*koin*) and staff (*shain*). Workers were paid a daily rate while staff were paid a monthly salary. Pay differentials were very large, and in some factories, there were separate entrances for workers and staff. It is not surprising, therefore, that early organizing drives at the grass roots were for separate blue- and white-collar unions. Both Asahi and Kondo were alarmed by this trend. Asahi thought, and Kondo concurred, that: 'Until the war ended, everyone believed that staff were on the company's side. But now we must do things with the staff and borrow their strength. Otherwise it would be difficult to carry out a big mission, such as to reconstruct the company and the country' (Matsushita Union 1966: 22). In order to reduce the distance between workers and staff, Asahi and Kondo proposed the abolition of the status distinction. Konosuke Matsushita was rather pleased with this proposal, which he believed would prevent the formation of radical worker-only unions, and incorporated it into the revision of the payment system in November 1945.

Although this helped to reform the feudalistic atmosphere in the company somewhat, labour leaders continued to debate the pros and cons of limiting the membership of such a union to shop floor workers. In fact, local momentum and opposition to an all-employee union led to the formation of establishment-level union organizations at shipyards and electrical machinery factories of Matsushita Konzern. Notable amongst them was a blue-collar union formed at Matsushita Shipbuilding under Shigeo Yamamoto leadership. Despite these moves, fierce debates within the preparation committee finally led to the view that all non-managerial employees should be organized into a single union.

In January 1946, 3,000 union representatives from Matsushita operations all over Japan gathered at Osaka's Nakanoshima Public Hall to found the Matsushita Industrial Labour Union (Zen Matsushita Sangyo Rodo Kumiai). By April 1946, all the establishments and subsidiaries of MEI were organized into forty-two branches with around 10,000 members (Matsushita Union 1957: 3). But the first major reorganization of the union structure came within seven months, when Matsushita Electric was deemed a Zaibatsu and was ordered by GHQ to abandon its holdings of subsidiary shares. The existing union was forced to dissolve itself formally, and a new Matsushita Electric Industrial Union was formed in January 1947 with twenty-eight branches (down from forty-two branches in April 1946). Membership fell from over 10,000 in late 1946 down to around 6,500. When ex-subsidiaries became independent companies, ex-union branches became independent unions. These unions were at such companies as Matsushita Denko, and later became federated as Matsushita Roren, a federation for unions at Matsushita Group companies.

Matsushita union leaders at the time were, by no means, ideologically homogeneous. But no one seriously questioned the wisdom of treating the entire Matsushita corporate group as the boundary of a unitary union organization. This structure, however, did not imply that the union branches (*shibu*) were passively taking orders from the centre. In fact, the 1950 annual conference saw a fierce debate over whether or not branches should be allowed to call a strike (Matsushita Union 1966: 175). In a tenth anniversary history of the formation of the union, one of the leaders reminisced that 'unlike now, the union was not so centralized, and each branch, with fresh memories of actually starting a union organization on its own, was very independently minded' (Matsushita Union 1957: 44)). But the overall consensus for a group-wide single union was reinforced by two related factors, namely the union's strategy to be deeply involved in the management of the company and the concentration of group-wide managerial power in the founder, Konosuke.

The Matsushita Industrial Labour Union demanded that it participate in managerial decision-making from the start (Matsushita Union 1957: 4). This was not the sort of checks and balances that the union might demand in the Anglo-American industrial democracy, but the sort that grants equal say to workers and management in the running of the company by granting co-decision and veto rights to workers. Workers' desire to institute this type of workplace democracy was fuelled by the union's call to abolish feudalistic status distinction between workers and staff, and to evict undemocratic top managers who subjected workers to oppressive discipline during the war. After a series of negotiations with management, the first collective agreement was signed in October 1946, which set up a Management Council (*keiei kyogikai*), formally endorsing the union's right to voice its views on management.

At the June 1947 Management Council meeting, management proposed a lay-off of 567 employees in order to weather the economic crisis. The union fiercely opposed this first post-war sacking attempt and forced management to withdraw its proposal. They were successful in forming a Matsushita Electric Reconstruction Study Committee consisting of seven managers and seven union leaders, to jointly consider the redeployment of workers (Matsushita Union 1957: 5). With the implementation of the Dodge Plan in 1949, however, management again proposed to lay off 890 workers (around a fifth of the total Matsushita Electric workforce) and to close the Osaka factory (Matsushita Union 1957: 7). This time, despite negotiations, the management won, laying off 900 or so union members and closing a number of factories including the Osaka factory (Matsushita Union 1957: 7).

In this climate of closures and redundancies, the MEI collective agreement was allowed to expire, and no new agreement could be established until 1956. The Trade Union Law was revised in 1949. Clause 15 of this law—stating that once expired, a collective agreement cannot be automatically renewed if one party objects to it—gave MEI management an excuse to repudiate the agreement that had bound them to obtain union approval for firings, transfers, and other personnel matters (Ohara 1952: ch. 7). The reassertion of managerial prerogative at Matsushita, as elsewhere in Japan, led to annulling the collective agreement in October 1949 (Matsushita Union 1957: 4).[5]

The disagreements between the company and the union were specifically over the following issues (Matsushita Union 1966: 296).

(1) The union wanted a union shop agreement, whereas management insisted on open shop.

(2) The scope of union membership: management insisted on excluding all security guards and all personnel department employees.

(3) Co-decision over factory closures, temporary shutdowns, mergers, hive-offs, downsizing, etc.: management wanted to concede notification only.

(4) The management council (*keiei kyogikai*): management wanted to replace it by joint consultation meetings (*roshi kondankai*) and a grievance procedure.

(5) Co-decision over all personnel matters (including redundancies): management preferred one-way notification.

(6) Wages and salaries: management wished to freeze pay for the duration of a multi-year collective agreement.

(7) Union activity within working hours: management wished to restrict it severely.

For the first few years, management saw the situation of no collective agreement as an advantage to them. Nevertheless, at the union's insistence, a total of seventy bargaining sessions ensued, but the company's stance guided by Nikkeiren (the Japan Federation of Employers' Associations) did not budge. The union branches then voted in favour of a 24-hour strike in October 1955, and the strike went ahead. One key point of disagreement until the last moment was on the management's right to manage around points 3–5 in the above list. In an attempt to thwart the strike, management first conceded to 'co-decision over firings due to company's management policy'. Once the strike started, it made a concession to the 'notification of personnel transfers and co-decision if the union has objections' (Matsushita Union 1966: 412–5). At last, in early 1956, a new collective agreement was signed at Matsushita, an entire decade after the previous one came into existence.

The 1956 collective agreement at Matsushita was a somewhat emasculated version of the 1946 agreement in so far as the union's voice in managerial decision-making was concerned. Instead of reviving the 1946 management council, the union had to acquiesce to a labour–management consultation committee (*roshi kyogikai*). This committee, however, evolved into a forum where union members voiced their views on issues of corporate strategy as much as on operational issues. A labour–management consultation forum is likely to become ritualized if it starts and ends with the union merely listening to management's presentation of its plans. Matsushita Union realized this danger, and in 1957, established a management countermeasure (*keiei taisaku*) committee as an advisory body to the union head office (Matsushita Union 1966: 613–14). The committee called upon various managers and supervisors to gather up-to-date information on corporate restructuring (e.g. hive-offs, reform of the sales network). The committee of union representatives then met to debate on a specific theme, and formulated concrete proposals in management policy at the divisional and subsidiary company levels.

Two decades of the Matsushita Union nurturing its capability to gather information and to make proactive suggestions towards management policy paid off in 1978, when the company agreed to formalize the system of participation in management strategy (*keiei sanka*) (Matsushita Union 1997: 149). This system enables the union to participate even more pro-actively in the process of management's strategic decision-making. A key institution in this system is the Management Council (*keiei iinkai*) (not to be confused with the 1940s Management Council (*keiei kyogikai*), which is a closed-door discussion forum between the company president and the top three officials of the union. By its very nature, it is difficult to give examples of how and why this forum is effective, but the union leaders who were interviewed valued this as an indispensable channel of communication, and a hallmark of Matsushita Union that distinguishes itself from other enterprise unions in the same sector.

3.2.2 Sansha Kyotei: Retaining a Single Union when the Company Hived off Divisions

We now turn to the second area of labour–management contest, namely the union's organizational responses to the corporate practice of hiving off internal divisions. The process of hiving-off potentially undermines union membership, particularly when the predominant form of union organization is enterprise-based. The Matsushita Union responded to this threat by negotiating that employees who had worked in internal divisions but were moved to hived-off companies should retain membership of the same union. Moreover, new employees recruited by the hived-off companies also became members of the same union.

Initially, the union's strategy was not so incompatible with the interest of the company, as the early hive-offs in electronics and telecommunications required the recruitment of high-quality workers and technologists for advanced technology. But the union's strategy to extend its boundary beyond hived-off divisions to regionally based production subsidiaries led to a clash of interests, with management wishing to benefit from lower regional wages for less-skilled routine production work.

As noted in Section 3.1, the first hived-off company was Matsushita Electronics, a joint venture with Philips. Matsushita Union agreed to this hive-off on the following four conditions (Matsushita Union 1966: 283):

(1) The joint venture shall not undermine Matsushita Electric's autonomy or suppress labour union activities.

(2) Existing employees who are to be transferred to the newly created joint venture company shall have an identical set of terms and conditions as set out in the collective agreement between MEI and the Matsushita Union.

(3) New employees to be hired by Matsushita Electronics should be seen as being on transfer from MEI.

(4) The employees of Matsushita Electronics should be members of the Matsushita Union, which shall remain a single unified organization.

The management of both MEI and Matsushita Electronics approved these conditions, and in 1952, an agreement was signed by the three parties concerned, namely the management of the two companies and the Matsushita Union. Remember that 1952 was still a time when no broader collective agreement existed between MEI management and union. When such an agreement was finally signed in 1956, the three-party agreement (*sansha kyotei*), which had hitherto been solely about identical terms and conditions of work, was extended to all terms in the collective agreement (Matsushita Union 1966: 419). This three-party agreement (*sansha kyotei*) came to be applied to subsequent cases of hive-offs. The employees of each hived-off company with such a collective agreement were then organized into a union branch (*shibu*). Thus, an enterprise union that draws its members from several legally independent companies was born out of this agreement.

Strictly speaking, the three-party agreement formally states that all employees of the companies with such an agreement (known as *sansha kyotei gaisha*) are to be recruited directly by a single company, MEI, which then allocate them to various hive-offs. These employees' contracts are with MEI, and their assignments (*haizoku*) are like internal job transfers. The ultimate 'employer' for all the members of the Matsushita Union is therefore MEI, regardless of their place of work. However, the fact that there exists a three-party agreement at all, which in effect recognizes the independence of subsidiary management from Matsushita Electric management, means that the immediate employer to whom employees can express their collective voice is the subsidiary management. The three-party agreement negates the right of the subsidiary company-level union organization (i.e. union branch) to collectively bargain over wages, hours, and all individual and collective issues that go into a collective agreement. The same collective agreement that is negotiated between MEI management and the union applies automatically to all companies with three-party agreements. But it still necessitates, and encourages, the union branch to obtain subsidiary-level management information so that it can effectively participate in strategic decision-making at the subsidiary level.

In 1985, the Matsushita Union signed a new type of three-party agreement (known as *shin sansha kyotei*) for group companies other than those that had been internal product divisions. For the Matsushita Union, this was the outcome of a long-fought battle since the 1960s. These companies were regional production companies set up by local entrepreneurs that were subsequently acquired by Matsushita, such as Matsushita Kotobuki Electronics Industries (Matsushita Union 1997: 168–70). As early as in 1966, the first so-called new regional union branch (*shin chiho shibu*) was established at one of the Kotobuki factories. They paid the going rate in Shikoku where they were located, which was lower than the Osaka-based MEI rates. The union organized them as union branches, not separate unions, with a policy to strive for three-party agreements in the future. By 1982 there were twenty such new regional union branches.

The 1980s also saw MEI's product divisions and hived-off companies establish their branch factories in the regions. Management initially had wished to hive off these factories as separate companies, but the union successfully opposed this. Thus, an anomalous situation was arising, in which employees at branch factories benefited from MEI conditions whilst those in regional companies in the same area did not. For example in Okayama Prefecture in West Japan, Matsushita Electronic Components, an old three-party agreement company, established Sashu Factory to make magnetic tapes, in commuting distance from Tsuyama Matsushita Electric, a regional company. The wages at Sashu were higher than at Tsuyama.

In 1983, MEI's motor division facing financial pressure decided to move the production of motors to Takefu Matsushita Electric, a regional company. This shift gave the union an opportunity to argue that Takefu's strategic position was similar to that of a branch factory, and successfully negotiated an identical set of labour conditions for the Takefu workers.

This presaged the concerted bargaining at all twenty new regional union branches in the autumn of 1985, which eventually led to the successful signing of the new three-party agreement. It took the union twenty years to obtain what they wanted. But management eventually gave in, presumably judging that the cost of continued disagreement would be too high.

The newness in the new three-party agreement is marked by the fact that although the wage rates are identical (amazingly) with the old three-party agreement companies, the company concerned is not a hive-off. It is also marked by the fact that the subsidiary company hires their employees locally, unlike for the old three-party agreement companies for whom hiring is centralized at MEI. This means that these employees are not asked to be on assignments beyond the bounds of a regional company. Moreover, some of the terms and conditions may differ slightly from the main collective agreement between Matsushita Electric and the Matsushita Union. Typically, the differences take the form of the non-application of some of the terms and conditions in the main agreement, such as welfare provisions and shift work patterns.

In 1997, there existed 28 three-party agreements, of which 19 were of the new types. In effect, there were twenty-eight limited companies, which were partially or wholly owned by Matsushita Electric, whose employees were organized into a single enterprise union. Over time, the Matsushita Union membership expanded from around 7,000 in 1947 to a peak of 90,000 (of whom half were MEI employees) in 1996, as did the number of branches from 28 in 1946 to 70 in 1996 (see Table 3.1).

3.2.3 Matsushita Roren: Sales Unions are In, Subcontractor Unions are Out

Apart from those hived-off and other companies whose management is bound by a three-party agreement, there are key Matsushita affiliates whose unions have come to form a networked *roren* organization. It is evident that the formation of a *roren* federation was in response to affiliated unions' desire for a group-wide solution to employment security and improvement in labour conditions. In drawing the boundary of the *roren*, both management and labour at Matsushita had a consensus that whilst unions at retailing outlets should be kept under close observation (and therefore part of the *roren*), unions at subcontractors should be kept out of the *roren* for having vastly different (i.e. inferior) conditions.

The origin of Zen Matsushita Roren may be traced back to 1956, when five enterprise unions at Matsushita Denko, Matsushita Reiki, Matsushita Seiko, Matsushita Boeki, and National Tire got together at the Matsushita Union head office for an informal coordination meeting (Zen Matsushita Roren 1996). By September 1966, this gathering grew to include twenty unions with 50,000 members, and formed a Committee of Matsushita Group Unions (Shorokyo). The mid-1960s were marked by the strengthening of *keiretsu* groups by many companies that wanted to defend themselves from the onslaught of the liberalization of international trade and capital markets. The greater formalization of the union organization from a coordination meeting to a committee may be interpreted as a labour response to tighter managerial control over the Matsushita Group. Although the outward appearance was autonomous management of separate companies and product divisions, it was perceived that everything moved according to the will of Konosuke Matsushita. Ultimately, strengthening union coordination was all about matching the level at which management's right to manage was exercised at the time.

In 1970, Keiichi Takabata, the Matsushita Union president at the time, put forward an ambitious vision for a confederation of Matsushita unions, Sorengo, that went well beyond the Shorokyo federation of only twenty unions at the core affiliated companies. The idea was to establish a large organization of enterprise unions at all Matsushita-related companies, including affiliates, subcontractors, and sales companies, an organization large enough to be a political force to unite the fragmented left-wing political parties in opposition at the time. Here, the large size in itself was attractive to achieve such a political end. The most obvious target for union expansion was in Matsushita's operations both upstream and downstream from the manufacturing operations. In particular, the Matsushita Union decided to pour resources into organizing the National brand retail shops downstream, in order to pre-empt leftist unions' attempts to target them. Consequently, two new union networks were founded in 1973, one for twenty unions at subcontracting companies (known as Shokan Rokyo) and another for fifty-eight unions at Matsushita sales companies (known as Hanroren).

Subsequently, Sorengo, encompassing the biggest possible boundary for an enterprise-based union, remained as a proposal to be discussed, but was abandoned by 1977. By 1985, the Plaza Accord led to the sharp appreciation of the yen and the fear of the hollowing out of the Japanese economy. Everyone at Matsushita felt the threat of job loss, and looked for a corporate group-wide response to securing employment. In response, Shorokyo established a Future Vision Committee in order to consider how it might be strengthened as a union organization. The committee posed two issues: first, why did the 1970 idea of Sorengo fail; and second, what did affiliated unions expect out of Shorokyo?

The diagnosis of the past failure was as follows: First, smaller unions had great expectations for Sorengo, but large unions saw little merit in it and even feared the undermining of their autonomy. Second, some Matsushita unions questioned whether the affiliation as a Sorengo group to Denki Roren, the industry-level federation, would be a good idea; in particular, this posed difficulty for some affiliated unions that already belonged to other industry-level federations such as Zenkin, the metalworkers federation. Third, affiliated unions wanted to retain the autonomy of enterprise-level industrial relations, and feared that it would be undermined by the formation of Sorengo. Fourth, it was thought that a clear future vision for the Sorengo movement was absent.

Through such reflection of past shortcomings, Shorokyo came up with the following five main items for a future agenda:

(1) that employment security is the most important issue for the Shorokyo labour movement;

(2) that members expect improvements in welfare and labour conditions;

(3) that there is an increasing need for union participation in managerial policy-making on a group-wide basis;

(4) that union members are demanding services that exploit the economies of scale of Shorokyo; and

(5) that Shorokyo must improve the overall living standards of members by strengthening its political and local activities.

In October 1989, Shorokyo was replaced by a tighter *roren* federation, Zen Matsushita Roren, with a view to implementing two concrete policies, the setting up of Matsushita Minimum Standards and a Matsushita Group-wide joint consultation system (see Section 3.3).

As of 2003, Zen Matsushita Roren (Matsushita Roren for short) is a federation of thirty-one enterprise unions headed by the Matsushita Union. The total membership stands at around 150,000, half of whom belong to the Matsushita Union. The other thirty unions may be classified into three groups: the largest six that are based at Matsushita affiliates (namely Matsushita Denko, Matsushita Refrigeration Company, Matsushita Seiko,

Kyushu Matsushita Denki, Matsushita Denso System, Victor Company of Japan); the twelve non-manufacturing unions; and the ten manufacturing unions. The sole criterion for affiliation to Matsushita Roren is that MEI owns the capital of the company at which a union wishing to affiliate is located. A minimum of 30 per cent ownership by Matsushita was mentioned as an informal rule of thumb. Unions that affiliated recently are in non-manufacturing sectors, such as financial services and software development. A major mechanism for developing candidate unions for affiliation is through organizing subsidiaries created by hived-off companies bound by a three-party agreement. For example, unions at West Denki and Toyo Denpa, both 100 per cent owned by Matsushita Electronics, are part of the *roren*.

Zenkoku National Hanroren (a grouping of 107 unions with 18,600 members at National Shops, the retailing outlets) is part of Zen Matsushita Roren, while Shokan Rokyo (with 20 unions and around 3,700 union members at key subcontractors) remains a separate organization. The latter was kept separate because the gulf in labour conditions between members in Matsushita Roren and Shokan Rokyo was considered too big to be bridged easily. This is an instance in which the interests of the focal union insiders and corporate management matched to keep the subcontracting workers out of the corporate and union boundaries.

3.2.4 Decentralization and the Breakup of the Multidivisional Union

The Matsushita Electric Union, although its membership declined from 90,000 in 1996 to 67,000 in 2003, is still the second largest enterprise union in Japan after the NTT Union. Apart from the size, the multiple companies that it organizes raise questions about the union's internal structure. How divisionalized is the Matsushita Union? How has the union coped with the administrative overload that comes with the growth in its size? And how centralized or decentralized is its internal governance? Is the degree of centralization determined only by the union's desire to mirror the corporate structure, or also by other considerations?

In the late 1990s, the union was organized into seventy branches (*shibu*), which in turn were classified into fourteen branch groups (*rengo shibu*). This consolidation of branches into groups was implemented in 1990, and was an attempt by the union head office to make coordination of an ever-increasing number of branches easier. At the same time, some of the headquarter responsibilities were devolved down the line to branch group offices, in particular the responsibilities for negotiating over rest days, some aspects of work hours (e.g. shift patterns, flexitime), and joint consultation over changes involving personnel transfers within the branch group arena (Matsushita Union 1990: 42). Thus, the introduction of *rengo shibu* in 1990 was not merely to reflect the three-tier corporate structure. It also facilitated a separate decision by the focal union, to start introducing a degree of decentralization in the union structure.

There has always been a rough correspondence between the company organization and the union organization, but more so since 1990. At the lowest level, the union branch (*shibu*) has typically taken the product division (*jigyobu*) as the unit of organization. As explained in Section 3.1, MEI reintroduced the three-tier structure in 1984, with headquarters, divisional groups (*jigyo honbu*), and product divisions (*jigyobu*) constituting the tiers. The Matsushita Union set up a committee to report on organizational reforms for the union in 1984, at the time that the managerial organization was being transformed through its ACTION 61 campaign. Although the union took a further six years to implement the structural reform, the changes applied to the union organization paralleled the changes in the management organization.

When the company created 'divisional companies' in 1997, the Matsushita Union responded by creating a branch group (*rengo shibu*) for each divisional company. According to the Matsushita Union president during 2002 and 2004, Yasuhiko Osamura:

It is natural for the union to try and match the management organization—to form a union branch group that corresponds to a new *bunsha*. This is because we have a system in which the union is quite involved in management decision-making. Once every month or two months, there are management council meetings and labour–management consultation meetings, at which labour can voice their views on management issues. So it is quite self-evident that the union must have a matching set of bodies to meet the management side at each level of the corporate organization.[6]

Thus, the union's need to mirror the management organization arises out of Matsushita Union's specific strategy in managerial participation. A divisional group, a divisional company, and a hived-off company are all treated at par by matching with a union branch group as the corresponding organization.

The 2003 corporate restructuring led to further rethinking of the focal union's internal structure, as it challenged the existing boundary between the focal union and Matsushita Roren. This is because as noted in Section 3.1, three affiliated companies (Seiko, Kyushu Matsushita Denki, Matsushita Denso System) were fully integrated into MEI. But unions at these companies belong to Matsushita *roren*, and are not part of the Matsushita Union. The corporation has therefore undermined the distinction between a branch group of the Matsushita Union and a separate union affiliated to the *roren*. In this situation, should this distinction be maintained or not? What should be the difference between the two?

Such questions led, in the Matsushita Union's 2003 annual conference, to a resolution to break it up into fourteen separate unions, each covering one of the fourteen business 'domains' defined by management (*Asahi Shinbun*, 10 September 2003). This structure will be adopted from 2006, and will give each union the right to negotiate over most conditions, as well as the right to call a strike. The fourteen unions will then become the core within Matsushita Roren. The breakup of the focal union heralds the death of a powerful inter-firm union that lasted for half a century. It is ironic that union decentralization was triggered by the company's move to refocus its business (hence recentralization in certain functions like technology and product development). In effect, although there is a general climate of decentralization in the Japanese industrial economy, the logic of decentralization for Matsushita's focal union appears to have come from within, as its organizational scope grew beyond a manageable size to maintain appeal for its membership.

3.3. How Corporate and Union Strategies Affect Labour Market Outcomes

Having spelt out the ways in which the corporate and union structures are derived from the interaction of respective strategies, this section examines specific ways in which those structures influence some key processes and outcomes. Here, we focus our discussion on (*a*) the impact of the extension of the focal union boundary to three-party agreement companies on the structure of the extended internal labour market, and (*b*) the role of Matsushita Roren in setting minimum standards and in facilitating intra-group movement of workers. It is argued that three-party agreements lasted for a few decades because they rested on incentive compatibility between the union and management, rather than because the union had an upper hand over management in drawing the boundary of the firm.

The union wanted uniform labour conditions as that was a mission most unions aspired to fulfil. The company management recognized that applying an identical human resource system to a core set of affiliated companies made sense for the efficient deployment of employees. The uniformity of labour conditions gave Matsushita Group the advantage of being able to move employees from one company to another according to demand fluctuations and company needs.

As discussed earlier, the instrument of 'three-party agreements' has extended the coverage from the focal firm, MEI, to as many as twenty-eight related companies encompassing 80,000 members. This means that the Matsushita Union headquarters negotiates the basic wage and bonus increases with the MEI management, on behalf of all the twenty-eight company management and labour representatives. Once a settlement is reached, the identical pay increase is applied to the same base pay levels to all the three-party agreement companies. Thus, a Matsushita factory worker in a low-cost location is paid exactly the same as a worker in metropolitan Osaka. Consequently, Matsushita Kotobuki Electronics Industries in Shikoku or Kyushu Matsushita Electronics in the southern island have been paying wages well above the local going rates for factory workers. What is remarkable about the MEI collective agreement is that it has been not merely pay and bonus but all other terms and conditions in the collective agreement that have been identical for all three-party agreement companies. They include such matters as working hours, shift patterns and premia, welfare provisions, and pensions.

The extended internal labour market that was created as a result of the three-party agreements gave MEI large scope for flexibility. Historically, the MEI head office hired all accounting and personnel management staff centrally for group companies in order to exercise management control. In the post-war period, as hive-offs were created, all university graduates and high school graduates were centrally hired by MEI, which then allocated new recruits to one of the old three-party agreement companies.[7] The latter companies did no direct hiring of these core categories of workers, relying on MEI's clout and reputation to attract better quality applicants than if they had hired directly. These employees, be they managerial track employees in various functions, engineers and technologists, or factory workers, could be asked to move from one hived-off company to another.

From the 1970s to 2000, an average of just over 8 per cent of all regular employees with over one year of service moved from one hived-off company to another every year. In the 1990s, for which internal company data are available, inter-company mobility (i.e. movement from one three-party agreement company to another) was higher, as expected, for personnel managers, accountants, and general managers, all at around 15 per cent per annum, than for those employed in sales (9 per cent), technology (6 per cent), or manufacturing (7 per cent). Thus, until recently, the uniform conditions within the extended internal labour market left open the option of flexible job assignments, often with geographical mobility. This mobility had the dual function of protecting employment security for regular workers and of facilitating technology transfer from mature to newer segments of Matsushita's diversified product portfolio.

More recently, however, there is less employment security and also less expectation of mobility between companies or locations. The fragmentation of the internal labour market through the decentralization of collective bargaining, though tempered still by an identical base wage system, will constrain the company's ability to redeploy workers when different sectors face differential business cycles. This theme will be discussed in greater detail in Chapter 8.

Outside the boundary of the focal union, the thirty or so unions affiliated to Matsushita Roren coordinate their wage and bonus negotiations closely, and settle soon after the focal union reaches a settlement. From 1991, Matsushita Minimum Standards have been set as targets for all affiliated unions to negotiate, so that their conditions would approach the MEI level in the near future. The Minimum Standards cover not only wage, bonus, premia (for overtime, night shift, etc), and work hours, but also pensions, retirement age, and other welfare and recreational provisions. Thus, the *roren* has clearly had a role in harmonizing labour conditions and standardizing personnel systems at companies of various sizes, as small as with fifty employees in some cases.

Apart from coordination among unions belonging to the *roren*, labour–management consultation at the *roren* level enhances its function in securing employment within the *roren*. In particular, as an extension of the Matsushita Union's participation in top-level management issues, Matsushita Roren (in effect, the presidents of affiliated unions) holds a non-public meeting with MEI top managers on a regular basis. This might be an occasion for smaller unions, such as at Shinto, to ask the MEI personnel director to give greater consideration to the sort of people MEI sends to affiliated companies as president; some MEI managers may work well in a large company setting but may not be so competent in leading a small company.

The forum may also be used to gauge the future of affiliated union members' job security. Matsushita Roren is known to have attempted to mediate movements of workers between companies through this forum. For example, in 1991, management at Matsushita Denso System (an affiliated company listed in Table 3.2) proposed to close its factory in Okayama, which was accumulating losses producing fax machine components. The union at the company, an affiliate of Matsushita Roren, responded that if a resolution within the company was not possible, it would be seeking a Matsushita Group-wide solution. At the union's request, Matsushita Roren set up a committee, and with the agreement of the Denso management, made efforts to find MEI internal divisions and other affiliated companies that might make use of the factory. In this case, the *roren* exhausted all possibilities, and the Denso Union in the end had to acquiesce to the factory closure in 1995.

Summary

The Matsushita case gives a clear indication of the utility of the SSI framework. First, corporate strategy affects its preferred structure. Second, union strategy affects its preferred structure. But third, it is the interaction between corporate and labour strategies that accounts for the realized structures and processes.

The company pursued a strategy of related diversification, and chose to create new divisions, bundle divisions into divisional groups, and to hive off divisions or divisional groups into affiliated companies. The resulting structure was half-functional and half-divisional, but the weight put on this mix fluctuated as the corporate head office tried to steer between relative autonomy of divisions in periods of steady growth and tight centralized control in periods of distress (caused either by war or by loss-making). Compared with other companies in the sector, however, Matsushita remained a relatively centralized company in strategy formulation, corporate finance, and personnel management.

The union recognized the centralized nature of corporate strategy and structure from the start. Consequently, the focal union chose the enterprise as its boundary, and extended it successfully through three-party agreements whenever internal divisions were hived off. The proliferation of these agreements was clearly the union's (but not management's) preference. The union also chose to be deeply involved in worker participation, and despite setbacks in the 1949–56 period, was able to revive and maintain its voice in strategic managerial issues.

By the 1990s, an 'inter-firm' union capturing as many as twenty-eight legally separate companies was suffering from bureaucratic burden, despite divisionalizing its internal structure. It is through this internal pressure that the focal union decided to break up into fourteen separate unions, just at a time when the focal firm recentralized and re-integrated some hived-off companies for the purpose of implementing its 2003 restructuring plan. Thus, the structural characteristics, summarized in Figure 3.2, with the focal union capturing within its boundary all the internal divisions, divisional groups, hived-off companies, and some affiliates, is about to be revised fundamentally.

The consequences of these structural changes are dealt with in Chapter 8. In this chapter, we concentrated on the relative stability of the criteria for corporate and union boundaries for half a century, which we argued was due to the compatibility of incentives. For unions, extending the boundary within which a uniformly good set of conditions applied was desirable as it signalled success for the focal union and the *roren*. For managers, it had the benefit of being able to move employees from company to company, either for transfer of know-how or to satisfy areas of labour shortage by shifting from areas of excess labour. A breakdown in this consensus for a homogeneous human resource system for the Matsushita Group is signalled by both corporate reforms and union reorganization.

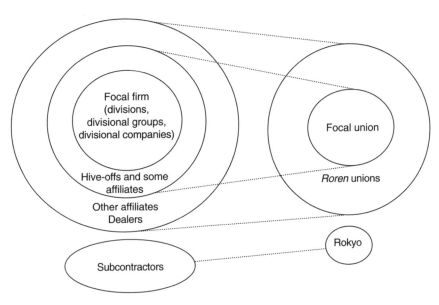

Figure 3.2 Comparing corporate and union boundaries at Matsushita Group

Notes

1. This is very similar to the situation in major US companies. In the Introduction to the 1990 edition of *Strategy and Structure*, Chandler wrote: 'Whereas before World War II the corporate offices of large, diversified, international enterprises rarely managed more than 10 divisions, the largest only 25 or so, by 1969 companies were operating as many as 40 divisions, some even more. For example, in that year the corporate offices of Borg-Warner, General Electric, and Bendix—firms whose products had some distant relationship with one another—administered 37, 46, and 53 divisions, respectively. Among the conglomerates—enterprises that grew wholly by acquisition of companies in unrelated industries—Gulf & Western administered 35, Textron 32, Walter Kidde 55, and Litton 70.'

2. Du Pont introduced the M-form in 1921, with seven to ten divisions during the 1920s and 1930s (Chandler 1962: ch. 2; Chandler 1991). There is no way of telling whether Konosuke knew of the developments in the United States (Kagono 1997: 64). In comparison, however, it is surprising that Konosuke felt the need for a multidivisional form with a mere 1,200 employees (cf. Du Pont employed 31,000 and General Motors just over 80,000 in 1920 (Chandler 1991: 50)). Perhaps Matsushita Konosuke anticipated, rather than felt, the management overload that would result from a strategy of product diversification.

3. The term 'division' or 'product division' is used throughout to refer to this organization unit at Matsushita. But as this account makes clear, the actual scope of functions contained within such as 'division' varied over time.

4. As a comparison, GE set up seventy autonomous product departments each with its own production, marketing, and engineering units in the 1950s. These were placed into divisions that, in turn, were administered by one of five groups (Chandler 1962: 369). In the late 1960s, GE had 190 product departments, 46 divisions, and 10 groups (Chandler 1991: 43).

5. The expiration of collective agreements was a widespread problem in Japan. The timing of the revision of the Trade Union Law coincided with Dodge Plan-induced dismissals and factory closures, for which management at many companies insisted they had the prerogative to decide without consulting their union. Thereafter, it was slow for new collective agreements to be signed. In May 1950, 44.9 per cent of union members and 37.2 per cent of unions had an agreement. In December 1952, only 55 per cent of union members and 57 per cent of unions were covered by an agreement.

6. Interview with Yasuhiko Osamura on 19 July 2002.

7. Under the new three-party agreement companies did their own recruitment. Over time, MEI devolved to old three-party agreement companies the recruitment of high school graduates around 1980 and that of technical college graduates from 1996, but their employment contract is with MEI head office.

4

Strategy and Structure at Toyota Group

This chapter traces developments in the interaction between Toyota Motor Corporation's (TMC) strategy and Toyota Union's strategy. TMC is Japan's largest and the world's third largest car manufacturer, offering a full range of models, from small passenger cars to large trucks. Besides its twelve plants in Japan, Toyota has fifty-six manufacturing companies in twenty-seven overseas locations, producing Lexus and Toyota brand vehicles. As of March 2002, Toyota had 355 domestic subsidiaries and 209 overseas subsidiaries, jointly employing 246,700 people worldwide. Although Toyota has significant international presence, this chapter is limited to a discussion of the domestic scene within Japan. Automotive business, including automotive sales and finance, accounts for more than 90 per cent of the company's total sales, which was 15.1 trillion yen in the 2001/2 fiscal year. The rest are diversified operations in telecommunications, prefabricated housing, and leisure boats.

As in Chapter 3, Section 4.1 outlines how TMC came to be as it is today, focusing on its corporate strategy and structure, starting with the textile machinery business from which the automotive business grew. Section 4.2 traces the origin of Toyota Union in factory-based organizations that became consolidated later at a time of deep corporate restructuring. It also looks at some of the key management–union interactions, both at the focal company level and at the level of the corporate group, before turning to the development of unions at two major suppliers, Toyota Automatic Loom Works and Aisin, in Section 4.3.

Compared with Matsushita, Toyota has a more focused product strategy in automobiles. Consequently, its organization has been primarily functional, with management focus on the implementation and the diffusion of the so-called Toyota Production System (TPS) at its factories and component suppliers. Toyota's focal union is a textbook-type enterprise union. Its strategy has been to improve conditions on the shop floor. The focal union boundary, covering the focal firm only, is narrower than at Matsushita. But Toyota's *roren*, covering around 100 supplier unions and nearly 180 dealership unions, is much broader than Matsushita's *roren* (see Figure 4.1).

These differences between Toyota and Matsushita boundaries are explained in part by differences in product type and the extent of diversification. Toyota by and large has focused on the production of vehicles with a manageable range of models, whilst Matsushita has a larger portfolio of electrical and electronic products. This difference led Toyota to choose a more functional structure, in contrast to Matsushita's multidivisional structure. Moreover, close coordination with suppliers is of central importance in manufacturing cars, which are more complex than electrical or electronic products. Consequently, component suppliers are deemed to be more a part of the core of Toyota's business group than Matsushita's.

At the same time, a difference in union strategy is also significant. Toyota Union's interest lay more squarely in improving working conditions and management methods on the shop floor—*genba*—at the heart of Toyota's corporate culture. By default, and due also to management stance, Toyota Union has less voice in managerial decision-making compared with Matsushita Union. The union and the *roren* focused their energy on seeking steady improvements in pay by contributing to modernizing management on the shop floor, particularly at owner-managed supplier companies. But this shop floor focus became inadequate since the 1990s when corporate restructuring came to involve dispersed factory locations and product diversification.

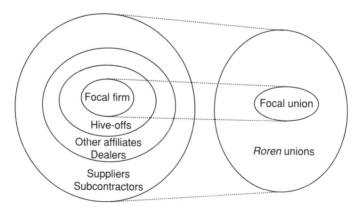

Figure 4.1 Comparing corporate and union boundaries at Toyota Group

4.1. Strategy and Structure of Toyota Motor Corporation

Toyota's strategy and structure are notable in the following respects. First, the original textile machinery business was superseded by the automotive business, leading to the child company (Toyota Motor Co.) (TMC) usurping from its parent (Toyoda Automatic Loom Works) the position of a focal firm heading a corporate group. Second, compared with MEI, the business of Toyota's focal firm has remained undiversified, concentrated around the design, production, and sales of passenger cars. Third, component suppliers, many without any shareholding links to TMC, are an important part of the Toyota group.

To explain how these structural characteristics came about, this section traces the corporate history with attention to five key periods during which Toyota group's strategic direction and structure changed: (*a*) the 1930s diversification into automobiles, (*b*) wartime integration and consolidation in the 1940s, (*c*) refocusing on automobile production in the immediate post-war period, (*d*) strengthening the functional organization during the rapid growth period, and (*e*) limited exploration into product diversification since the 1990s. The evolution of Toyota's structure is important for understanding not only the development of the business group, but also the influence it has had on Toyota Union's structure. As in Chapter 3, the key contribution of this chapter is in clarifying the ways in which the evolution of corporate strategy and structure influenced, and was influenced, by, union strategy and structure.

4.1.1 Diversification Strategy: From Textiles to Automobiles in the 1930s

Sakichi Toyoda and his son Kiichiro, the founders of the textile machinery and automobile businesses, respectively, had one thing in common, namely the mentality of an inventor with a preference for in-house technological development and constant innovation. Sakichi had to fight against commercial interests to reserve funds for R & D, and this experience shaped his preference for internal business expansion with tight family control.

From the time Sakichi Toyoda succeeded in taking out his first patent for a manually operated wooden loom in 1891 to the time a licensing agreement was signed with Platt Brothers of Britain for Toyoda's G-type automatic loom in 1929, he had a clear objective: to secure enough funds towards inventing better looms. Sakichi's early commercial activities were directed to this end. In 1895 he founded Toyoda Shoten to sell a yarn-reeling machine that he had invented, 'thinking of inventing a machine which would be simple and have a high sales potential so as to generate research funds' (Toyoda Boshoku 1996: 6). But he soon realized that invention and commercial profit making were not easily reconcilable goals and decided to withdraw from the latter. As a commercial enterprise, Fujihachi Ishikawa a local financier, helped establish the first weaving factory using Toyoda's power looms. But as output grew, Sakichi realized the difficulty of carrying out experimental research in a factory managed as a commercial enterprise. Hence, he sold his share of this company and set up his own experimental factory.

This episode was repeated on a larger scale, when in 1899, Mitsui established Igeta Shokai to manufacture the looms, after signing a ten-year agreement with Sakichi for the exclusive rights to his power looms. At first, the company prospered, but when the recession following the Sino-Japanese War hit the company, its research budget was cut, and Sakichi resigned his position as chief engineer in 1902. He returned to his firm, Toyoda Shoten, and turned it into a limited company, Toyoda Loom Works, in 1907. But again, Sakichi's desire to maintain a large research budget led to a conflict with other investors, and he resigned from the company in 1910.

By now suspicious of outside capital, Sakichi raised his own financing in 1911 for a cloth mill, named Toyoda Automatic Weaving Factory. In improving his automatic looms, he encountered the problem of not being able to distinguish the cause of yarn snapping, between a defect in the loom and bad-quality yarn. To tackle this problem, Sakichi resolved to establish his own spinning operations with the financial help of Mitsui managers, Kamenosuke Fujino and Ichizo Kodama.[1] In 1918, the company, now consisting of both spinning and weaving operations, was renamed Toyoda Boshoku (Toyoda Spinning and Weaving Co.). While becoming a limited company with 5 million yen capital, all shares were controlled by the Toyoda family and its close allies (Toyoda Boshoku 1996: 19). At the time, it employed 1,000. Subsequently, when Toyoda's G-type automatic loom was perfected, Toyoda Boshoku decided to hive off its automatic loom division as an independent manufacturing and sales company. This was Toyoda Automatic Loom Works, founded in 1926 with 1 million yen capital, 60 per cent of which came from Toyoda Boshoku (Toyoda Boshoku 1996: 34).

The Great Depression in the 1920s affected the Toyoda companies badly. The number of machines sold by Toyoda Automatic Loom Works fell by 35 per cent from a high of 4,132 units in 1928 to 2,590 units in 1929; then in

1930, sales fell to a mere one-third of the 1929 figure (Wada and Yui 2002: 203). They launched a programme of rationalization and diversification, notably by founding Shonaigawa Rayon Company, and Chuo Boshoku, a joint venture company with Toyo Menka. By 1935, the Toyoda Group consisted of eight companies headed by Toyoda Boshoku, with a total capital of approximately 35.6 million yen, employing 12,800 workers (Toyoda Boshoku 1996: 45). The eight companies were as shown in Table 4.1.

It was in the recessionary climate of the late 1920s that Kiichiro entertained doubts about the future of the cotton and textile machinery industries and developed an ambition to go into the automotive business. This idea appears to have already entered Kiichiro's mind during his travels to the United States and Europe, ostensibly to sell the use of the Toyoda Automatic Loom Works' patents, but also to study assembly-line production and precision machining (TMC 1988: 39; Mass and Robertson 1996). As soon as he returned, an automobile research room was secretly set up inside the machine shop at Toyoda Automatic Loom Works in 1930. Experiments in making the Smith Motor to power bicycles were soon bearing fruit, as were attempts at making high-grade cast iron, using an electric arc furnace, to produce cylinder blocks for future automobiles as well as the automatic loom frame. Conquering these technical challenges led the Board of Directors of Toyoda Automatic Loom Works to decide to add to its operations the manufacturing of automobiles in 1933. Thereafter, Chevrolet-like cars were built at an experimental factory within the grounds of Toyoda Automatic Loom Works in Kariya from 1934, leading to the first trial model of the A1 passenger car and a G1 truck in 1935. Then in 1936, Kiichiro established an automobile research laboratory in Shibaura in Tokyo, and the first mass production assembly plant in Kariya to produce the Model AA passenger car and the Model GA

Table 4.1 Toyoda Group companies around 1935

	Year of establishment	Employees	Capital (thousand yen)
Toyoda Boshoku	1918	4,218	15,600
Toyoda Automatic Loom Works	1926	2,020	6,000
Toyoda Boshoku Shanghai	1921	4,370	5,000
Toyoda Oshikiri Spinning and Weaving	1929	496	2,000
Toyoda Spinning and Weaving Kikui Factory	1918	300	Unknown
Chuo Boshoku	1929	504	3,000
Shonaigawa Dye Factory	1928	185	1,000
Shonaigawa Rayon Company	1932	711	3,000

Source: TMC 1967: 16.

truck. Toyota reached this stage of development without any licensing agreements with existing auto manufacturers.

Toyota Motor Co. Ltd. (TMC) was founded in August 1937 with a capital of 12 million yen. The promulgation of the Law Concerning the Manufacture of Motor Vehicles in 1936 made automobile manufacturing a government-controlled industry; production was allowed only with government permission. It was evident that only a limited number of domestic companies would be authorized to produce automobiles. Thus, Toyoda Automatic Loom Works rushed into the incorporation of TMC before Komoro plant was completed, although this plant's capacity was necessary to meet the government production target of 3,000 units per month for Toyota. Toyota was also spurred on by the success of Tobata Foundry Co. to facilitate a merger of truck makers (Ishikawajima Automobile Works and DAT Automobile Manufacturing Co.) to manufacture the small Datsun passenger cars as early as in 1933 (Wada and Yui 2002: 237). Moreover, ongoing merger talks amongst Platt Brothers, Toyoda Loom Co., and Toyoda Automatic Loom Works, though it did not result in any merger, must have made the Toyoda family focus their mind on the success of their next core business in automobiles (Wada and Yui 2002: 228).

4.1.2 Wartime Integration and Consolidation

TMC responded to the start of the war in 1939 and a complete stop to the flow of imported vehicles and materials in two major ways, which enabled it to scale up vehicle production.

First, as the internal organization expanded rapidly, TMC added one more layer—section (*ka*) between department (*bu*) and subsection (*kakari*)—to the management hierarchy, in order to limit the span of control of each manager. At this time, all department heads were also directors. At the same time, functional departments were redefined, by separating out the accounting department and the purchasing department to strengthen TMC's ability to manage funds and materials. Moreover, TMC merged production and process technology departments into a manufacturing department, within which a section was created for each process such as casting and forging (TMC 1967: 167). Thus, TMC remained essentially a functional organization.

Second, TMC decided to address problems related to the quality of automobiles by vertically integrating upstream. Most immediately, these problems were traced back to the quality of steel and machine tools. The expectation that the domestic (or overseas) market would eventually deliver these inputs was crushed by the wartime exigency. Thus, Toyoda Steel Works (later known as Aichi Steel Works) was established in 1940 by consolidating the steel mills that belonged to the Steel Works Division of Toyoda Automatic Loom Works. Just as with vehicle production, steel production was also restricted to those with government permission under the Law Concerning the Manufacture of Steel. TMC would not have been able to benefit from this law had steel production remained part of an operation for automatic looms (TMC 1967: 199). Similarly, in 1941, the Machine Tool Department of Toyota Motor Co. Ltd. was hived off to establish Toyoda Machine Works, again so as to obtain government approval under the Law Concerning the Manufacture of Machine Tools (TMC 1967: 199–226; Monden 1983: 51; Wada and Yui 2002: 296). Thus, Toyota's hive-off structure evolved because of legal requirements, not because of its strategy for product diversification as such.

Product diversification occurred also, however, within the framework of the government's Munitions Companies Law promulgated in 1943. First, at the request of the military government, Tokai Hikoki Co., an aircraft manufacturing joint venture with Kawasaki Aircraft Co., was established in 1943.[2] Second, just before the end of the war, Toyota Auto Body Co. was created to manufacture truck bodies, as the military government finally approved what TMC had wanted to do since 1940 (TMC 1967: 226).

In the inter-war years, the relative fortunes of the textile and automobile sectors changed in Japan, as elsewhere. By the 1940s Toyota's textile operations were forced to contract while automobile production expanded. However, the corporate structure to manage this decline in textiles was controlled by the military, whose intention it was to rationalize the spinning industry by forming larger blocs of companies and closing smaller firms (Toyoda Boshoku 1996: 61). This meant that within Toyota Group, Chuo Spinning Co. was established in 1942 by merging Toyoda Boshoku with two other Toyota companies (Toyoda Oshikiri Spinning and Weaving and Chuo Spinning and Weaving). Then in 1943, again by government fiat, the merged company became part of TMC, so as to focus on munitions production (TMC 1967: 212). In effect, Toyoda Boshoku was acquired by its grandchild company, TMC. This firmly established automobile manufacturing as the main business of the Toyota Group. During the war, however, automobiles were restricted to trucks, and the three main factories (Kariya South, Kariya North, and Nakagawa) inherited from the textile business were all converted to aircraft-related production.

As the war drew to a close, TMC was engaged in the production of trucks and aircraft totally for military use. Production was also controlled by the military, whilst Kiichiro was responsible and accountable to them. Apart from six internal factories, the Toyota Group also had three hive-offs (Toyoda Steel Works, Toyoda Machine Works, Toyota Auto Body) and one joint venture (Tokai Hikoki). In 1942, Toyota Finance Ltd., established in 1936 to engage in hire-purchase business, was renamed Toyoda Sangyo and made into a holding company for the Toyota Group.

4.1.3 Post-war Refocusing on Automobiles by Hiving off Nippondenso and Toyota Sales: 1945–52

At the end of the war, TMC was capitalized at 91.5 million yen and had six plants: the Komoro plant, Kariya plant, Shibaura plant, and the three aircraft plants that had been part of Chuo Spinning Co. Komoro and Kariya plants were engaged in making military trucks, while Shibaura plant, originally established as a research laboratory, was engaged in storage battery research, the inspection and testing of externally procured parts, and the building of special vehicle prototypes. The three aircraft plants were in Kariya North, Kariya South, and Nakagawa. Of these, GHQ gave immediate permission for the following four factories to resume civilian production: Komoro plant to make trucks and truck components, Kariya South and North to make auto components, and Nakagawa factory to engage in the production of various parts including radiators, exhaust pipes, and pumps. Thereafter, TMC eliminated the manufacturing and sale of aircraft from its article of incorporation at the November 1945 shareholders meeting, thus placing automobiles as *the* core business of TMC.

As early as in 1946, TMC had an internal management plan, to hive off the sales, electrical parts, and textile operations so that the company could refocus on its core auto business. However, it took five years for TMC to realize this objective due to government restrictions and policies. In particular, the Zaibatsu dissolution and the 1949/50 financial difficulties influenced the future direction of management and union structure. These are discussed in turn.

IMPACT OF ZAIBATSU DISSOLUTION

TMC was not listed officially as a Zaibatsu. But in anticipation, the 1945 TMC shareholders' meeting appointed presidents and vice-presidents of group companies other than Kiichiro Toyoda and Risaburo Toyoda, in order to disperse the concentration of managerial power (TMC 1967: 258). In March 1946, when GHQ revised the Regulations Affecting Restricted Concerns to include more companies, TMC was also designated as a Mitsui-affiliated restricted company.[3] This meant that TMC had to seek the approval of the Minister of Finance and the Minister for International Trade and Industry before implementing any corporate restructuring.

DODGE PLAN IMPACT

Even before the Dodge Plan, TMC was in a financially delicate position, as its borrowing was about eight times its capitalization of 91.5 million yen in November 1948. When the deflationary macroeconomic policies were implemented in 1949, demand for automobiles fell and the price of raw materials rose, plunging TMC into the most unstable period in its history. TMC was making an operating loss of 34.6 million yen in November 1949, increasing nearly sixfold to 198.8 million yen by December 1949. In the midst of this financial distress, the Toyota Union agreed to a 10 per cent wage cut on the condition that management would never resort to redundancies as a means of overcoming corporate crisis. But this promise was soon reneged upon when management announced the retrenchment of 1,600 workers in April 1950, leading to an all-out strike that lasted until 10 June. How this strike and the subsequent labour–management relations were settled is discussed in the second half of this chapter.

Here, we focus on corporate restructuring. In November 1949, the government finally approved the Toyota Rationalization Plan devised by Toyota management in 1946 to hive off three product areas. As a result, in December 1949, the Kariya North factory was hived off as Nippondenso, with 15 million yen capitalization and 1,500 employees, to produce electrical components including radiators. This was followed by hiving off the Nakagawa factory as Aichi Horo, and the Kariya South factory as Minsei Spinning.[4] TMC intended to de-merge these non-automotive business units as early as in 1945, but the long delay caused by the government approval system contributed to financial distress.

By December 1949, TMC, in the midst of huge accumulated losses, was rescued by a group of twenty-four banks headed by Mitui Bank and Tokai Bank that raised sufficient funds to cover the losses for a while. Then early in 1950, a consortium of banks proposed a revival plan, involving amongst other things the separation of the sales operation from manufacturing. TMC had been keen to resume its pre-war hire-purchase plans as a means of improving TMC's cash flow, and was therefore ready to take on this plan. In April 1950, Toyota Motor Sales Co. was established. It took the form of a new company with a new set of shareholders, rather than formally hiving off and handing over the TMC sales operations, which would have been subjected to the long approval process by virtue of TMC being a restricted concern. Toyota Motor Sales (TMS) continued to be a separate company working closely with TMC, until the two were merged in July 1982 as Toyota Motor Corporation.

4.1.4 Managing Rapid Growth by Strengthening the Functional Structure

In late 1949 and early 1950, TMC made only around 1,000 units per month, mostly trucks. From 1947, TMC resumed the production of passenger cars in a small way, and production volume grew at a spectacular rate in the 1950s, from 7,400 units in 1955 to 42,000 in 1960, 236,000 units in 1965, and 1 million units in 1970 (TMC 1988: 461). During the decade from 1955 to 1965, sales turnover grew fifteen times to 123.5 million yen, employees quadrupled from 5,162 to 22,595, and paid-in capital increased from 1.672 billion yen to 38.25 billion yen (TMC 1967: 493).

The most visible part of this rapid expansion was the construction of new plants, starting with Motomachi Plant in 1959. Toyota built Kamigo Plant, Takaoka Plant, and Miyoshi Plant in the 1960s, five new plants (Tsutsumi, Myochi, Shimoyama, Kinu-ura, Tahara) in the 1970s, and two further plants (Teiho, Hirose) in the 1980s. Thus, by the end of the 1980s, there were twelve plants, all located in and around Toyota City, including the oldest Honsha Plant (known earlier as Komoro Plant) that dates back to 1938. In 1992, TMC's domestic production capacity increased further by establishing plants in Kyushu in the south and Hokkaido and Tohoku in the north, although these plants were incorporated as separate companies.

The spectacular scaling up of production in the 1960s was made possible by the implementation of a number of managerial and organizational reforms. Perhaps the most well known is the perfection of the so-called Toyota Production System (TPS), involving just-in-time (JIT), *jidoka* (automatic defect detection), and *kaizen* (continuous improvement) (Ohno 1978; Monden 1983; Fujimoto 1999). This was later lauded as lean production, an alternative paradigm to mass production (Womack et al. 1990). Less well known is the role Total Quality Control (TQC) played in not only the rapid diffusion of TPS across Toyota factories, but also in linking shop floor processes and targets to the policies of higher-level management (Nemoto 1983). TQC systematically instilled top-down and cross-functional coordination within the company. TMC won the Deming Award in 1965 and set out to work with six other group companies

(Toyoda Automatic Loom Works, Toyoda Machine Works, Nippondenso, Aisin Seiki, Toyota Auto Body, and Kanto Auto Works) to continue its efforts towards 'all Toyota quality assurance'. The synergy generated in the simultaneous application of TPS and TQC in the 1960s was enormous (Shimokawa et al. 1997: 23) (see Chapter 6 for more details).

The 1960s also saw a whole series of organizational reforms to strengthen top management's decision-making capacity. TMC President Tatsuzo Ishida (who took over after the death of Kiichiro Toyoda in 1952) gave way to Fukio Nakagawa in 1960, just when Japanese markets were being opened up for international trade. This concentrated the minds of TMC's top managers, for whom the image of foreign giants taking on the Japanese market was combined with the fresh memory of Toyota's financial crisis a decade earlier. The issue at hand was how to make agile and timely strategic decisions, whilst at the same time consulting the views of middle and lower managers, when the company was expanding rapidly.

This resulted in three initiatives in the 1960s. First, TMC created a *jomukai*, an executive directors' meeting, to discuss specific policy issues in detail, and seven planning committees (*kikaku kaigi*) in new products, new production lines, production planning, equipment and machinery, cost, make-or-buy decisions, and quality control (TMC 1967: 517). The committees were chaired by board directors, so that the board and committee meetings tended to happen on the same day. Second, as part of the implementation of TQC, corporate policies were formalized, including, for the first time, a long-term (five-year) management plan that spelt out not only production and investment plans but also future sources of profitability. Third, cross-functional cooperation was found to be lacking as each department argued for its own interest only in order to cope with day-to-day demands of mass production. To address this problem, a function-based management system (*kinobetsu kanri*) was in place by the mid-1960s. In this system, around ten managerial functions were identified, for example in planning, quality control, cost control, personnel, technology, purchasing, sales, and production. Each of these functions became the responsibility of a group of directors. At the same time, the headquarters organization consisted of an ever-increasing number of departments (*bu*)—twenty-three in 1960, fifty-four by 1967—each of which was assigned to a director (TMC 1967: 672).

Despite these reforms, TMC remained essentially a functional organization throughout its history. But this structure went hand in hand with great attention given to cross-functional coordination, the essence of TQC. It is the combination of TQC, cross-functional coordination, and the ability of the shop floor to engage in continuous improvement that constitutes Toyota's management system. Thus, lean production on the shop floor is seen as a practice that is part of this larger system.

4.1.5 The 1990s and Beyond: Diversification or Strategic Focus?

Toyota's product strategy throughout the 1950s into the 1980s was focused on pursuing what it does best, i.e. automobile production. As an extension of this strategy, TMC expanded by investing overseas, without much thought for product diversification. But some signs of change started to appear in the 1990s, particularly after the appointment of Hiroshi Okuda as TMC president in 1995.

The second half of the 1990s saw a combination of factors that led TMC to reconsider its strategy. First, domestic competition was getting tougher, not only because of the prolonged recession but also because of threat from competitors, notably Honda. Consequently, Toyota's domestic market share dipped below the 40 per cent target for a few years. Second, part of the reason for this decline in domestic share was attributed to Toyota's image for being sober, sound, and conservative, but neither exciting nor challenging, thus leading to car models that appealed to those over fifty but not to the younger generation. Third, M & A and strategic alliances, most notably the creation of DaimlerChrysler, posed a threat to TMC retaining the third position in the global ranking in the auto industry. In response, TMC under Hiroshi Okuda sought to revive the company in various ways. One idea for rejuvenation was product diversification and the adoption of a pure holding company structure. The discussion over this idea was accompanied by the rhetoric of introducing Western-style 'logic of capital' to supplant the sort of paternalism that had hitherto governed Toyota's business group (*Chunichi Shinbun*, 11 February 1999).

TMC did not adopt a holding company structure, but decided to enter some new markets in the late 1990s. Thus, TMC classifies its operations into seven divisions besides its automotive business, namely in housing, information and communications, financial services, industrial equipment, GAZOO (an Internet site), marine, and biotechnology & afforestation. Each division consists of one or more companies: for instance Crest Homes in housing, KDDI in telecommunications, and Toyota Financial Services Corporation in financial services. Despite such diversification, 90 per cent of Toyota's total sales remain in the automotive business. TMC's financial base is strong, thus evoking the label 'Toyota Bank'. But unlike GE Capital, TMC has extended its car loan business to cover housing loans, insurance, and credit card business only in so far as it promotes TMC's core business in automobiles (Nikkei 1999). Thus, although further product diversification is a possibility in the future, TMC remains largely a company with a functional structure, focused on the production and sales of automobiles.

4.1.6 Development of the Toyota Group

Throughout its history, TMC has drawn multiple rings of inner and outer boundaries in its corporate grouping. Within the group, there are two major groups of companies, one consisting of core TMC affiliates and a second group consisting of supplier companies. The first group is based on shareholding links just as at Matsushita Group, whilst the second group is based on trading links. There is some overlap between the two groups.

The inner core of Toyota's corporate group consists of companies that were hived off or created by group companies. In the post-war period, this inner group has been a relatively stable core of about a dozen companies, including TMC, Toyoda Automatic Loom Works, Aichi Steel Corporation, Toyoda Machine Works, Aisin Seiki, Toyota Auto Body, Nippondenso, Toyoda Boshoku, Toyoda Tsusho, Toyota Central Research Laboratory, and Towa Real Estate (TMC 1967: 683). In the 1960s, the prospect of the liberalization of trade and capital markets led to the strengthening of this inner group to survive international competition. Notably, a presidents' club was established to discuss production plans and long-term strategic plans, an All Toyota Technical Committee to share technological know-how, and the All Toyota QC Coordination Committee to promote the implementation of TQC (TMC 1967: 684). The core shareholding-based group expanded when TMC took an equity stake in Hino in 1966 and Daihatsu in 1967.

Over time, a pattern of cross-shareholding developed amongst these core Toyota affiliates. TMC's ownership of the core group companies often goes hand in hand with the transfer of directors from TMC to these core companies. In the late 1990s and early 2000s, the degree of cross-shareholding and interlocking directorship increased (*Asahi Shinbun*, 13 June 2000). Tighter coordination is considered essential for survival in tough global markets, and Toyota stands out as exceptional in not seeking strategic alliances with other automakers. Moreover, TMC increased its shareholding control over large component suppliers such as Denso and Aisin. This was done in order to ensure the suppliers' allegiance to Toyota, even as their technological capabilities in specific areas have come to surpass those of TMC (Ahmadjian and Lincoln 2001). Table 4.2 shows the core group companies and their shareholding links to TMC, as of fiscal year 2003.

The second type of corporate group at Toyota is based on trading linkages. By far the most significant is the group of component suppliers, often described as 'cooperating factories' (*kyoryoku kojo*). This nomenclature is quite common in other Japanese companies. Nevertheless, it underlies Kiichiro Toyoda's instruction to Toyota buyers to think of the suppliers as their own arms and legs, and thus take care of them by giving technical and managerial guidance (TMC 1967: 692). The most visible of various associational networks for suppliers is the supplier association, Kyohokai. This dates back to 1939, during the wartime control regime, when Kyohokai worked as a materials supply channel to nominated suppliers (Kyohokai 1967: 10). After 1945, Kyohokai's major task turned to upgrading Toyota suppliers' technological and managerial capabilities, spurred on by the prefectural government's free factory benchmarking and advisory service in 1953 (Kyohokai 1967: 24; Wada 1991*a*). The association, for example, became a channel for diffusing TQC. These activities instilled a general sense of solidarity and loyalty between Toyota and its suppliers.

By April 2002, Toyota had expanded its supplier association membership to 211 parts suppliers. They account for 98 per cent of TMC's parts purchasing expenditure. However, these companies are no longer a homogeneous group of locally based 'cooperating factories'. They now include not only those component-making companies whose primary loyalty is to Toyota, but also other firms, including large companies that supply to automakers other than Toyota. As the boundary of the group of suppliers with trading linkages grew, the group became increasingly heterogeneous. Toyota therefore has come to make a more explicit distinction between the inner core of suppliers to whom Toyota's know-how in Toyota Production System is taught, and the rest (see Chapter 6 for more details on supplier development).

4.1.7 Summary

In summary, Toyota Motor Corporation has pursued a strategy to be a top player in the automobile industry. The resulting structure has been functional, giving much regard to cross-functional coordination to facilitate continuous improvement and effective decision-making. TMC has treated the shop floor—*genba*—as central to the effectiveness of its operations, but its success is underpinned by a high degree of top-down and

Table 4.2 Toyota Group companies in 2003

Company name	Main products/ activities	Established	Equity share by TMC (per cent)	Capital (million yen)	Number of employees
Toyota Industries Corporation[a]	Manufacture and sales of spinning and weaving machines, industrial ve- hicles, and automobiles	Nov. 1926	24.67	68,046	9,899
Aichi Steel Corpor- ation	Manufacture and sales of specialty steel and forged steel products	Mar. 1940	24.72	25,016	2,622
Toyoda Machine Works Ltd.	Manufacture and sales of machine tools and auto parts	May 1941	24.98	24,805	4,252
Toyota Auto Body Co. Ltd.	Manufacture of auto and special vehicle bodies and parts	Aug. 1945	47.10	8,871	8,086
Toyota Tsusho Cor- poration	Import, export, and trading of raw materials and products	July 1948	22.99	26,748	2,067
Aisin Seiki Co. Ltd.	Manufacture and sales of auto parts, household appliances, and die-cast parts	June 1949	24.55	41,140	10,305
Denso Corporation	Manufacture and sales of electric auto components and household appliances	Dec. 1949	24.52	173,105	33,998
Toyoda Boshoku Corporation	Manufacture and sales of cotton thread, cotton cloth, auto parts, and household appliances	May 1950	15.56	4,933	2,039
Towa Real Estate Co. Ltd.[b]	Real estate development, management, and rental	Aug. 1953	49.00	23,750	80
Toyota Central Research & Development Laboratories Inc.[b]	Fundamental technical research for the Toyota Group	Nov. 1960	54.00	3,000	895
Kanto Auto Works Ltd.	Manufacture of auto bodies and parts and equipment for housing construction	Apr. 1946	48.95	6,850	5,500
Toyoda Gosei Co. Ltd.	Manufacture and sales of synthetic resin, rubber, and cork products	June 1949	41.79	25,138	5,490
Hino Motors Ltd.	Manufacture and sales of large trucks and buses	May 1942	50.11	72,717	8,693
Daihatsu Motor Co. Ltd.	Manufacture and sales of automobiles	Mar. 1907	51.19	28,404	10,583

[a] renamed from Toyoda Automatic Loom Works.
[b] As of the end of fiscal year 2002.

Note: Data are as of the first half of fiscal year 2003 for each company.
Source: Company website www.toyota.co.jp/Irweb/corp_info/profile/manufac_j.html (accessed April 2003)

cross-functional communication within the company. In many ways, this mode of intense communication extends to Toyota's corporate group, facilitating the diffusion of Toyota's management methods. The group consists of an inner core of companies listed in Table 4.2 with cross-shareholding linkages involving TMC, and a second group of component suppliers that belong to the supplier association, Kyohokai. These boundaries are signposts for union organizing, to which we will now turn.

4.2. Strategy and Structure of Toyota Union

Compared with Matsushita Union, Toyota Union started as a more decentralized collection of factory-based units, has always drawn a narrower boundary for its organization, and has been less involved in managerial decision-making. A major trigger for the shift from factory-level to enterprise-level organization was the Dodge Plan-induced deflation and the resulting need to restructure the company in 1949 and 1950. There then followed a decade of turbulent industrial relations when the union struck in 1950 and then again in 1953, until a peace pact was signed in 1962.

This section goes beyond recounting this drama and focuses on Toyota Union's strategy and its structural consequences. First, the origin of Toyota's labour movement is traced to factory-level activities, but corporate restructuring, particularly the creation of TMS, triggered a move to unite factory unions into an enterprise union. Second, after 1950, the reassertion of managerial prerogative and the absence of a formal collective agreement for two decades resulted in a union with centre of gravity on the shop floor (*genba*) and a weak voice in strategic management decisions. Third, Toyota Roren came to be established in 1972 with its boundary drawn to include unions at supplier and dealer companies. This structure facilitated the diffusion of Toyota Production System and the modernization of suppliers' management and work organization. Fourth, we analyse Toyota Union's response to pressures for internal diversity as the corporation diversifies its locations (e.g. by creating a factory in Kyushu) and its business to non-automotive areas.

The complicated vertical articulation of union organization within the Japanese automobile industry is set out in Chapter 7. Here, it suffices to note that, between 1947 and 1951, Toyota's factory unions affiliated to Zenji, a short-lived industrial union for the automotive sector. Zenji was destroyed and dissolved after a prolonged strike at Nissan in 1953. Thereafter, Toyota Union was a branch of Jidosha Tokai, an interim federation of unions in the central Japan, which then became part of Zenkoku Jidosha (All Japan Federation of Automobile Workers Unions, JAWU) in 1962. This was the major federation for Toyota Union until 1972, when finally a single auto industry confederation, JAW, was established. With the decision to make *roren* the unit of affiliation to this confederation, Toyota Union established its own *roren* federation of enterprise unions, Toyota Roren. Although these developments at the industry level are pertinent, this chapter concentrates mainly on enterprise-level factors that affected the nature of Toyota Union and its *roren*.

4.2.1 From Factory Unions to Enterprise Union in the Aftermath of the Second World War

On 15 August 1945, all wartime production of trucks and aircraft stopped at Toyota factories. Until the GHQ gave permission to resume civilian production at TMC's plants, no one knew whether automobiles would be viable as an industry in peacetime. TMC announced that the company was entering a difficult period and might not be able to pay wages and therefore asked workers to think of their own future (TMC 1967: 234). In summer 1945, the Komoro plant alone had a labour force of around 9,700, but it declined to 3,000 in a matter of a few months as workers left both voluntarily and involuntarily in a mood of confusion, turmoil, and disillusion.

In this situation, workers at Toyota chose the factory as the unit of union organization. Of the six main TMC plants at the time, the Toyota Motor Kariya South Factory was the first to be organized by an employees' union in December 1945. This electrical parts operation was later hived off as Nippondenso in 1949. The union initially resisted the hive-off plan due to the uncertainty over the financial viability of Nippondenso on its own (Nippondenso Union 1996: 33–4).[5] Next, the Komoro plant was unionized in January 1946, laying the foundation of the core of the later Toyota enterprise union. Its mission, according to union documents at the time, was '(a) to build a democratic society by destroying the military, capitalist, and financial cliques; (b) to defend the factory with friendship and solidarity by establishing a basis for organizing workers, and (c) to stabilize people's livelihood by signing a collective agreement, establishing a minimum wage, and enhancing welfare facilities, thus contributing to the healthy development of the union' (Toyota Union 1966: 6).

As at many other Japanese unions, the key debate at Toyota unions initially was over whether factory workers (*ko-in*) and staff (*shokuin*) should join the same union. Given a large gap in status between blue- and white-collar at the time, Communist activists found no difficulty in arguing for an exclusive blue-collar union, by portraying white-collar workers as instruments of capitalism. But through much debate, key individuals in the supervisory middle-management layer at Toyota were instrumental in persuading union leaders to settle for a single employees union, initially with section chiefs (*kacho*) included in the membership (they were subsequently excluded with the revision of the Trade Union Law in 1949).

Amongst the other four TMC plants, Kariya South was in the process of resuming a spinning and weaving operation, and was organized by a union in July 1946 (Toyoda Boshoku 1996: 114). TMC's spinning and weaving department considered it wise to manage industrial relations separate from the automotive department, if it was to obtain the GHQ and governmental approval for its hive-off plan. Thus, apart from its own trade union, a separate collective agreement and a labour–management council for the department were in place by 1947. The Kariya South Factory Union also joined Zensen Domei, the textile industry union federation, in March 1948, preceding the hiving off of the plant as Minsei Spinning by two years. By December 1948, TMC consisted of six factories, each with its own union, as shown in Table 4.3. Of the total of 8,929 workers in TMC, 63 per cent were at the Komoro plant, which accounted for 85 per cent of the company's production capacity by value.

As early as in February 1946, Toyota Group unions formed a Unified Coordination Committee (Toyota Union 1966: 7). In February 1947, six key Toyota Group unions (at Kariya Koki, Automatic Loom Works, Toyoda Auto Body, Aichi Steel Corporation, Toyota Komoro plant, and Toyota Kariya South plant) met to discuss the possibility of forming an all-Toyota union federation. But the voice of those advocating the autonomy of individual unions won out, thus thwarting a path towards a united group-based federation (*Rodo Jiho* (Toyota Union Journal), 19 February 1947). Thus, in December 1949, when Nippondenso was established by hiving off the Kariya Denso factory, the factory union there became Nippondenso Union. The Kariya South factory had a separate union from the Komoro plant, and continued to be a separate union when the corporate hive-off took place. No discussion appeared to have taken place on whether or not the two factories should be covered by the same union.

In December 1949, the Komoro Factory Employees Union agreed to a 10 per cent across-the-board wage cut on the condition that management would not resort to making redundancies. But management soon reneged on this promise due to the deteriorating financial situation and by using

Table 4.3 Toyota Motor Company factories and unions in the late 1940s

Plant name (date of establishment)	Number of employees (Dec. 1948)	Date union was formed	Company name (date of hive-off)
Komoro (1938)	5,640	Toyota Komoro Factory Employees Union January 1946	This became the main TMC factory
Kariya Denso (ex-Kariya North) (1943)	1,298	Toyota Motor Kariya South Factory Employees Union December 1945	Nippondenso (December 1949)
Nakagawa (1943)	700	Zenji chapter existed[a]	Aichi Horo (December 1949); closed April 1949[b]
Shibaura (Tokyo) (1937)	129	Zenji chapter existed[a]	Closed April 1950
Kamata (Tokyo) (1946)	184	Zenji chapter existed[a]	Closed April 1950
Kariya South (1943)	978	Toyota Motor Kariya South Factory Union July 1946	Minsei Spinning (1950) Renamed Toyoda Bohoku (1967)

[a] Date the union was formed is not known.
[b] Two sections (auto repair and printing machine) closed in April 1949. The rest was sold to Aichi Horo in December 1949.
Source: TMC 1967: 264; Toyota Union 1966; Toyoda Boshoku 1996: 115.

the courts to question the legality of the memorandum on which this agreement rested (Gankoji 2003). Toyota announced 1,600 redundancies and the closure of Kamata and Shibaura factories in April 1950, provoking a strike that lasted until 10 June. The end of this two-month strike was marked by the management proceeding with the dismissal notices, some targeted at union activists, and the resignation of Kiichiro Toyoda as company president.

It was in the midst of this strike that Toyota announced its intention to create a sales company. In reaction, the Komoro Factory Union considered it essential to keep a unitary union encompassing both TMC and TMS and passed a motion to this effect at its annual conference in September 1950. The justification for this enterprise union encompassing two limited companies was that: 'if not left as before (i.e. without a link between sales and manufacturing), it would be difficult for the union to grasp the overall picture of the company, and the union would not be able to maintain its members' living standards' (*Rodo Jiho*, 10 September 1950). Thus, management's action to change the corporate boundary triggered the creation of a union encompassing two limited companies, TMC and TMS, in August 1951. This replaced a loose collection of factory and establishment unions, to give labour a stronger voice in times of redundancies and closures, which had already caused workers to move from one location to another.[6] It was therefore an attempt by union leaders to provide a united front to defend employment security.

4.2.2 Strong Presence on the Shop Floor, Weak Voice in Managerial Decision-Making

Toyota's Komoro Factory Union had signed a collective agreement in 1946. As at many other companies, the agreement contained provisions for a management council (*keiei kyogikai*) that gave much power to the union. Article 5 of the agreement stated that (*a*) issues concerning production technology and efficiency, (*b*) issues relating to pay and other working conditions, and (*c*) issues concerning welfare benefits and education were to be discussed at the council meetings (Toyota Union 1996: 260). Moreover, Article 13 spelt out that all discussion items (*kyogi jiko*) must be decided with unanimity, giving the union in effect the right to co-decide (*doui*) on certain issues. The union version of the agreement explicitly stated that individual items for union approval (*shounin*) should be itemized in subsequent agreements (*Rodo Jiho*, 1 October 1946).

However by 1950, when the unsuccessful strike to protest against 1,600 redundancies ended, the management council was already emasculated. The union was then made to sign an end-of-dispute memorandum, including a clause that amended every mention of co-decision (*doui*) or approval (*shounin*) to mere discussion (*kyougi*) (Toyota Union 1996: 262; Gankoji 2003). Not surprisingly, when the collective agreement came up for renewal in 1951, it was not extended. The reasons at Toyota were similar to those at other companies, as the union would not agree to management's reassertion of its prerogative over personnel issues. Toyota's management wanted to abolish the management council in favour of a discussion forum, and to disallow union-led political protests even during rest time (Toyota Union 1976: 26). This is the context in which much of the subsequent developments in industrial relations at Toyota should be understood.

The 1950s were a decade of turbulent industrial relations when Toyota Union, under the direction of Zenji (the industrial union in the auto sector), operated on a principle of economic and political struggle, engaging for example in a fifty-five-day strike over wages and bonuses in 1953 (TMC 1967: 416). However, by the late 1950s, efforts by personnel managers to encourage shop-level discussion within self-managed groups were bearing fruit in transforming Toyota's industrial relations towards one based on mutual understanding (Yamamoto 1982). The culmination of this ethos was the 1962 Labour–Management Declaration based on three principles, namely Toyota's contribution towards national prosperity, industrial relations based on mutual trust, and joint efforts towards productivity improvements.

Somewhat surprisingly, an entire decade went by after this declaration before another collective agreement was signed. Toyota lived through two decades with no collective agreement, and the union's *de facto* power to participate in managerial decisions was severely curtailed during this period. A labour–management discussion forum (*roshi kondankai*) existed after 1962, but a formal labour–management consultation forum (*roshi kyogikai*) came into existence only after a collective agreement was finally signed in 1974. Unlike the labour–management council (*keiei kyogikai*) that met during 1946–50, this consultation forum is primarily for negotiating over working conditions such as pay and hours. In fact, Article 25 of the collective agreement effective since 1974 states that the consultation forum is for the purpose of negotiation on the basis of mutual trust. Moreover, Article 28 states briefly that items for discussion and negotiation at the consultation forum are 'problems that the company and the union face; pay, hours, and other working conditions; and other items deemed necessary for discussion by both parties.' This situation is in stark contrast to the proactive stance adopted by Matsushita Union to exercise voice in management policy, after a much shorter six-year period with no collective agreement (see Chapter 3).

Thus, Toyota Union has grown into a textbook-type enterprise union. Its structure for the purpose of the collection of union dues and wage bargaining is centralized at the enterprise level. But the company's rapid growth, its culture of emphasis on the shop floor, and the absence of a formal agreement over labour–management consultation resulted in a union that had its centre of gravity on the shop floor and a weak voice in strategic management decisions. In one sense, this did not matter as long as TMC's business was focused on automotive product lines.

In the 1960s, the internal structure of Toyota Union was remarkably simple, with just three branches, one for TMC in central Japan with 18,200 members, another for TMC Tokyo with 100 members, and the third for TMS with 2,000 members. But as the total membership grew to 30,000, the union leadership considered it necessary to bring union activities closer to its members. Thus, at the 1970 conference the internal organization was revised, first by separating out the TMC Union from the TMS Union, and second by making each of the six plants a formal branch of the TMC Union (*Rodo Jiho*, 15 May 1970). No such branch was considered necessary up to this point, and, although the number of manufacturing plants was growing, they were all located close to each other.

Whilst efforts were under way to devolve some activities to the union branches, Toyota Union had an incentive to retain central control over bargaining. The 1950s and 1960s saw a rapid increase in membership as the number of Toyota employees grew from around 5,000 in 1955 to over 40,000 in 1970. As early as in 1956, the company began to take on seasonal and temporary workers (*rinjiko*) as a way of coping with the increase in production volume whilst being cautious about taking on new regular employees after the early 1950s strife. In the 1960s, some of these workers were given an opportunity to become regular employees.

Parts of Toyota's shop floor, particularly in processes such as machining, paint, and casting, were still controlled by foremen and workers with a craftsman mentality, who were slowly being transformed into multi-skilled operators. Around five or six workers were organized into a team led by a team leader (*hancho*); three or four team leaders reported to a group leader (*kumicho*), and around four group leaders in turn reported to a supervisor (*koucho*). All these supervisory ranks were union members. The factory manager appointed group leaders and supervisors, but from around 1953, such appointments came to be made by the corporate headquarters. This greater centralization in the supervisory appointment system gave an incentive for the union to centralize its bargaining structure at the corporate level. But Toyota's personnel function remained close to the shop floor, dispatching personnel managers to each factory where they were in close touch with supervisors. At the same time, group leaders were empowered to make decisions over job rotation within, and even between, factories (Yamamoto 1982). This sort of devolution of power underlies the importance of the shop floor in Toyota's corporate culture, making union presence on the shop floor an important factor for its survival.

Since the 1990s, however, the union's focus on the shop floor became a constraint as TMC began to consider product diversification and business rationalization. Toyota Union was used to seeing its members move from factory to factory as part of the normal routine for job rotation and reallocation. But it was not prepared to facilitate the movement of its members to another company in the corporate group, for instance, as a result of TMC hiving off its internal division. Again, a contrast with the Matsushita case is evident here. The first such major case happened in

2001 when TMC's forklift truck sales division was absorbed by Toyoda Automatic Loom Works that had hitherto designed and manufactured the trucks.

In April 2000, the news about TMC's plan to hive off the forklift truck division, known as L & F, was leaked to the press, before Toyota management could formally announce the decision to the union. During 2000 and April 2001 when the hive-off was actually executed, management and the union met three times on this issue. In particular, Toyota Union argued that the L & F workplace was in turmoil due to the absence of timely communication about the company's future plan on forklift truck business. Worker morale was adversely affected, the union argued, as members at the division were given no reassurance beyond the company statement that the normal rule on temporary transfer (*shukko*) would be applied. Workers feared that whilst the formal rule on transfers was for a maximum of three years, they would not have a real option to return to TMC at the end of the transfer period.

Initially 175 members were transferred to Toyoda Automatic Loom Works. By 2004, cumulatively, around 300 employees were transferred from TMC's L & F division on *shukko*. Many chose to return to TMC, and only a small number were transferred permanently to Automatic Loom Works. This was an outcome based on a new agreement on inter-company transfers signed at TMC, with *shukko* to be always time-limited with an initial period of three years plus one further year of extension, and with *tenseki* (permanent transfer) to take place only with the worker's consent.

The L & F episode illustrates how unprepared the company and the union were in handling corporate restructuring that required shifting a large group of workers from one company to another. It also illustrates the limitations of Toyota's labour–management consultation forum that focuses primarily on operational issues at the exclusion of strategic issues. As the following statement by a Toyota union official reveals, however, the labour–management relations philosophy at Toyota remains unchanged: labour essentially trusts management to manage, and the union is there to check any infringement of what is acceptable.

It is questionable whether or not we as a union should say yes or nay to the company's strategy. The union puts emphasis on first seeing if the rationale behind the proposed strategy is sound, so if it is a hive-off proposal then we examine if its future is viable. And once we are reassured that it is, then we insist on exercising a strong voice to maintain the working conditions of union members who are to work in the new workplace.[7]

4.2.3 Toyota Roren Contributed to the Diffusion of Toyota Production System

The same philosophy of operational focus and strategic acquiescence pervades the activities of Toyota Roren (Federation of All Toyota Workers' Unions), a *roren* federation of unions at Toyota's suppliers and dealers led by Toyota Union. Toyota Roren has contributed to standardizing pay and other conditions through coordination during the Shunto bargaining round and by setting minimum standards known as Toyota Minimum. It also harmonized the group-wide system of labour–management relations, and facilitated the diffusion of Toyota Production System to supplier companies.

Toyota Roren is essentially an umbrella organization that brings together unions at companies connected with production, transportation, and sales of Toyota products. In 1994, this *roren* had 283,000 members, and consisted of 258 unions, of which 9 unions were at assemblers, 70 at parts suppliers, 9 at equipment manufacturers, 8 at transportation and other services, and 162 at dealers. By December 2002, there were a total of 284 unions, of which 106 were in manufacturing and 178 at dealers.

Comparing the boundary of Toyota Roren with the corporate boundary indicates that nearly all the unions at the core Toyota Group companies (listed in Table 4.2) belong to the *roren*. Exceptions are Hino and Daihatsu, which have their own *roren*; also Toyoda Automatic Loom Works (renamed Toyoda Industries Corporation) had belonged to the metal industry union federation Zenkin until 1988 (see Section 4.3). Beyond the core corporate group, Toyota Roren's reach in the broader grouping is significant but not extensive. Of the 144 Tokai Kyohokai member companies in 1993, only 52 had unions that belonged to the *roren*. At other companies, unions may exist but remain unaffiliated. There is a trade-off here for Toyota Roren. On the one hand, Toyota Roren wishes to grow in size to enhance its bargaining power in Shunto wage bargaining, and to exploit economies of scale in the mutual help and welfare programmes that it runs for Roren affiliates. On the other hand, however, Toyota Roren does not wish to dilute its standards by admitting unions that it cannot look after. Thus, it retains a few 'probationary' status unions at smaller suppliers, which will be admitted fully once they satisfy a certain minimum standard in working conditions.

The history of Toyota Roren as a formal organization is quite recent, dating back to 1972 when it was created in order to affiliate to Jidosha Soren (JAW). JAW decided to have *roren* as the unit of affiliation.

No *roren*-like organization existed for the Toyota group before 1972, although the Tokai regional branch of Zenkoku Jidosha (JAWU) functioned somewhat like a *roren* by coordinating Shunto wage negotiations. Unions affiliated to JAWU were enterprise unions of the textbook type, organizing workers from one corporation, typically at a medium to large supplier. There was little thought within the JAWU movement to extend the boundary of the union beyond one enterprise (as in the case of Matsushita (see Chapter 3) or Nissan (see Chapter 7)).

Internal critics who opposed the formation of Toyota Roren, such as Hisashi Sawada (Zenkoku Jidosha Tokai branch president at the time) considered a corporate group-based *roren* a heresy. In particular, they feared that the unions would be engulfed in 'enterprise consciousness' (*kigyo ishiki*) deriving from Toyota's purchasing policy (Zen Toyota Roren 2003: 36). The early 1970s was still a time when it was common for the make-or-buy decision to fluctuate with demand, bringing work back in at times of low demand, thereby favouring employment at Toyota at the expense of suppliers. At times of growth, Toyota employees benefited from higher pay, but supplier workers continued to suffer from lower wages due to Toyota's pressure to reduce component prices. Thus, uniting workers at Toyota and suppliers, whose interest conflicted, was not a straightforward matter.

But one factor was decisive in swinging the general opinion in favour of establishing a *roren* at Toyota Group. This was the felt need for unions to respond with one voice to Toyota management's tighter control over suppliers as they implemented TQC and TPS. According to Shiro Umemura:

There was a strong sense that management was intent on standardizing parts supplier companies' management methods and capabilities.... At the time, Nippondenso was a large enterprise, but other firms with only 400 or 500 employees were no more than workshops (*machi koba*). Management recognized, as we did as unions, that the Toyota Production System would not become effective unless the situation in which the owner-manager did things at his whim became subjected to systematic management like in a limited company. Various problems occurred in the process of improving the quality of management. We felt that unless the unions were strong, we would not be able to respond.[8]

In practice, union leaders such as Hisashi Sawada faced supplier owner-managers who would defer wage increases, and who did not comprehend why they had to discuss production and investment plans or the need to do overtime with workers. Whenever unions demanded pay increases, these owner-managers refused on the pretext that Toyota's purchasing manager would then demand a reduction in component prices. At times, Toyota Union facilitated a three-way discussion between the supplier company management, a Toyota purchasing manager, and Toyota Union, at which Toyota was made to explain its purchasing policy. At other times, the union targeted particularly backward suppliers for strike action. According to Hisashi Sawada:

With international competition, prices may have to come down. But productivity must also increase, and in order to increase productivity, labour and management must talk in depth in order to avoid pushing the burden of adjustment onto workers. We were for ever preaching along these lines. But we faced bottlenecks whenever people's attention was directed merely to owner-managers evading pay increases or Toyota purchasing demanding price reduction.[9]

Thus, the precursor to Toyota Roren played an important role in facilitating the diffusion of the Toyota Management System (including TPS and TQC) to supplier companies. There were two major obstacles to smooth diffusion: first, the labour-boss type supervisors, both within Toyota and supplier factories; and second, the owner-managers of small supplier companies. First, multi-skill training for TPS and the switch from recruiting middle school to high school graduates undermined the power of labour-boss-like foremen exercising unilateral discretion in work methods. In the process of creating tight control by first-line supervisors educated in TPS, various problems and grievances arose within Toyota factories, and it was evident that they would spread to supplier companies as Toyota was diffusing TPS to them. The union leaders sought to maintain a well-functioning shop floor by increasing the frequency of shop floor discussion meetings, and by policing the shop floor at supplier companies. Second, as explained above, in response to Toyota demands for lower prices, owner-managers at smaller supplier companies were prone to press for wage cuts. Toyota Roren countered this by putting pressure to bear on these managers to regard paying a wage comparable with Toyota's as concomitant with the adoption of TPS (Zen Toyota Roren 2003: 89). Thus, the *roren* foreclosed the cheap labour route, biasing supplier choice towards the high road to better wages through productivity improvements.

Toyota Roren has played a role, not only in bringing about near-identical percentage increases for all unions at Shunto wage bargaining rounds, but also in standardizing other working conditions. In 1976, a system of Toyota Minimum was established, specifying a *roren*-wide guideline on a minimum acceptable level in nine areas, namely overtime premium, rest day premium, night shift premium, shiftwork allowance, mandatory retirement age, retirement pensions, occupational accident aid, commuting accident aid, and paid holiday days. In 1992, four new areas were added, namely assistance for home ownership, commuting subsidy, subsidy for car ownership, and business expense claims within Japan. Apart from these labour conditions, Toyota Roren also concerns itself with instructing small and medium unions to meet the 'Activity Minimum' (*katsudo minimum*), by developing a labour–management relations system with key institutions such as a consultation forum, a union executive meeting, and a production committee. The Toyota Roren headquarters provides the know-how in creating and running these meetings, devising an action plan and monitoring progress.

Thus, Toyota Roren has worked within the Japanese norm that the bargaining unit is at the company level. But it has contributed towards harmonizing labour–management systems within Toyota's corporate group by diffusing the focal union's know-how to other affiliated unions. The *roren* has also contributed to Toyota Group-wide informational efficiency, particularly where it concerns production plans that affect manning levels and members' job transfers most directly. The TMC production planning information passes from the focal union to *roren*-affiliated unions as fast as from TMC's purchasing department to supplier management, thus giving supplier unions a head start in anticipating supplier management's manpower requirements. There are also discussion meetings once a month for top management and labour leaders from a dozen or so companies in each geographical area, under Toyota Roren's auspices. The supplier association representatives and Toyota's purchasing and personnel managers also meet with Toyota Roren leaders twice a year. These are occasions to share views about general aspects of Toyota's competitiveness and labour conditions.

4.2.4 Sources of Emerging Diversity: The Case of Toyota Motor Kyushu Inc. and TMC's Non-Automotive Business Units

Since the 1990s, Toyota Union's policy to apply uniform working conditions at its twenty branches was challenged by the geographical dispersion of new factory locations and product diversification. This section examines Toyota Union's response when a new assembly plant was built in Kyushu. It also takes a brief look at the state of union organizing at TMC's non-automotive business units.

Toyota Motor Kyushu Inc. was established in 1992 to assemble Mark II saloon cars and Harrier SUVs. This was one of three plants built by Toyota Motor Corporation outside central Japan around Toyota City.[10] TMC management initially considered building the Kyushu plant as a branch plant of TMC, but in the end decided to set it up as a separate limited company. Reasons were multiple, in turn rendering union responses complex. First, TMC management saw that Toyota's contribution to Kyushu's regional development—building a Kyushu plant for Kyushu people, using locally based suppliers—as an important aspect of this project. A separate company would underpin locally made decisions. Second, TMC management evidently wanted to benefit from low-cost labour in Kyushu, made easier by setting up a separate company than facing public criticism for introducing differential conditions for employees within the same company, not an accepted norm at the time. Third, Kyushu plant was seen as a good experimental ground for innovative practices—such as shorter assembly lines with buffers in between, the consecutive two-shift pattern that avoids the unsocial shift that starts at midnight, an environmentally friendly and quiet factory—that might later be adopted for organizational revitalization in the rest of Toyota.

Initially, a team consisting of 17 managers and 100 supervisors were sent to Kyushu on temporary transfer (*shukko*) from TMC. TMC carefully chose people who had some connection with the Kyushu region, including the first plant manager, Mr Nakamura, who had been the Motomachi plant manager. By 1998, an accumulated total of 700 were transferred to Kyushu from various Toyota factories to occupy all the supervisory and managerial positions, whilst a further 1,300 workers were recruited locally. From the start, a letter of intent was signed between Shoichiro Toyoda (TMC president at the time) and Nakamura that Toyota Kyushu is a spin-out company (*bunshin gaisha*), with totally open sharing of information between the two companies. To all intents and purposes, except in formal corporate form, Toyota Kyushu is treated as a branch plant with no other staff function except personnel. Product planning and parts purchasing for Kyushu are done out of the TMC head office in Toyota City. TMC can phone Toyota Kyushu using an internal telephone directory.

In preparation for organizing the Kyushu operation, Toyota Union held a review of its organization in 1991. The resulting report spelt out three options: (*a*) to make Kyushu a branch of Toyota Union, (*b*) to establish an independent union that would affiliate to Toyota Roren, and (*c*) to establish an independent union that would be part of a new Toyota Kigyoren (consisting only of unions at the core Toyota

Group subsidiaries). The report recommended the third option. Once management decided to set up Kyushu as a separate company, discussions took place between TMC management and Toyota Union. The union considered organizing the Kyushu site as a branch of Toyota Union, but was uncertain over whether or not members would acquiesce to different conditions for different plants. Significantly, there was no debate within the union about equal pay for equal work for Kyushu workers, but only a fear that incorporating a plant with lower wages would cause major concerns among members.

In the end, Toyota Union decided to create a separate union and to provide guidance and financial assistance to it. In February 1992, when new recruits were being hired, the Toyota Kyushu union was launched with eleven members led by a president who had been the Miyoshi factory branch leader. Toyota Union donated 40 million yen to the Kyushu Union ostensibly to transfer the subscription fees paid by the 700 or so transferees from TMC to Kyushu. Thereafter, Toyota Union established Torenkyo, a federal committee of unions at TMC, Kyushu, Hokkaido, and Tohoku, as a continued means of redistributing resources from Toyota Union to these smaller unions to fund full-time union officials and other activities. Toyota Kyushu Union later became an affiliate of Toyota Roren. In effect, Toyota Union came to acquiesce to a degree of diversity in working conditions within the core set of final assembly plants at Toyota.

At the same time that Toyota Union had to tackle the challenges brought about by organizing new plants in low-cost locations far from Toyota City, it also faced the problem of incorporating members who were in businesses other than automobiles. For example, at Toyota Finance, with just less than 1,000 employees, there is no union. There are, however, a handful of TMC employees—in the finance and accounting department—on temporary transfer (*shukko*), who retain their membership of Toyota Union. The other divisions, such as in housing and telecommunications, are treated in a similar manner, with Toyota Union looking after only members on *shukko*, whilst not attempting to organize workers hired directly by these non-automotive operations.

4.2.5 Summary

In summary, Toyota Union started as a collection of factory unions, but quickly became united into an enterprise union in 1951. It played an active role in modernizing the shop floor, and in diffusing the Toyota Management System to Toyota factories and supplier companies. Toyota

Roren, as a federation of unions at suppliers and dealers, came into existence only in 1972, but since has played a significant role in standardizing working conditions and the system of labour–management relations within the Toyota group. At the same time, Toyota Union and Toyota Roren's focus on shop floor activities has been at the expense of exercising voice in strategic management decisions. Toyota Union has respected the management's right to manage, and a weak form of joint consultation has become institutionalized. This had suited both Toyota Union and management until recently, when greater product diversification beyond the automotive business might make the existing union stance more constraining than in the past.

4.3. Perspectives from the Periphery: Toyoda Automatic Loom Works and Aisin Seiki

This section turns to the development of unions at two of Toyota Group's affiliated companies, namely Toyoda Automatic Loom Works and Aisin Seiki. Both unions are now part of Toyota Roren. But the Automatic Loom Workers Union is interesting as it is a recent joiner, having started as a union for textile machinery workers. The Aisin Workers Union (AWU) is interesting for being a union that encompasses multiple group companies, much as in the case of Matsushita Union but on a smaller scale. Both companies are owned partially (around 25 per cent) by Toyota Motor Corporation, but the boundaries of the union developed in different ways.

4.3.1 Toyoda Automatic Loom Workers Union

The shifting affiliation of the union at Toyoda Automatic Loom Works is useful in understanding the bases for uniting in a labour movement at the Toyota Group. Toyoda Automatic Loom Works was the original parent company from which Toyota's automotive business was hived off in 1937. Whilst retaining a close shareholding linkage with TMC, it had engaged in textile machinery operations unrelated to the automotive sector. Thus, Toyoda Jidoshokki Union (TJU) had been affiliated to the metalworking federation, Zenkoku Kinzoku, until 1989 when it switched to Toyota Roren. In effect, TJU strengthened its coordination with the core Toyota group unions only after the company became a supplier of key components (e.g. engines) and vehicles (e.g. pickups and trucks) for TMC. This suggests that trading linkage, rather than shareholding linkage, with the focal firm is a more important criterion for affiliating to Toyota Roren.

TJU started out as a set of factory-based unions. As soon as the wartime Sanpo organizations were disbanded in 1945, Toyoda Jidoshokki Employees Union was formed at the headquarters Kariya factory. The first union president was Katsuro Ooshima, a section chief (*kacho*) in the factory's production control department. Around the same time, separate employees unions were formed at the other two factories, Oobu and Sakou (TJU 1996: 36). But by 1946, these employees 'unions gave way to workers' unions, in part to conform to the Trade Union Law of that year. In effect, managers from the factory manager down to departmental and section managers were obliged to resign from union posts and give up their union membership.

The three factory unions acted separately at the start, but the Kariya factory union came to take a lead, given its relatively large size (2,650 members compared with Oobu's 600 and Sakou's 400). In particular, the Kariya Union took part in Toyoda Renkyo's coordinated struggle to establish a common retirement pay for factory workers (TJU 1996: 39–40). Moreover, the Kariya Union was the second largest union in an industrial union, Zensenki, the All Japan Textile Machinery Workers Union Federation, founded in 1948 with twenty unions. Zensenki was short-lived due to disagreements over political affiliation, and disbanded itself by 1953, when the Kariya factory union in effect affiliated to Zenkoku Kinzoku, the left-wing metalworkers' federation under the influence of Sohyo.

The political leadership of Sohyo's Zenkoku Kinzoku was essential to cope with the post-Korean War recession, which hit the cotton spinning industry most severely. The Japanese government (specifically the Ministry of International Trade and Industry) put forward in 1955 a draft of an emergency measure for the textile industry, which required the compulsory registration of all spinning machines and prohibited producing any machinery not approved by the government. Anticipating a severe restriction in output and the damaging effect on employment, the textile machinery section of Zenkoku Kinzoku staged an all-out opposition campaign in various parts of Japan (TJU 1996: 64).

The structural decline of the textile industry also necessitated the three factory-based unions to coordinate with each other, eventually leading to their unification at the enterprise level. Toyoda Automatic Loom Works management foresaw the need to diversify into areas other than textile machinery. This diversification policy led to the building of new factories. One such factory was Kyowa Factory, built in 1952 initially with the intention of undertaking the repair of heavy goods vehicles for the

Tachikawa Air Force Base. But with the end of the Korean War and given the union's ideological opposition to taking on munitions-related production, Kyowa Factory focused on civilian production, assembling bus chassis and S-type engines for TMC. This was the beginning of the auto-related business by Toyoda Automatic Loom Works (TJU 1996: 67).

The rise of the automotive business paralleled the decline of the textile machinery business. In 1955, management asked workers for a 12 per cent pay cut in exchange for the reinstatement of a six-day working week (TJU 1996: 62). The three factory-based unions formed a joint committee to negotiate hard with management, and eventually settled for unpaid overtime in exchange for a commitment of no lay-offs and a pay increase in the following year. By this time, the three factory unions felt the need to form a unified organization to negotiate with company management, and in 1957 a federation of the three unions took formal responsibility to negotiate with management. Perhaps the biggest trigger to forming a single enterprise union was the closure of Sakou Factory in 1957. At one time, this factory boomed with the assembly of spinning machines, employing 600 regular workers supplemented by temporary workers. But with the onset of a declining demand, workers were transferred to Kyowa Factory in stages. With the factory closure, the Sakou Factory Union was absorbed into the Kariya Union, and an enterprise union was formed in October 1958 by merging the existing three factory unions. The unified TJU had 3,180 members at the time of its formation.

Thereafter, TJU's membership expanded to over 9,000 in the mid-1990s, with the establishment of new factories at Nagakusa in 1968 to assemble Publica pickups, at Takahama in 1970 to produce fork lift trucks, and at Hekinan in 1982 to make C-type engines. The company's diversification policy led to a major shift in the nature of business at Toyoda Automatic Loom Works, to the extent that by the mid-1990s, over 90 per cent of its business was in automotive-related products. This position of the company as a component supplier and a subcontract assembler to TMC led TJU to suggest a change of affiliation from Zenkoku Kinzoku (the metalworkers' federation) to Toyota Roren in 1988.

Changing the affiliation to a higher-level body is not a decision to be taken lightly. Particularly when differences exist in the stance and policy of such bodies, the enterprise union may split and lead to the creation of a second union. TJU avoided such eventuality by judging that the time was ripe to propose the switch. Aside from the change in the nature of business from textile machinery to vehicle components, there were other factors that contributed to the membership's perceived need to become part of

Toyota Roren. First, Zenkoku Kinzoku was full of smaller unions whose demands were always lower than what TJU could afford to demand. Second, Zenkoku Kinzoku's ideology for a political struggle that transcends enterprise-level labour–management negotiations was felt to be increasingly at odds with the members' sentiments. Third, with the formation of Rengo in 1989 and the dissolution of Sohyo to which Zenkoku Kinzoku belonged, prospects for a rapprochement between the left wing and the right wing of the labour movement became clear. TJU thought that its request for withdrawing from Zenkoku Kinzoku would be handled quietly without accusation of defection.

4.3.2 Aisin Workers Union (AWU): An Inter-firm Union

AWU, an affiliate of Toyota Roren, is itself an organization encompassing workers from a number of related companies within the Aisin Group. AWU, with 19,140 members in 1995, is therefore an inter-firm union, like at Matsushita but on a smaller scale. Aisin management's decisions over spin-outs and mergers, combined with the union leaders' belief in standardization, triggered such a union structure.

The corporate origin of Aisin firms may be traced back to Tokai Hikoki, a wartime joint venture between Toyota Motor Co. and Kawasaki Aircraft Co., set up in 1943 to produce aircraft engines. The war ended, however, before engine manufacturing could begin, and by December 1945, Tokai Hikoki was renamed Aichi Kogyo (TMC 1988: 79). Soon after, in February 1946, Aichi Kogyo workers formed an enterprise union.

A few months later in May 1946, another enterprise union was established at Shinkawa Sangyo, which started as a subcontractor to Tokai Hikoki but soon switched to auto components manufacturing with the end of the war (AWU 1986: 26). Shinkawa Sangyo had the policy of diversification by spinning out internal divisions. In 1952, the sewing machine division was hived off to establish Hekinan Kogyo. In 1960, the casting division was hived off to set up Takaoka Kogyo. Thus, by 1960, the Shinkawa corporate group consisted of three companies: Shinkawa Kogyo (renamed from Shinkawa Sangyo), Hekinan Kogyo, and Takaoka Kogyo.

The immediate reaction by union leaders to hive-offs was to establish a separate enterprise union at the newly independent firms. However, frequent personnel transfers among the three related companies engendered a demand to harmonize working conditions throughout the corporate group. Thus, the three company-based unions eventually merged to create a unified single organization, Shinsan Union, in 1962. This marks the beginning of the Aisin unions' principle that a union may cross the boundary of a firm.

The next challenge for the unions was posed by management's decision to merge Aichi Kogyo and Shinkawa Kogyo in 1965, as part of a rationalization policy to prepare for trade liberalization at the time. The newly merged company was called Aisin Seiki, and to reflect this name change, the Aichi Kogyo enterprise union immediately changed its name to Aisin Seiki Union. For the workers at Shinsan Union, the inter-firm union of the Shinkawa corporate group, there was a choice: either to faithfully follow the changes made by management in redrawing its organizational boundary, or to impose its own new boundary. The former meant that the union unit at Shinkawa Kogyo had to detach itself from those at Hekinan and Takaoka, while the latter meant a complete merger of Aisin Seiki Union and the inter-firm Shinsan Union. The two unions, after much discussion, opted for the latter, to form a unified AWU in February 1966. The organizational principle adopted at this time was to let each firm be organized as a union branch of AWU. There were originally three branches, at Aisin Seiki, Takaoka Kogyo, and Hekinan Kogyo; a fourth branch was added when Aisin Warner, a joint venture between Aisin Seiki and Borg Warner, was formed in 1969.

What have been the major achievements of AWU as an inter-firm union? In the 1960s, AWU set out to harmonize the wage system for all workers within the union (AWU 1986: 30). The union negotiated with the three companies' management to create a single wage and benefit system out of two pre-merger systems that differed in the composition of basic pay, productivity-related pay, job-related pay, and various benefits. In the 1970s, AWU was able to sign a central collective agreement with all the company management teams put together, thus imposing common rules in regulating industrial relations (AWU 1986: 68). Moreover, AWU created a *roren*-like federation of eleven unions at Aisin Seiki's subsidiaries, Aisin Rokyo, to extend its policy of coordination and standardization (AWU 1986: 163).

4.4. Summary and Conclusions

In summary, Toyota Motor Corporation was born out of a major diversification from a textile machinery company into an automotive business. Toyota's product strategy has been focused on the auto sector, with only minor diversification in recent years. The resulting structure has been largely functional, with much cross-functional coordination to sustain the principles of Toyota Management System (i.e. a combination of TPS and TQC). In order to deliver continuous cost reduction and quality improvement, managing the supply chain has occupied an important place. Thus, Toyota has invested resources in developing its core suppliers. The resulting boundaries are fourfold: a narrowly defined focal firm, a core group of affiliates some of which were hived off from the focal firm, a group of locally based suppliers that depend heavily on Toyota for their survival, and a group of more independent suppliers.

Toyota's unions have mirrored the corporate structure well. They started as factory unions, but were quick to organize themselves at the enterprise level. Hive-offs (e.g. Nippondenso) and new subsidiaries (e.g. Toyota Kyushu Inc.) were typically organized as separate unions. The geographical concentration of Toyota's operations facilitated close coordination between unions in the 1960s, but it was not until 1972 that a *roren* based on the corporate group, Toyota Roren, was formally established. With this relatively recent history, Toyota Roren has had a hand in diffusing modern management methods to supplier companies. Toyota unions' strategy has been to improve members' conditions by proactively participating in productivity-enhancing measures on the shop floor. This production focus, without a strong voice in long-term business plans (including on diversification), has not been perceived to be a problem as long as TMC remains largely a single product company. Recent diversification and corporate restructuring have, however, begun to pose some challenges to this unchanged union stance.

The logic of shareholding within the Toyota Group may grow in importance as TMC diversifies into housing, financial services, and telecoms. At the same time, the logic of trading links may become diluted with the diversification of customer base at supplier companies. So far, however, as the case of the union at Toyoda Automatic Loom Works shows, trading linkages continue to be more important than shareholding linkage in defining the boundary of affiliation to Toyota Roren.

We will now turn, in Chapter 5, to assessing alternative principles applied by various *roren* federations to draw their boundaries.

Notes

1. Kodama was manager of Mitsui's Nagoya branch, whose younger brother, Risaburo, married Sakichi's daughter, Aiko, and became Toyota Group's chief executive working closely with Kiichiro.

2. In the post-war period, Tokai Hikoki was renamed Aichi Kogyo and then Tokai Kogyo, which in turn merged with Shinkawa Kogyo in 1965 to establish Aisin Seiki.

3. At the time, Mitsui and its affiliates owned 14 per cent of TMC (TMC 1967: 259). TMC's links with Mitsui date back to very early days of Toyoda's textile machinery business.

4. After a brief post-war boom in the spinning industry, Minsei Spinning struggled with diversification into synthetic fibre and woollens, renaming the company to Toyoda Boshoku in 1967. Subsequently, the Japanese textile industry faced a secular decline, resulting in the Toyota Group placing orders for automotive work to its textile grandparent and parent, which gave birth to TMC. By the mid-1990s, automotive-related business accounted for over 90 per cent of Toyoda Automatic Loom Works' sales and around 80 per cent of Toyoda Boshoku's sales.

5. By the time Nippondenso was hived off, the operations moved from Kariya South to Kariya North (TMC 1967: 246–7).

6. For example, when Nakagawa factory closed, 400 workers were transferred to Komoro plant.

7. Interview with Shinya Kono, Director of Planning and Public Affairs, Toyota Union, 19 June 2003.

8. Interview with Shiro Umemura, 8 April 1997.

9. Interview with Hisashi Sawada, 8 April 1997.

10. Kyushu is the southern island of Japan. The other two plants were in Hokkaido, the northern island of Japan, and in Miyagi Prefecture in the north of the main island.

5

Inter-Industry Differences: Criteria for Union Boundary Decisions

How typical is the union strategy and structure at Matsushita or Toyota of the industry it represents? Are the sort of differences found between Matsushita and Toyota also reflected more generally in differences between the electrical machinery and automotive industries? This chapter examines these questions by analysing a questionnaire survey conducted by the author.

Table 5.1 summarizes the structural characteristics of *roren* organizations at Toyota and Matsushita, which were the subject of the previous two chapters. It also presents corresponding characteristics at Nissan and Fujitsu. There are notable differences between the two automotive union federations and the two electrical union federations. First, the focal union in the *roren* organization has a much bigger presence in the electrical machinery industry than in the automotive industry. In particular, Matsushita Union and Fujitsu Union capture 47 per cent and 58 per cent, respectively, of total membership of the *roren* organizations that they lead. The proportions are much smaller, at 22 per cent for Nissan Roren and 23 per cent for Toyota Roren. This is partly because at Matsushita and Fujitsu, the focal enterprise union had extended its organizational boundary by signing three-party (*sansha kyotei*) agreements when new subsidiaries were created, whereas such an arrangement is rarely found in the car industry.[1] As we saw in Chapter 4, a more typical arrangement at Toyota was to organize a separate enterprise union at a new subsidiary, such as Toyota Kyushu, which in turn affiliates to Toyota Roren.

Second, the organizational boundary of the *roren* is more encompassing in the automotive industry than in the electrical machinery industry. In the case of Matsushita Roren, the criterion for affiliation is shareholding

128

Table 5.1 Structural characteristics of four *roren* federations in the late 1990s

	Toyota Roren	Nissan Roren	Fujitsu Roren	Matsushita Roren
Total membership	282,730	324,985	100,000	166,000
Focal union	Toyota Union	Nissan Union	Fujitsu Union	Matsushita Union
Membership	65,700	71,909	58,100	78,216
Per cent of total members	23 per cent	22 per cent	58 per cent	47 per cent
Number of branches	19	10	14	69
Sansha kyotei companies[a] within focal union	None	None	72	28
Number of unions, of which	251	548	34	30
Parts	81	168		
Dealers	157	286		
Other comments	CND was established in 1988 as an association of unions at dealers, and this unit in turn affiliates to Toyota Roren.	The units of affiliation to *roren* are Hanro for dealer unions, Buro for parts maker unions, and Minro for miscellaneous category of unions.		Hanroren, established in 1996 with 107 unions at retail outlets, affiliates to Matsushita Roren. Shokan Rokyo for 20 unions at subcontractors remains a separate organization.

[a] *Sansha kyotei* companies are firms whose management has agreed to be covered by the collective agreement signed between the focal firm and the focal union (see Chapter 3 for details).

Source: Author interviews at *roren* offices; Denki Rengo (1996); Jidosha Soren (1994).

linkages with Matsushita Electric (30 per cent or more capital participation was said to be the rule of thumb for affiliation). By contrast, in the case of Toyota Roren, the criterion for affiliation includes shareholding links but also trading links. Thus, well over half of Toyota Roren's members are employees working at supplier companies that are independent of Toyota in terms of ownership.

The nature of *roren* activities is grounded in these structural characteristics of *roren* organizations, with the focal union being bigger at Matsushita than at Toyota, and the *roren* boundaries being drawn more narrowly by shareholding links at Matsushita than at Toyota. For instance, Matsushita Roren, led by Matsushita Union, has much scope for participating in, and coordinating over the consequences of, strategic managerial decision-making by the focal firm, MEI. By contrast, the focus of Toyota Roren's activity has been more operational. The automaker and supplier companies are highly integrated through the adoption of JIT delivery and production. Consequently, Toyota Roren's focus of activity is to antici- pate production plans that have important consequences for union mem- bers' working time and job transfer. At the same time, Toyota Roren has less scope than Matsushita Roren to participate in the focal firm's strategic decision-making. We saw in Chapters 3 and 4 that such focus in union activity derived in part from the union's own philosophy, as well as from corporate strategy. In particular, Matsushita's strategy is centred on prod- uct diversification, whilst Toyota's strategic focus hinges on 'make or buy' decisions and supplier relationships.

The rest of this chapter analyses the questionnaire survey data in order to gauge the extent to which the Matsushita–Toyota contrast drawn above can be extended to a contrast between the two industrial sectors. Specif- ically, are *roren* organizations structured differently by sector, and do structural differences lead to different functions, either fulfilled or expected by members? Section 5.1 describes the survey methodology and sample characteristics. Section 5.2 identifies and attempts to explain the key difference in the way *roren* boundaries are drawn and the way the *roren* organizations are structured internally. *Roren* organizations are clas- sified into those based on capital affiliation and those based on trading links. Capital affiliation is more important as a sole criterion in electrical machinery *roren*, whilst trading links (principally with parts suppliers and dealers) are found to be more important in drawing the boundary of *roren* in the automobile industry. Section 5.3 explores the consequences of such structural differences for the role that *roren* fulfils in wage bargaining during the Spring Offensive (Shunto), employment ad- justment, and worker participation. Section 5.4 focuses on sectoral differ- ences in the vertical articulation of union structure, in particular the articulation between the *roren* and the industry-wide union federation or confederation.

Our working hypothesis is that *roren* organizations vary in structural form by sector, and that their function varies according to their form. Thus, this chapter takes up the 'labour structure affects labour strategy' part of the Strategy–Structure–Institutions (SSI) framework presented in Chapter 1. More precisely, what the survey questionnaire is able to do is (*a*) to examine the structural characteristics of *roren* organizations, in terms of their boundaries and internal structure, (*b*) to analyse what sort of roles and functions are fulfilled by, or expected of, *roren* organizations, and (*c*) to gauge the underlying strategy of *roren* and focal unions that remain unobservable in the questionnaire by correlating (*a*) and (*b*). This functionalist focus on the structural dimension of trade unions is not meant to ignore the fact that the existing *roren* boundaries have, in most cases, emerged as a result of political contestation and compromise. Moreover, social identity and ideology, as much as strategic calculations in labour markets, would have played a part not only in determining union boundaries but also in the relative emphasis placed on various types of union activities including collective bargaining and worker participation. Chapter 7 gives a striking example of such political processes that led to intra-sectoral differences in union strategy and structure in the car industry.

All reported differences between the two industries are significant at the 5 per cent level, unless stated otherwise. Although inter-sectoral difference is the focus of analysis in this chapter, attention will be drawn, where relevant, to company- or union-specific factors that might account for intra-sectoral variations. This anticipates the discussion in Chapters 6 and 7.

5.1. Survey Sample Characteristics

Exploratory semi-structured interviews were conducted initially at the industry-level union federations in the automotive and electrical machinery industries, followed by some at *roren* organizations and their affiliate unions in each of the two industries. On the basis of these interviews, a questionnaire survey was devised (see Appendix). We decided to target all unions affiliated to five major *roren* federations in the automotive industry and six such federations in the electrical machinery industry. They were the *roren* federations for Toyota, Nissan,[2] Honda, Mitsubishi Motors, and Mazda in automobiles, and those for Hitachi, Matsushita, Fujitsu, Toshiba, NEC, and Mitsubishi Electric in electrical machinery.

As in previous chapters, the questionnaire survey called a parent firm in a corporate grouping a 'focal firm' (e.g. Toyota Motor Corporation for the Toyota group). Correspondingly, a union organized at the focal firm is called a 'focal union'. A focal union is part of the *roren*, and is considered to be in a leading position to decide the policies and practices of the *roren*. Since the questionnaire asked about the role of the focal union in the *roren* as much as about the function of the *roren*, focal unions were excluded from the sample.

The survey sample includes all the manufacturing-based unions affiliated with the eleven *roren* federations. This meant that the survey excluded those unions organized at dealerships or retail shops even if they were part of the *roren*. In the electrical machinery industry, we occasionally found cases in which there were other more loosely organized union networks for smaller subcontractors, known as *rokyo*. To make the task manageable, this survey excludes such networks and does not attempt to cover every type of union network organized around the focal union. The survey therefore gives a comparative, but by no means comprehensive, view of the relationship between the structural characteristics of *roren* and its functions.

In order to achieve a good response rate, we sought permission to conduct the survey from each of the eleven *roren* headquarters offices. All offices, when approached, agreed to take part, and provided a comprehensive mailing list. The sole exception was Toyota Roren, which restricted our access to a sample of only twenty unions out of a population of over 100 parts supplier unions affiliated to the *roren*. All respondents were also promised a report summarizing the results of the survey. Such a report was sent out to the 340 respondents, and was published in Japanese as Sako and Sato (1999).

In November 1997, the questionnaire was distributed to union presidents either directly by post or through the *roren* headquarters office, with a request to return the filled questionnaire to the Institute of Social Science at the University of Tokyo by December 1997. A reminder was sent to non-responding unions after that date. A total of 227 questionnaires were sent and 168 were returned in the auto industry (a response rate of 74.0 per cent). In the electrical machinery industry, 264 were sent and 172 returned (a response rate of 65.2 per cent) (See Table 5.2).

The average size of the responding unions is quite small with 948 members, but the unions in the electrical machinery industry were more than twice as large as those in the auto industry (an average of 1,337 members as compared to 549 members). This is in part because the electrical *roren* exclude unions at smaller subcontractors and suppliers with no shareholding links to the focal firm. The oldest unions were established in 1945, the newest in 1997. But unions have been in existence much longer in the auto industry than in electrical machinery, reflecting the relative age of the industry. The median year of establishment was 1962 in automobiles and 1972 in electrical machinery. The median year in which sample unions affiliated to the *roren* was 1972 for automotive unions and 1983 for electrical unions. The year 1972 was when the Confederation of Japan Automobile Unions (JAW) was finally formed, after the coexistence of multiple bodies claiming to be industry-wide federations (see Chapter 7 for details). The survey respondents are either presidents or general

Table 5.2 *Roren* questionnaire survey sample

Roren name	Questionnaires sent	Valid responses	Response rate (per cent)	Union size (average number of members)
Toyota	20	20	100	981
Nissan	98	72	73	516
Mitsubishi Motors	51	36	71	402
Honda	21	16	76	816
Mazda	37	24	65	340
Automotive subtotal	227	168	74.0	549
Matsushita	30	21	70	3,095
Fujitsu	34	27	79	1,219
Mitsubishi Electric	49	26	53	828
NEC	27	22	81	1,089
Hitachi	70	36	51	1,378
Toshiba	54	40	74	895
Electrical machinery subtotal	264	172	65.2	1,337
Total	491	340	69.2	948

secretaries of the unions. The majority of the respondents have had rich experience in union activity. The average length of time they spent as a member of the union's central executive committee or in a higher official position is 7.8 years (6.8 years in the auto industry and 8.6 years in the electrical machinery industry).

5.2. Structural Characteristics of *Roren* Organizations

This section concentrates on two structural characteristics of *roren* organizations: first, how the external boundaries are drawn, and second, the nature of internal structure of the *roren*.

5.2.1 Criteria for Organizational Boundaries: Capital Affiliation versus Trade Linkage

The headquarters of a *roren* federation stipulates membership criteria, although the criteria may not be stated formally in a written constitution. One such criterion is whether the firm organized by a union has a capital or trading linkage with the focal firm. The questionnaire investigated both types of linkages between the focal firms and the firms where *roren*-affiliated unions were organized. Most of the electrical unions (80 per cent) said that their firm was owned in part by the focal firm, while less than half (44 per cent) of those in the automotive *roren* said so. Analysing a subset of firms with a share ownership rate of 50 per cent or more makes the sectoral contrast even sharper. Specifically, the percentage of unions at firms with 50 per cent or more share ownership by the focal firm drops to 14 per cent in the auto industry, while that for the electrical machinery industry remains as high as 66 per cent.

Strong capital linkages make it more likely that focal firms send their employees as directors to the firms organized by *roren*-affiliated unions exist. Seventy-four per cent of electrical unions, as compared to 45 per cent in automotive unions, received directors from the focal firm. The average number of directors received per firm is 5.4 in the electrical machinery industry and 4.3 in the auto industry. Generally, capital affiliation is highly correlated with top management transfers (Lincoln and Gerlach 2004). The current survey findings confirm this, since, regardless of sector, a great majority (i.e. 92 per cent) of the firms whose capital is more than 50 per cent owned by their focal firm have also received directors from the same source.

Next, the questionnaire asked about the nature of business transactions between the focal firm and its group companies. At one extreme, around a quarter of the firms organized by the responding unions in both sectors were reliant on the focal firm for nearly all (i.e. between 90 and 100 per cent) of their sales turnover. At the other extreme, around 15 per cent of the firms with the responding unions had 10 per cent or less of their transactions with their focal firm. Nevertheless, trading linkages were stronger in the automotive industry than in electrical machinery. In particular, 74 per cent of the automotive unions said that their firm's business dealings with the focal firm accounted for 50 per cent or more of their total sales, while 65 per cent of the electrical unions said so (this inter-industry difference was significant at the 10 per cent level according to the Chi-square test).

Let us call a *roren* that draws its organizational boundary mainly in terms of capital affiliation a 'capital affiliation type', and a *roren* that defines its boundary mainly in terms of trading links a 'trading linkage type'. From the analysis so far, it may appear that membership of the *roren* in the auto industry tends to be based more on trading linkages than on capital affiliation, and that in the electrical machinery industry more strongly on capital affiliation. However, what distinguishes automotive *roren* from electrical *roren* is the extent of the overlap between capital and trading linkages, as the cross-tabulation of capital and trading linkages in Table 5.3 shows. In the auto industry, the majority of *roren*-affiliated

Table 5.3 Capital and trading linkages between focal firms and firms with *roren*-affiliated unions

Automotive industry (*N* = 145)

		Trading linkage	
		Less than 50% of sales	50% or more
Capital affiliation	Less than 50% of shares	34 (23.4%)	91 (62.8%)
	50% or more	4 (2.8%)	16 (11.0%)

Electrical machinery (*N* = 137)

		Trading linkage	
		Less than 50% of sales	50% or more
Capital affiliation	Less than 50% of shares	18 (13.1%)	11 (8.0%)
	50% or more	31 (22.6%)	77 (56.2%)

Note: Figures in parentheses are percentages of total sample.

unions (63 per cent) are at firms with a relatively weak capital linkage but a strong trading linkage with the focal firm, whereas in the electrical machinery industry, the majority of unions (56 per cent) are at firms with both strong capital affiliation *and* strong trading linkages with the focal firm.[3] Within-industry dispersions in these patterns exist, but they are dwarfed by the inter-sectoral differences noted above.

Why should such a sectoral difference emerge in the way *roren* boundaries are drawn? Explanations may be found on both corporate and union sides of the picture. First, differences in the nature of the product have led to different criteria for drawing corporate boundaries. In particular, the automobile is a much more complex product, requiring more strategic contribution in the development and production of components from suppliers, than a typical electronic product. Consequently, the degree of integration of parts suppliers and subcontractors has been of greater strategic importance in the automotive industry than in the electrical machinery industry. Since it is relatively more important that supplier relationships are stable and reliable in producing automobiles than electrical and electronic goods, focal firms have crafted supplier associations and other mechanisms for stabilizing supplier relations. This is also reflected in the way *roren* boundaries are drawn, with automotive *roren* incorporating unions at suppliers more than in electrical *roren*.

Second, electrical and electronic products depend more than automobiles on rapid introduction of diversified products, requiring more agile responses to the need for new suppliers of technology and parts. This puts another pressure on supplier turnover, making shareholding linkages a more stable basis for product diversification. Consequently, capital affiliation is a relatively more important criterion for drawing the corporate group and *roren* boundaries in electrical machinery than in automobiles.

Third, all *roren* federations aim to protect and improve the working conditions of union members, and this frequently involves attempts at narrowing the gap between the standard enjoyed by the focal union members and the lower standards of members at smaller supplier companies. Automotive parts unions are part of the *roren* whereas electrical assembly subcontractor unions are not. As in the case of Matsushita, the latter are typically organized as a separate association, *rokyo*, which was not included in this survey. These unions are kept separate because the wage gap between the focal firm and these subcontractors are considered too large for the *roren* to attempt to close. One key reason for this large wage gap is because the proportion of female workers is much higher in electronic assembly subcontracting than in the automotive industry.

To summarize, trading linkage is a salient criterion for drawing *roren* boundaries where stable supplier relations deriving from the complexity of the product are important. Capital affiliation is prominent where corporate diversification strategy is prevalent. Moreover, the exclusion from *roren* of unions at firms with trading linkage but low capital affiliation appears to be due to the wish to access low-cost labour (e.g. female workers) at subcontractors.

5.2.2 Degree of Centralization in Roren's Internal Hierarchy

Having gauged the external boundary of *roren* organizations, we will now turn to the internal structure of *roren*. In particular, how centralized or decentralized are the financial and personnel resources that *roren* organizations command? Also, how strong is the *roren* headquarter *de facto* influence over the affiliated unions' decisions? This subsection investigates the extent to which these dimensions differ between the two sectors under investigation. Following Pugh et al. (1968: 76), centralization refers to the locus of authority to make decisions affecting the organization. These dimensions parallel those identified in the typology of enterprise unions presented in Chapter 1.

The union subscription level is higher, at 4,595 yen per month on average in electrical machinery, than in automobiles where the monthly average is 3,861 yen. But a higher percentage of this lower sum—29 per cent in autos compared with 17 per cent in electrical machinery—is handed over to the *roren* federation to support its activity. This suggests that *roren* headquarters are better resourced in the automobile industry than in electrical machinery. Moreover, a greater proportion of automotive unions—55 per cent compared with 23 per cent in electrical unions— thought that the *roren* has a strong or moderate *de facto* influence on the level of subscription that it could set. This sectoral difference is in part due to the fact that the automotive *roren* take on much of the role of an industry federation, whereas the electrical *roren* sit side-by-side in competition with the industry federation (see Section 5.4 for details).

The greater degree of centralization of automotive *roren* in terms of financial resources, as shown above, is also reflected in personnel resources. One in ten unions in the sample had at least one union official who was based at the *roren* headquarters office, but the proportion was as high as 20 per cent in automobiles compared with a mere 3 per cent in electrical machinery. Automotive *roren* have a much stronger *de facto* influence on the process of nominating such officials than electrical *roren* (56 per cent in autos compared with 44 per cent in electrical machinery). Moreover, 69 per cent of automotive unions, compared with 21 per cent of electrical unions, said that there is someone at the *roren* headquarters or regional office who is in charge of looking after the union and visiting the union once a month (compared with only five times a year in electrical machinery).

Also a higher proportion of automotive unions—60 per cent as compared to 40 per cent of electrical unions—thought that the *roren* federation had a strong or moderate *de facto* influence on their decision to call a strike. That is, although the formal right to call a strike rests with individual enterprise unions, the *roren* has an influence in the exercise of such right. There is some evidence that tighter trading linkages with the focal firm increase such *de facto* influence, but no evidence that higher capital affiliation does.

To summarize, on average, the *roren* federation is better resourced in financial and personnel terms and has stronger *de facto* influence on affiliated unions in the automobile sector than in electrical machinery. Given this difference, it is not surprising that a higher proportion of automotive unions (34 per cent) than electrical unions (17 per cent) felt that their resource contribution to the *roren* was greater than the services they received from the *roren*. The higher degree of centralization of automotive *roren*, compared with electrical *roren*, may be explained only when this is set in the full picture of vertical articulation with the industry-level union federations. Section 5.4 details this picture, which shows that *roren* organizations in automobiles are powerful relative to the industry-level confederation, JAW, whilst electrical *roren* organizations are in a weaker position relative to the industry-level union federation, JEIU.

5.3. What Do *Roren* Federations Do?

Given the above differences in the organizational structure of *roren* in the two sectors, in what ways do their functions vary? In short, what do *roren* federations do? This section examines their role in three key areas: first, in improving and standardizing working conditions; second, in facilitating employment adjustment; and, third, in promoting worker participation at both the corporate and *roren* levels.

5.3.1 Standardization of Working Conditions and Coordination in Wage Bargaining

A large majority (80 per cent) agreed or strongly agreed with the statement 'Our union has been able to improve members' working conditions more by belonging to a *roren* federation than by negotiating on its own.' There was no significant difference between the industries. At the same time, only a very small number of unions (2.4 per cent) agreed with the statement 'Our union would be able to improve members' working conditions more freely if it had not affiliated to a *roren*.' Four in every five unions surveyed disagreed or strongly disagreed with this statement. The first significant thing that a *roren* does, then, is to improve unions' bargaining power vis-à-vis management by joining forces as a federation. The actual negotiated outcome of such enhanced bargaining power is the subject of Chapter 8. Here, the discussion focuses on specific mechanisms that are being used to improve conditions generally and to standardize (i.e. narrow the dispersion of) achieved conditions within a *roren*.

One such mechanism is for a *roren* to coordinate enterprise-level negotiations on working conditions by establishing a common achievement target or a guideline for a broad range of conditions to be improved. Various *roren* federations have a stated goal to better working conditions through this mechanism, as we saw in the case of the Matsushita Minimum (in Chapter 3) and the Toyota Minimum (in Chapter 4). When asked whether their *roren* provides specific targets and guidelines for conditions other than wages, as many as 86 per cent of survey respondents said yes. This was the case for a slightly greater percentage (93 per cent) in the automotive industry than in the electrical machinery industry (79 per cent).

Of those unions that have *roren*-defined targets and guidelines, 78 per cent (82 per cent in electrical machinery, 74 per cent in autos) said that they have, indeed, achieved better working conditions through this arrangement in the last five years. More specifically, when asked which aspects of the work environment were improved successfully, the top four issues most frequently mentioned were shorter working hours, pension provisions, accident compensation, and the number of rest days, in descending order of importance. Electrical unions were more likely to make improvements in shorter working hours, whilst automotive unions focus more on pensions and accident compensation.

Next, we turn to examine the role of *roren* in Shunto wage negotiations. Shunto—the Spring Offensive—is a highly coordinated wage bargaining round, which has been in existence in Japan since 1955 (see Sako 1997*b*). Typically, the process involves unions in each major industry coordinating over a wage demand and the precise date (and sometimes time) at which settlements are to be reached. The survey asked about the degree of substantive influence that the *roren* federation had on the affiliated unions' wage demand and settlement. To this question, 80 per cent of the unions surveyed responded that *roren*'s influence was 'very strong' for wage demands, suggesting the existence of a highly concerted wage demand process in Shunto. *Roren*'s influence declines somewhat when it comes to actual settlements—52 per cent said that *roren* had very strong influence—because unions are meant to use their own judgement ultimately to settle at the enterprise level. *Roren*'s degree of influence does not vary much between the two industries for wage demand. But for wage settlements, a greater proportion of electrical unions (65 per cent) than automotive unions (39 per cent) felt that *roren*'s influence was very strong. This perception may be due, in part, to the importance of *roren*'s head office influence relative to other channels (see below), and the dominance of the focal union membership in the total *roren* membership in electrical than in automotive sectors.

In what ways do *roren* get involved in, and influence, the wage negotiation process? The survey asked respondents to identify all the organizations and individuals that have frequently given direct advice or support to them during Shunto wage negotiations. The most frequently consulted (mentioned by 70 per cent of all unions) was 'the *roren* federation headquarter', followed by 'other unions in the same *roren*' (mentioned by 30 per cent), 'the *roren*'s local organizations' (29 per cent), 'the focal union of the *roren* federation' (20 per cent), and 'retired union officials' (11 per cent). It is possible that with multiple responses, respondents that ticked the *roren* headquarter imputed in this response the influence that the focal union exerts via the *roren* headquarter.

One significant difference between the two industries was in the relative importance of *roren*'s headquarter and its local organizations. Unions in electrical machinery, compared with those in the auto industry, rely more on *roren*'s central office and less on its local organizations (see Table 5.4). Conversely in the auto industry, *roren*'s local offices perform a greater advisory role than in the electrical machinery industry, despite the fact that unions in the auto industry are not necessarily more geographically dispersed. Note that the percentages of unions that have received frequent advice and support from the headquarter and local organizations, when combined, show little difference between the automotive and electrical machinery industries (see (a) in Table 5.4). In fact, in each sector, nearly all affiliated unions deal with *roren* offices of some description. One can say that the aggregate level of advice or support by the *roren* for affiliated unions is quite similar in the two industries.

Table 5.4 Sources of direct advice during Shunto negotiations

	(Per cent of respondents)	
	Automotive industry	Electrical machinery industry
Ranking		
1	Roren headquarters (58.3)	Roren headquarters (82.0)
2	Local organizations of roren (41.1)	Other unions of roren (34.9)
3	Other unions of roren (25.0)	Focal union of roren (19.8)
4	Focal union of roren (20.8)	Local organizations of roren (16.3)
5	Retired officials of the union (11.3)	Retired officials of the union (9.9)
6	Local organizations of industry-level federation (4.8)	Local organizations of industry-level federation (9.9)
7	Others (2.4)	Industry-level federation head-quarters (8.7)
8	(1.2),	Others (2.9)
9	Local organizations of Rengo (1.2)	Local organizations of Rengo (2.3)
10	Rengo headquarters (0.6)	Rengo headquarters (0.6)
(a) Roren headquarters + local organizations (1 + 2)	99.4	98.3
(b) All roren-related units (1 + 2 + 3 + 4)	145.2	153.0

Note: Multiple responses allowed. For (a), if we adjust for double-counting resulting from multiple responses, the percentage is 99.4 − 18.5 = 80.9 in autos, and 98.3 − 15.1 = 83.2 in electrical machinery.

The differences that exist in the exact routes through which such advice or support is channelled, with greater reliance on regional offices in automobiles, may well be due to the sheer size of the *roren* at some automakers, such as Nissan and Toyota. There is survey evidence that the larger the *roren* size, the more likely the reliance on local offices, in accordance with the organization theory of administrative control.

Otherwise, the two sectors are remarkably similar in a number of respects. Notably, in both industries, other unions in the same *roren* are a more important source of advice than the focal union. Even if we allow for the fact that much of the focal union's influence might be perceived to be exercised via the *roren* headquarters this points to the importance of lateral communication in the information and advice networks of affiliated unions, relative to the more hierarchical guidance from the focal union. Moreover, Table 5.4 indicates that *roren*-affiliated unions receive little direct advice or support from industry-level federations in the Shunto negotiation process. This indicates that *roren* are fulfilling a complementary, rather than an overlapping, role to the industry-level federations (see Section 5.4 for further discussion).

5.3.2 Roren's Role in Employment Adjustment

Business diversification and spin-outs have led to temporary and permanent transfers of union members to subsidiaries and affiliated firms. Consequently, as discussed in Chapter 2, union members have come to rely increasingly on a corporate grouping, rather than a firm, to deliver security of employment and income. What role have *roren* federations played in extending union members' career span within corporate groups? When asked whether or not their '*roren* performs an indispensable role in securing employment stability for union members in the face of corporate restructuring', a majority of survey respondents (56 per cent) agreed or strongly agreed with the statement. But the extent of agreement was greater in the electrical machinery industry (66 per cent) than in the auto industry (46 per cent). This inter-industry difference is due in part to the fact that employment adjustment was more prevalent in electrical machinery than in automobiles.

In the last five years, union members have rarely been made redundant, but 64 per cent of unions experienced temporary transfer (*shukko*) or permanent transfer (*tenseki*) of regular employees, and 56 per cent experienced transfers of middle managers. More than half of the unions (62 per cent) also received employees on transfer from other unions within the same *roren*. If we compare the two industries, electrical unions experienced more employment changes than automotive unions (see Table 5.5). For instance, nearly double the proportion of unions in electrical machinery— 81 per cent compared with 46 per cent in automobiles—experienced 'temporary and permanent transfers of regular union members'. Similarly, three-quarters (73 per cent) of electrical unions, compared with 50 per cent of automotive unions, received transferees from the focal firm or from other firms within the corporate group. This sectoral difference is in part due to the fact that electrical unions are more likely to be tied to the focal union through ownership linkages. As shown in Table 5.5, regardless of sectors, when the sample is divided into those at firms with high capital affiliation (50 per cent or more owned by the focal firm) and low capital affiliation (less than 50 per cent owned), employment transfers were much higher for the former group than for the latter group.

How do unions secure the destinations for those employees to be transferred? The survey asked the unions what they did (or would do) in response to a management proposal for manpower reduction due to worsening corporate performance. The most popular measure was 'to seek support and advice directly from the *roren* headquarter' (70 per cent), followed by 'exchanging information with unions at affiliated companies' (36 per cent), 'asking *roren* headquarters to coordinate and mediate

Table 5.5 Employment adjustment in the last five years (Per cent of respondents)

	Industrial sectors		Capital affiliation	
	Electrical machinery unions	Automotive unions	50% + ownership	Less than 50% ownership
Transfer of union members to other firms within *roren*	81.4**	46.4**	74.6**	52.2**
Transfer of middle managers to other firms within *roren*	68.6**	43.5**	63.8**	47.2**
Voluntary early retirement of union members	19.2**	11.9**	10.1	15.6
Compulsory redundancies for union members	0.0	1.2	0.0	1.1
Temporary transfer of union members to the focal firm or its affiliates	60.5**	35.7**	64.5**	35.0**
Receiving transferees from the core firm or its affiliates	73.3**	50.6**	82.6**	46.7**
Increase in non-regular employees	51.7	50.6	49.3	50.6

*Note:*** Differences are significant at 1% level;* significant at 5% level.

the process of finding the destination for surplus workers', (22 per cent), and 'finding firms that can employ surplus workers through discussion with other unions in the same *roren*' (18 per cent). The first two measures have been used (or are expected to be used) more often in the electrical machinery industry than in the auto industry (see Table 5.6). The reason why electrical unions are more likely to seek advice from the *roren* headquarters than auto unions is due to the aforementioned differences in the information network, whereby automotive unions have regional offices and other unions to talk to. The reason why electrical unions are more likely to exchange information with unions at affiliated companies than automotive unions appears to be compositional; in fact, automotive unions whose firms are 50 per cent or more owned by the focal firm are just as likely to engage in such information exchange as electrical unions whose firms have the same ownership characteristics.

5.3.3 Labour Participation in Management at the Corporate and Roren *Levels*

The *roren* federation may be regarded as a forum for affiliated unions to exchange information with each other in order to improve working conditions and to cope with employment adjustment. There is evidence that

Table 5.6 Union responses to management proposal for manpower reduction
(Per cent of respondents)

	Industrial sectors		Capital affiliation	
	Electrical unions	Automotive unions	50% + ownership	Less than 50% ownership
Seek support and advice directly from *roren* headquarters	76.7**	63.1**	72.5	65.6
Exchange information with unions at affiliated companies	41.3*	30.4*	44.2**	28.3**
Ask *roren* headquarter to coordinate and mediate the process of finding the destination for surplus workers	22.7	20.8	27.5*	18.3*
Find firms that can employ surplus workers through discussion with other unions in the same *roren*	16.3	19.0	16.7	18.9
Find the reason for the firm's deteriorating performance through other unions in the same *roren*	5.8	10.1	7.2	7.8

Note: Multiple responses allowed. Differences are** significant at 1% level;* significant at 5% level.

the extent of such information exchange is greater in the electrical ma-chinery than in the auto industry. Whilst 61 per cent of electrical unions strongly agreed with the notion that 'by belonging to the *roren*, it has become easier to exchange information and to engage in mutual learning with other unions in the same *roren*', less than half (47 per cent) of the automotive unions did. Also, to the notion that they can engage in 'hon-est heart-to-heart information exchange with officials of other affiliated unions', 26 per cent of the electrical unions agreed strongly compared with 15 per cent of the auto unions. Finally, when presented with the view that the union 'can obtain information about the focal firm's manage-ment trends more quickly by belonging to the *roren*', 65 per cent of the electrical unions agreed strongly, compared with 41 per cent of automo-tive unions. These sectoral differences underlie the fact that the firms that electrical unions organize are more likely to be linked to the focal firm by capital affiliation.

While it may seem from the above that information exchange within a *roren* federation is based on informal personal networks, such connections quite often originate in formal meetings. These meetings and gatherings take place at different levels within the *roren*, but the survey focused on two types of gatherings. One is a forum in which *roren*-affiliated union leaders meet with the focal firm's top management, as Matsushita Roren does with Matsushita Electric top management. The other is a gathering in which *roren*-affiliated union leaders meet with managers of firms in the corporate grouping, as Toyota Roren does with the supplier association, Kyohokai. According to the survey, around two-thirds of all unions have both these types of discussion forums. Inter-industry difference was not significant for the first type of meeting, but the second type—group-wide meeting on both sides—was more prevalent in the automobile sector than in electrical machinery. Evidently, the management side is more formally organized in the auto sector in the form of a supplier association than in electrical machinery.

Moreover, a significantly larger proportion of automotive unions than electrical unions were not satisfied with the current state of affairs, calling for strengthening the role of such meetings (see Table 5.7). This difference is likely to be related to the fact, noted earlier, that automotive unions find it more difficult than electrical unions to make use of the *roren* federation as a means of obtaining valuable information about the focal firm's man-agement trends. Such information is crucial for securing union members' mid- to long-term employment stability. The demand for a more effective forum for discussion between the *roren* federation and the focal firm's top

Table 5.7 Nature of labour–management consultation (Per cent of respondents)

(a) *Roren*-wide consultation
Is there a forum for labour–management consultation or discussion at the following levels?
Meeting between *roren*-affiliated union leaders and:

	Electrical unions	Automotive unions
Focal firm's top management	65.7	68.5
Yes, satisfied with current state	27.3	18.5
Yes, but should be strengthened	38.4	50.0
Managers of firms in the corporate grouping	54.1	84.5
Yes, satisfied with current state	24.4	19.6
Yes, but should be strengthened	29.7	64.9

(b) Enterprise-level consultation
In the last five years, has your union had occasions to discuss the following matters with company management?

	Electrical unions	Automotive unions
Annual business plan (involving investment, marketing, etc.)		
Yes	97.1	85.8
Yes, and the union modified the plan	12.8	4.8
Monthly production plan and manning level		
Yes	86.7	91.7
Yes, and the union modified the plan	25.6	40.5

management reflects, at a minimum, the unions' wish to achieve employment security for members.

The survey also asked about the current state of labour participation in management at the enterprise level. Some *roren*, such as Toyota Roren, as discussed in Chapter 4, formulate guidelines on the structure, process, and content of labour–management consultation at firms where *roren*-affiliated unions are organized. This hints at the possibility of standardizing these aspects of labour–management consultation within each *roren*. However, it is difficult for an outsider to judge whether these guidelines have been implemented successfully or not because, unlike working conditions, they are less transparent, less easily quantifiable, and less comparable between unions. Thus, labour–management consultation is most likely to vary widely in its substance and procedure. The questionnaire addressed this difficulty by selecting two specific items for labour–management consultation, namely the annual business plan and the monthly production plan. It asked the unions whether consultation had indeed taken place over these items, and if so whether they influenced the outcome of consultation.

The annual business plan includes strategic issues such as investment and marketing. The survey asked whether labour–management discussion ever occurred over this item in the last five years. A larger proportion of electrical unions (97 per cent) than automotive unions (86 per cent) said yes, which is not surprising given the prevalence of ownership links in electrical machinery. Moreover, electrical unions were more likely to have influenced the outcome: 13 per cent, compared with only 5 per cent of automotive unions, made management revise the plan as a result of the consultation (see Table 5.7).

The other item is more operational and concerns the monthly production plan and the corresponding plan for manning levels. An overwhelming majority (92 per cent of automotive unions and 87 per cent of electrical unions) said they discussed this item with management, but the inter-industry difference was not significant. However, the percentage of those unions that have successfully made management revise the plan in accordance with the union's wish is higher in the auto industry (41 per cent) than in the electrical machinery industry (26 per cent). These results underlie the central importance of supplier relationships for the well-being of *roren* union members in the automotive sector.

In summary, the survey identified variations in the nature of labour–management consultation at the enterprise level within a *roren* federation and within each industry. But on the whole, electrical unions tend to exercise effective voice on strategic plans. By contrast, automotive unions effectively influence production planning and other shorter-term operational issues. This inter-industry difference at the corporate level appears to be reflected in labour–management discussion at the federation level. Unfortunately, this survey did not ask about the content of *roren*-level discussion. But the fact that auto unions are less satisfied than electrical unions in *roren*-wide consultation appears to suggest a widening gap between the expectations of *roren*-affiliated unions to have a greater voice and the reality of little talk about strategic planning issues at the *roren*-wide consultation in automobiles. For now, auto unions get less out of *roren* than electrical unions, with a lower likelihood of getting access to valuable information about the focal firm's management trends. Of course, given corporate strategy to date, with less product diversification in the auto sector than in the electrical sector, automotive unions also have had less need and motivation to engage in participation at the strategic level.

5.4. Division of Labour between Industry-Level Federations and *Roren*: An Aspect of Vertical Articulation

What *roren* federations do must be set in the context of the vertical articulation that links individual members at the workplace to enterprise, industry, and national levels. The survey found, as discussed in Section 5.2, that the automotive *roren* typically had more financial and personnel resources than electrical *roren*. But this gives a partial view, unless the role of the industry-level union federations is taken into account. The conventional view of vertical articulation is that the national confederation, Rengo, coordinates industry-level union federations, to which enterprise unions affiliate. Where does the corporate group-based *roren* fit into this picture of three-level articulation? It depends on the industry, each captured by different ideologies that are either in favour of or hostile to *roren*-type union structures (more on this in Chapter 7). However, even in automobiles and electrical machinery in which unions are governed by the same philosophy of International Metalworkers Federation—Japan Council (IMF-JC), the resulting structures have been quite different.

The questionnaire is able to shed light on how affiliated unions think about the division of responsibilities between the corporate grouping-based union federation and the industry-level union federation. Thirty-six per cent of the unions surveyed agreed or strongly agreed with the statement that 'there is an overlap in activity between the *roren*- and the industry-level federations', while a total of 29 per cent disagreed or strongly disagreed. A greater proportion of electrical unions (41 per cent) perceived this overlap in activity than the automotive unions (32 per cent), but this sectoral difference was not statistically significant.

This result, with an even balance between those that agree and those that disagree, reveals a degree of unresolved ambiguity in the division of labour between *roren*- and industry-level union federations. Formally, the relationship between *roren*-affiliated unions and industry-level federations (known as *sanbetsu*) differs between the automotive and electrical machinery industries. In the automotive industry, there is a clear hierarchy, with

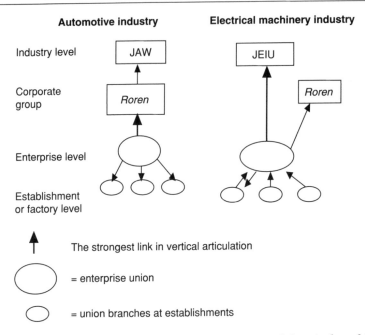

Figure 5.1 Vertical articulation of unions in automotive and electrical machinery industries

Note: Arrows indicate the direction of flow of resources in terms of money and people.

enterprise unions organizing themselves into corporate grouping-based *roren*, which in turn affiliate to JAW (see Figure 5.1). JAW is therefore a confederation at the industry level, and some *roren* came into existence so as to affiliate to JAW.

By contrast, electrical unions are vertically articulated in different ways, so that the overall picture is much messier than in the automotive industry. Some enterprise unions directly joined Denki Rengo (JEIU), the industry-level federation. Others remain unaffiliated to any industry-level federations but are affiliated to a *roren*. Still others are affiliated with an industry-level federation other than Denki Rengo such as Zenkin Rengo (now part of the Japanese Association of Metal, Machinery, and Manufacturing Workers, JAM). According to the questionnaire survey, 42 per cent of electrical unions also affiliate directly to a higher-level organization other than their *roren*; and every four in five of these were affiliated to Denki Rengo, the industry-level federation. By contrast, as expected, only 10 per cent of automotive unions said they affiliated to organizations other than their *roren*.

Thus, as shown schematically in Figure 5.1, the *roren* is a powerful organization in the automotive industry, in the sense that a significant proportion of financial and personnel resources flow from enterprise unions to the *roren* offices. But because the *roren* federation satisfies much of the role of the industry-level federation, JAW is relatively weak. JAW in fact receives only 230 yen per union member as subscription, and all JAW officials are on temporary transfer from the *roren*. By contrast, electrical unions contribute more—500 yen per member—to JEIU, the industry-level federation, which has resources to employ some union officials directly (Sanken Sentaa 1995). This means that electrical *roren* federations are in an awkward relationship to JEIU, being a poor cousin in terms of financial and personnel resources. Generally, however, the financial base of industry-level federations is limited, as enterprise unions keep the lion's share of union dues, passing on average 9.9 per cent of the total dues (or 512 yen out of 5,177 yen per month) to industry-level federations (Rengo 2003).

In sum, enterprise unions believe that *roren*- and industry-level federations overlap in activity. The complex union structure in the mezzanine level is an outcome of a compromise between different organizing principles, not just between the two sectors, but also within the same sector. Chapter 7 discusses the historical context in which the existing division of responsibilities emerged in the automobile industry. It represents a sector with one of the most drawn-out battles between unions with different strategies. Here we suggest that the structures finally emerged from two decades of political contestation between large and small unions, and between unions that regarded corporate group-based *roren* as promoting the transition to industrial unions and those that saw it as a hindrance to the creation of industrial unions.

5.5. Conclusions

This chapter presented the results of a questionnaire survey of enterprise unions that are affiliated to *roren* federations organized along the lines of corporate groupings. The survey identified *roren*'s role in three functions, namely in improving and standardizing working conditions, in coordinating employment adjustment within the boundary of the *roren* federation, and in facilitating information access and the exercise of worker voice through labour–management consultation. First, the automotive *roren* are more likely to issue targets or guidelines for improving working conditions than electrical *roren*. But during Shunto wage negotiations, *roren's* influence on affiliated unions was seen to come more directly from its headquarters in the case of electrical *roren*, whereas it was more dispersed via its regional offices in the case of automotive *roren*. Second, electrical unions experienced more employment adjustment than automotive unions, and they looked to the *roren* headquarters to coordinate and mediate the movement of union members between firms within the *roren* boundary. Third, electrical unions were more satisfied than automotive unions with the *roren*-wide labour–management consultation meetings as a way of gauging the focal firm's management trends. The electrical unions also exercised more effective voice vis-à-vis their company management on strategic issues such as the annual business plan, whilst automotive unions were more geared to exercising effective voice on operational issues such as the monthly production plan.

These generic functions of *roren* derive from significant structural differences between the automotive and the electrical machinery industries. First, unions affiliating to *roren* federations in electrical machinery tend to be at firms with both high capital affiliation and trade linkage with the focal firm, while unions in automotive *roren* were bound mainly by trading linkages. Second, automotive *roren* federations were found to be more centralized in financial and personnel resources than electrical *roren*, and had greater *de facto* influence over their decisions. The apparent contradiction—that automotive *roren* command more resources and *de facto* influence whilst being internally less cohesive—is explained in part by the fact that automotive *roren* partially satisfies the role normally undertaken by industry-level federations.

These different principles for drawing *roren's* organizational boundary and for the degree of centralization in the internal structure are consistent and complementary with the existing functions of *roren*. In this sense, labour strategy influences structure, which in turn facilitates the persistence of existing labour strategy. However, boundaries are not static. Automotive unions fear fluidity in the boundary and the internal cohesion of *roren* organizations in the future, due to greater instability of supplier relationships. Electrical unions also face changes in capital affiliation linkages, as firms engage in M & A and corporate restructuring, as we saw in the case of Matsushita in Chapter 3. We will analyse such interaction between union structure and strategy in Chapter 8, i.e. the ways in which structural characteristics of *roren*-type union networks facilitate, and constrain, labour strategies to secure jobs and improve working conditions.

Notes

1. As noted in Chapter 3, a three-party agreement is signed between the focal union, the focal firm, and the newly created subsidiary management, in order to apply the collective agreement for the focal firm to the subsidiary firm. This, in effect, extends the focal union membership to incorporate employees at the subsidiary firm.

2. Nissan Roren has a different formal structure from others, with three main 'inter-enterprise' unions, Hanro for dealers, Buro for parts makers, and Minro for a miscellaneous category. Each of the three unions is organized into branches at the enterprise level, corresponding to enterprise unions in other cases (see Chapter 7 for further details). It is Buro, the parts makers union, that is the subject of this survey. For the sake of comparability we treat Nissa Roren Buro as the *roren* organization, and its branches as enterprise unions, in this survey.

3. 'Strong' here is defined as 50 per cent or more share ownership or 50 per cent or more sales going to the focal firm.

6

Intra-Industry Differences I: Why Companies Differ

The previous chapter dealt with inter-sectoral differences in union structure and strategy, comparing the automotive and the electrical machinery sectors. This and the remaining chapters turn to an analysis of why firms and unions in the same sector differ, and why the differences matter. Differences between firms are the key focus for students of business strategy who are interested in identifying the sources of competitive advantage in distinctive and difficult-to-imitate capability. The key aim in this chapter is to unpack the question 'why do firms in the same industry differ and how does it matter?' (Nelson 1991) by comparing supplier development activities at Honda, Nissan, and Toyota. Supplier development is a company's undertaking to improve its supplier's capabilities, and has been taken for granted in the Japanese automotive industry for several decades.

As discussed in Chapter 1, national institutions affect corporate structures by providing legitimacy to particular patterns of authority. They also affect corporate strategy via the degree of investments that actors are willing to make in relation-specific assets. But institutions and market environments are largely controlled as sources of variation when examining firms in the same industry in the same country.

Thus, national institutions are the same for all automobile companies in Japan. For instance, certain corporate governance characteristics, such as long-term stakeholding, make it easier for firms to engage in know-how exchange and joint capability development between customer and supplier companies, each with long-term employed workers. These institutions therefore facilitate greater permeability of know-how between legally distinct units of financial control. Despite an identical institutional environment, Toyota has developed a distinct strategy and internal structure for engaging in capability enhancement activities, as compared with Nissan and Honda.

The aim of this chapter is to analyse the causes and consequences of the differences between Toyota, Nissan, and Honda. Section 6.1 discusses the organizational capabilities approach in so far as it is relevant to the topic of supplier development. Section 6.2 surveys the range of supplier development activities at each of the three automakers. The empirical work is based on interviews conducted with key respondents (managers in purchasing and supplier development engineers) at Honda, Nissan, and Toyota, and at some of their suppliers. Both historical and contemporary documents provided by the companies were consulted. Section 6.3 compares the three companies' structures and processes for supplier development, and discusses the issue of replication of such structures and processes outside of Japan. The chapter concludes by drawing broader theoretical implications concerning capabilities, governance, and the boundary of the firm.

6.1. Supplier Development as an Organizational Capability and a Mechanism for Replicating It

This chapter concerns itself with both (*a*) companies' organizational capabilities to develop their suppliers, and (*b*) organizational capability as a subject taught to suppliers. It sets out to answer the following question: what factors facilitate and constrain a firm's attempt to replicate its organizational capabilities at suppliers, within the intended boundary whilst preventing leakage to competitors? This question may be addressed by distinguishing among different types of capabilities, by identifying internal organizational structures that facilitate the transfer of new capabilities, and by linking organizational capabilities to corporate governance considerations. Supplier development may be positioned as a capability-enhancing activity that fits neither 'market' nor 'hierarchy'. But without invoking the governance question—who makes decisions about what resources to commit to what investment—the notion of organizational capability alone ironically does not give guidance as to what constitutes an organization.

Supplier development is a procedure by a company to help improve its suppliers' capabilities. More specifically, it may be interpreted as a firm's attempt to transfer (or replicate) some aspects of its in-house organizational capability across firm boundaries. The ability to replicate such capability is, in itself, also a capability. In the automobile industry, automakers may send their own engineers to the supplier's shop floor to help solve a problem with a specific component in order to meet the product launch date. They may provide training courses for suppliers' employees in techniques such as TWI, Quality Circles, Value Engineering, and simultaneous engineering. They may also ask a supplier to work on a specific production line for an extended period with a view to learning heuristics to achieve cost reduction, inventory reduction, or quality improvement.

The organizational capabilities that are being replicated at suppliers consist of a hierarchy of practiced routines that are coherent (Nelson 1991: 68). 'Routines' refer broadly to the way things are done in an organization, and may include not only well-specified technical routines but also 'the relatively constant dispositions and strategic heuristics that shape the approach of a firm to the non-routine problems it faces' (Nelson and Winter 1982: 15). In so far as such routines involve an important element of interaction and coordination between individuals, organizational capabilities are not fully reducible to individual skills. Knowledge is typically distributed in different parts of the organization.

One important capability in supplier development is continuous improvement (or *kaizen*). In a Schumpeterian or evolutionary context, firms may satisfice, in response to an uncertain and complex world. Such satisficing behaviour is dislodged by heightened performance aspiration and by re-igniting learning through continuous improvement (Winter 2000). The practice of continuous improvement amounts to an effort to re-ignite the quest for improvement in organizational routines 'so frequently that the flame burns pervasively and continuously' (Winter 2000: 993), rather than starts and stops in relation to the identification and solving of a specific problem (Winter 1994: 103). Continuous improvement is inherently firm-specific in its application and results, and therefore is part of the intangible assets for which no ready market exists. The distinctive and difficult-to-replicate character of such assets is central to the sustenance of a firm's competitive advantage. It also explains why firms differ, even in the same industry in the same country (Nelson 1991).

The organizational capabilities framework makes it possible to classify the content of supplier development programmes along the following two dimensions:

(1) *Type of capability*, classified into three levels: first, the most basic level of 'maintenance capability' (i.e. the ability to maintain a particular

level of performance consistently); second, 'improvement capability' (Fujimoto 1997: 12),[1] which affects the pace of performance improvements; and third, the highest level of 'evolutionary capability' (i.e. capability for capability building) (Fujimoto 2000: 246). The last is to be distinguished from 'dynamic capabilities' (Teece and Pisano 1994) to the extent that the emphasis is less on 'adapting, integrating, and reconfiguring internal and external resources in response to changing environments' (Teece 2002) and more on the sustained accumulation of the other two capabilities. This, then, resembles dynamic capabilities in moderately dynamic markets, rather than in high-velocity markets, as elaborated by Eisenhardt and Martin (2000).

(2) *Scope of activity*: ranging from supplier development activity focused around a model-specific component to that for the whole factory or the whole company. The broader scope implies not just an expansion from a specific production line to a larger production area, but also an expansion to non-production areas (such as product development and capital investment decisions).

The most limited aim of supplier development is to intervene in order to teach 'maintenance capability' with respect to a specific component. At the other extreme, the most ambitious aim is for a company to replicate at its supplier a whole set of organizational 'routines' underlying its own evolutionary capability.

In Japan, key suppliers are given a consistent set of *incentives* to learn and acquire organizational capability from their customer companies. Suppliers benefit from relationships that are variously characterized as relational, obligational, trust-based, and voice-based (Dore 1983; Macneil 1985; Helper 1990; Sako 1992; Adler 2001). Long-term trading induces investment in relation-specific skills (Asanuma 1989), a joint problem-solving approach adopted in developing 'black box' parts (Clark and Fujimoto 1991; Fujimoto 1997), and a clear rule for sharing gains between the automaker and the supplier (Smitka 1989; MacMillan 1990). Less noted in the literature, but clearly demonstrated in the empirical section of this chapter, is that the automaker's transfer of its capability requires not only resource commitment but also a distinctive internal organizational structure. Despite these incentive-structuring mechanisms, there remain at least three obstacles to the replication of automakers' organizational capability by suppliers. Consequently, incentive structuring is a necessary but not a sufficient condition for facilitating suppliers to acquire organizational capability. Differences in core capabilities to overcome these barriers to replication explain why firms in the same industry differ despite similarities in incentive-structuring mechanisms.

First, the replication of organizational capability may be difficult due to the tacit nature of the knowledge to be transferred to suppliers. Manuals (i.e. for standardization and codification) may exist, but typically, hands-on instruction must accompany classroom teaching, which makes the process of replication labour-intensive (e.g. sending engineers to spend a significant amount of time on the supplier's shop floor) and expensive (because economies of scale are difficult to exploit). In this study, we may conjecture from the chosen mode of supplier development (e.g. shop floor visits vs. seminars) what the automaker's presumed degree of tacitness is concerning that which it is purporting to teach. The more automakers rely on teaching through the practice of routines rather than the representation of routines, the more complete the replication process is likely to be. Moreover, doing and teaching are different things. In a craft skill context, some are excellent at doing but are *unwilling* to teach a trick or two because that would undermine one's power. More noted in the recent management literature on knowledge is the fact that some are excellent at doing but are *unable* to teach because of the tacit and complex skills involved: 'we know more than we can tell' (Polanyi 1967: 4). How can the amount of 'telling' be increased to match the level of 'knowing'? This study shows empirically that the firm's teaching capability is enhanced when there are opportunities for it to practise in different settings.

Second, replication may be problematic because of a high degree of interdependence among a firm's supplier development process and other processes in the organization. It has been noted that: 'Recognizing the congruences and complementarities among processes, and between processes and incentives, is critical to the understanding of organizational capabilities' (Teece and Pisano 1994: 544). Consequently, partial imitation of a few elements in a successful model may yield little benefits (Milgrom and Roberts 1995). For example, the 'lean production' model is essentially interpreted to apply to the shop floor. But 'lean production requires distinctive shop floor practices and processes as well as distinctive higher-order managerial processes' (Teece and Pisano 1994: 543). This implies that as a cumulative process, there is an inbuilt bias towards automakers' strategy to broaden and deepen the scope of supplier development, as they extend their activities beyond shop floor improvement procedures.

Third, this strategy to extend the coverage of capabilities in supplier development programmes is at loggerheads with certain modes of corporate governance. A system of corporate governance shapes who makes investment decisions in corporations, what types of investments they make, and how returns from investments are distributed (O'Sullivan 2000*b*). Supplier development involves the supplier company deciding to allocate resources for new physical investments and for learning new skills. But since the voice and the input of the customer company as a teacher are pertinent in such decisions, the notion of the supplier company as an autonomous unit of organizational control is potentially undermined. When supplier development concerns basic 'maintenance capability' for a specific component, the customer company's input tends to be clear, and a rule for sharing gains from a joint performance improvement effort eliminates the need to negotiate each time gains are made. But when it concerns the teaching of 'evolutionary capability' with a wide scope for activity over a long period of time, the customer company's contribution becomes less easy to specify. In such cases, even among innovative enterprises, the notion of the customer company as a semi-insider stakeholder in the supplier company has to be accepted for such supplier development intervention to be considered not too intrusive. In the absence of legitimacy of such customer company role, the replication of organizational processes across legally distinct units of organizational control may be constrained by the fear that suppliers' financial (and more broadly managerial) autonomy may be compromised in the process of replication.

6.2. Case Studies at Toyota, Nissan, and Honda

6.2.1 Toyota

Toyota is noted for two things that distinguish it from Nissan and Honda. First, its internal organization for providing supplier development is decoupled. TPS and TQC activities are taught to suppliers by different parts of the company. This bifurcated internal structure facilitates suppliers to accumulate their 'evolutionary capability' (i.e. capability for capability building) and lower-level capabilities at the same time. Second, through Jishuken Groups (self-study groups), Toyota relies not just on one-to-one teaching of suppliers, but also on lateral learning amongst suppliers through the practice, rather than the mere representation, of capability.

ORIGIN OF SUPPLIER DEVELOPMENT

Toyota Motor Corporation's purchasing philosophy is enshrined in the 1939 Purchasing Rules, which state: 'once nominated as Toyota suppliers, they should be treated as part of Toyota (as branch plants); Toyota shall carry out business with these suppliers without switching to others, and shall make every effort to raise the performance of these suppliers' (TMC 1988: 76; Kyohokai 1994: 18). But the post-war trigger for thinking more concretely about supplier development was the so-called enterprise group diagnosis (*keiretsu shindan*) conducted by the Aichi Prefectural Government during 1952–3 (Kyohokai 1967: 24–5; Wada 1991*a*; see also Nishiguchi 1994: 65; Fujimoto 1997: 76, 212). The public-sector consultancy chose the Toyota *keiretsu* (in practice Toyota and its twenty-one key suppliers) as the unit to evaluate along four criteria, namely the existence of a management policy, productivity improvement, quality improvement, and the fulfilment of production plans (Kyohokai 1967: 24). The consulting exercise resulted in a heightened expectation that Toyota provide assistance to improve suppliers' company-wide managerial capabilities.

In the 1950s, lectures, seminars, and training courses for Toyota employees were made available to core supplier employees. For example, a 30-day lecture course on production management, organized by the Japan Management Association, was first held in 1955 for Toyota and supplier employees, and was repeated twenty times until 1967, producing 372 graduates (excluding Toyota employees) (Kyohokai 1967: 32). These supplier employees learnt from others' factories: 'we made a round of Kyohokai member companies as well as Toyota's internal factories in order to conduct research into improving work methods. Task improvements helped anticipate repeated pressures for cost reduction. So companies vied with each other to open up their own factory as a study site, and were eager to polish each other's skills' (Kyohokai 1967: 32). There were also a whole series of lectures and seminars on quality control aimed at top and middle managers of supplier companies in Kyohokai, which eventually established its Quality Control Committee in 1961.

Despite these efforts, when Toyota won the Deming Award in 1965, the Japanese Union of Scientists and Engineers (JUSE) pointed out the sizeable gap in quality standards between Toyota and parts suppliers (Nemoto 1983: 151). Masao Nemoto was appointed to head the Purchasing Control Department (*kobai kanribu*), newly created in 1965, preceding the establishment of Taiichi Ohno's Operations Management Consulting Division (OMCD) (*seisan chosabu*) by five years. While Ohno's mission was to promote TPS among suppliers, his lesser-known counterpart, Nemoto, was to diffuse TQC to the suppliers. This is the origin of the bifurcated responsibilities for supplier development within Toyota (see Figure 6.1).

It is well understood that TPS, a system relentlessly focused on the elimination of waste, exposes quality problems through line stoppages and forces management to fix the root cause of the problem (Ohno 1978; Monden 1983). Less noted in the literature is the contribution TQC has made to the rapid diffusion of TPS across Toyota factories, not only by educating middle managers in quality control techniques but also by using Hoshin Kanri (policy deployment) to link the shop floor processes to the policies of higher-level management. (Nemoto quipped that lean production is the Toyota way minus TQC (Shimokawa et al. 1997: 7).) By extension, Toyota's suppliers benefited from the synergy resulting from combining TQC and TPS. The teaching of TPS led to suppliers accumulating their 'maintenance capability' and 'improvement capability', whilst the simultaneous teaching of TQC enabled them to make TPS sustainable throughout their operations, leading to a form of 'evolutionary capability'.

OMCD'S DIFFUSION OF TOYOTA PRODUCTION SYSTEM

TPS was initially introduced to all Toyota factories in the 1960s. These factories demanded JIT delivery of parts, but a real effort to implement JIT production within supplier factories did not begin until the 1970s (Kyohokai 1994: 91). The OMCD, established in 1970 as part of Toyota's production control function, facilitated a seamless transfer of knowledge about TPS between Toyota and its suppliers. Because OMCD is in charge of implementing TPS both within Toyota factories and at its core suppliers,

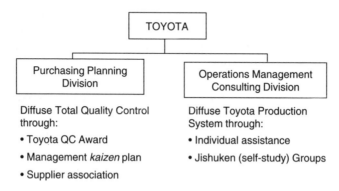

Figure 6.1 Bifurcated structure for supplier development at Toyota

the same methods, procedures, and heuristics are applied to internal and external factories by putting the same set of engineers in charge of both. The OMCD employs around fifty supplier development engineers, who have come up the ranks after in-company training placements in Toyota factories. Within Toyota, Factory Jishuken (*kojo jishuken*)—an autonomous study group—takes place as a culmination of education and training for Toyota's middle managers and first-line supervisors. They are considered the most important repository of *kaizen* know-how on the shop floor (Nemoto 1995; Ishida et al. 1996). Supervisors are given an incentive to make continuous improvements with concrete results, as they are required to regularly present *kaizen* ideas in front of factory managers and top management (Ishida et al. 1996).

Jishuken Groups for suppliers to improve their shop floor by refining the application of TPS came about in the early 1970s, but were kept under wraps from external eye for a decade or two. By all accounts, Jishuken seems to have had an informal beginning with some suppliers requesting help from OMCD. By the late 1990s, there were nine Jishuken Groups in all, two for body makers (nine factories) and seven for parts manufacturers (forty-seven factories). The total is therefore fifty-six factories belonging to fifty-two enterprises, accounting for 80 per cent of all purchasing spend by Toyota. Interestingly, some of these suppliers also have an OMCD-like operation in-house, cascading downwards the practice of diffusing TPS within the company and to smaller second-tier suppliers (Imai 1985). Toyota has given regard to geographical proximity and the absence of direct competitors in forming these groupings. Such considerations are deemed important for intensive interaction and sharing of know-how during Jishuken sessions.

Every calendar year, Jishuken activities are carried out within the broad policy direction issued by OMCD (the 1998 focus, for instance, was to adapt to model mix changes and output fluctuations in the age of low demand). Within such a framework, each Jishuken company chooses a specific theme in discussion with OMCD, and identifies a specific factory area for study by the Group (JECO, a medium-sized instrumentation supplier, chose to focus on parts and finished goods logistics). Every year, each supplier company hosts a study over a two-month period. The study session begins by setting concrete performance targets in terms of shop floor indicators, such as productivity (in terms of the number of process steps), cost reduction, and inventory turns (e.g. JECO's targets were to reduce the inventory to meet order fluctuations by 54 per cent (from 0.65 to 0.30 days) and to reduce the inventory of rotors by 95 per cent (from 0.67 to 0.03 days)). The senior OMCD engineer in charge visits a supplier company under study around three times during the two-month period and generally makes severely critical observations, whilst more junior OMCD engineers visit the company at other occasions to give more detailed guidance. Jishuken Group members meet once a week to put forward concrete *kaizen* ideas. A typical Jishuken gathering would consist of around thirty people, as each supplier company nominates five participants. Most of the ideas are implemented by the host company before the two months are up (e.g. at JECO, 222 of the 248 *kaizen* ideas put forward in total were implemented, an implementation rate of 90 per cent). Many of the ideas concerned the use of Kanban and the clarification of rules, for instance, when defects were discovered at the point of shipment. Of the 222 implemented ideas, 85 originated from within JECO, whilst 135 came from other companies within the same Jishuken Group. Some of the unimplemented ideas are taken up by JECO's in-house shop floor study groups, evidence that Kaizen activity is sustainable within JECO beyond the stimulation given by the Jishuken Group. At the end of the year, all the Jishuken Groups gather in one location to make presentations of their year's achievements. Written documents of these achievements are compiled and handed out to all participants.

Besides Jishuken, Toyota's OMCD also provides individual assistance to suppliers on an if-and-when-necessary basis. For instance, the purchasing department may request assistance for a supplier with a pre-production problem in fixing its component quality. What are the relative advantages and disadvantages of bilateral assistance and group activities like Jishuken? An OMCD manager gave the following eloquent answer.

Individual assistance is good whenever we are looking for quick results. When a supplier's profits have plummeted suddenly, or when a supplier is not keeping up with the launch of a new model, we send in our trained experts and tell everyone to watch quietly. But this short-term, yet deep, intervention requires a tremendous amount of resources on our part. More likely than not, suppliers feel they have improved by doing what they are told, but do not understand why, and things come to a halt when the experts go home. By contrast, Jishuken is good for developing and training people, both at the suppliers and at Toyota. In order to make improvements towards a set of targets by everyone putting their ideas forward, there are various obstacles to be overcome along the way. It would most certainly be quicker for an expert to take a lead and provide answers, but this would not result in developing the skills of those who are led. The strength of the Toyota Production System lies in creating as many people who can implement and put into practice the TPS on their own as possible. So the most important thing for the survival of TPS is human resource development. But also there is no point in holding study group sessions without concrete results, because then companies would not be profitable. So we do put serious pressure for Jishuken Groups to meet the targets.

Thus, Jishuken is a closely knit gathering of middle-level production technologists from a stable group of companies, who jointly develop better capabilities for applying TPS through mutual criticism and concrete application. The two modes of delivery by the OMCD, namely the Jishuken Group activities and individual assistance, are synergistic, in that the former gives suppliers the space to experiment and explore on their own while the latter provides a top-down quick solution by Toyota experts, which on its own may discourage learning. Jishuken also has the benefit of developing Toyota's own personnel in teaching tacit skills. Both modes of supplier development give Toyota enormous access to the detailed cost structures of its main suppliers. This contributes to the sustenance of Toyota's core capability to engage in target costing, and to the retention of manufacturing know-how for components that Toyota does not produce in-house. Thus, there is a fine line to be drawn between monitoring and learning (Beaudet 1998).

THE PURCHASING DEPARTMENT'S DIFFUSION OF TQC

Like the OMCD, the Purchasing Department also relied on bilateral and multilateral modes of supplier development. In the multilateral mode, the department has been in charge of the supplier association, Kyohokai, which, despite its ever-expanding membership, remains a forum for imparting and sharing information in the supplier community. They hold regular seminars, study group meetings, training courses, exhibitions, and presentations of members' achievements in various matters including cost, quality, delivery, and development (Kyohokai 1994; Sako 1996).

More concrete individual guidance is given to suppliers that aspire to obtain the Toyota QC Award, established soon after Toyota won the Deming Award in 1965 to motivate suppliers to adopt TQC (Nemoto 1978; Kyohokai 1994: 74–5). As of September 1996, a total of forty-four suppliers obtained the Toyota QC Award. The Quality Technology Section of the Purchasing Planning Department offers hands-on guidance in Hoshin Kanri, quality assurance, cost control, Genba Kanri, delivery management and so on. Because of this traditional TQC focus, the Purchasing Planning

Department defines supplier assistance to be about capability enhancement (*taishitsu kyoka*, 'the strengthening of one's constitution' in a literal translation). This is necessarily a long-term undertaking, involving assistance in marketing, cost and investment planning, cost control, process improvements, and quality improvement.

More recently, however, an urgent task surfaced with the recession in the 1990s. Whereas in 1988, fifty-seven out of the seventy-seven major suppliers (with 20 per cent or more sales dependence on Toyota) saw their revenues and profits increase, by 1993, only three were experiencing increases while fifty-seven were facing declining revenues and profits. Toyota responded by creating in 1993 a Kaizen Promotion Section within the Purchasing Planning Department, staffed by twenty-one employees (fifteen of whom came from factory-level production engineering sections, while the rest had cost and accounting expertise). The main task of this new section is to help suppliers secure profits in the short run by various means including cutting pay and freezing investment. In effect, the Purchasing Planning Department's supplier assistance is two-pronged, one aimed at the short-term recovery of loss-making suppliers and the other for longer-term capability enhancement regardless of profitability problems.

The account so far leads to a question about how the OMCD relates to the Purchasing Department when dealing with the same set of core suppliers. The nature of coordination between the OMCD and the Purchasing Planning Department is informal, based on personal networks. No organizational procedures exist for informing each other's work. According to an OMCD manager:

When we go to a supplier, we do not put the purchasing function at the forefront. We can see everything at the supplier company including the detailed breakdown of costs. If rationalization is for the sole purpose of passing on the gains to the purchasing department, suppliers would rather not make any improvements. So we do not let the purchasing department know how much productivity improvements a particular supplier has made as a result of our intervention.

Similarly, a Purchasing Planning manager was confident that most suppliers are reassured of the absence of a direct link between supplier assistance and price negotiations:

No supplier would do Kaizen if such a link is made. Within Japan, we tell the suppliers, don't worry, there is no need for such fear. If improvements were made with OMCD assistance, the OMCD would never pass on to purchasing the information with a view to reflecting it in component prices.

A supplier, participating in Jishuken and receiving assistance from the Purchasing Planning Department, reinforced this view:

There are occasions, like with VA, when Toyota says let's split the gains where they relate directly to markets. But we feel that Toyota provide guidance, quite consciously bringing our attention to other aspects from which we can gain for ourselves regardless of Toyota. They tell us from time to time to direct our Kaizen effort to these aspects.

In effect, the supplier in question is allowed to keep the gains from an OMCD intervention.

To summarize, Toyota's OMCD has a separate existence from the Purchasing Department, facilitating a smooth transfer of know-how between internal factories and supplier factories, and giving suppliers an incentive to enhance their 'evolutionary capability' for the long term rather than to seek a quick fix for commercial advantage. The OMCD and the Purchasing Department, separately, emphasize the need for both short-term fixing of problems and long-term capability enhancement. The resulting array of supplier development channels, from group-based activities to individual assistance, enables Toyota to ensure that both explicit and tacit knowledge is communicated to its core suppliers (Dyer and Nobeoka 2000). Moreover, suppliers, by being taught TPS and TQC at the same time, are able to exploit the synergy in sustaining continuous improvement.

6.2.2 Nissan[2]

Like Toyota, Nissan's Yokohama plant received an enterprise group diagnosis in 1953. The diagnosis revealed that many of the owner-managers of Nissan's subcontracting firms came from technical backgrounds, and lacked interest in management issues. The diagnosis report recommended that Nissan provide guidance for its suppliers in 'clearer management direction, better organization structure, managerial planning and scientific management principles, improved time management, and more attention to production management' (Ueda 1997: 226). In reality, however, Nissan's assistance was initially restricted to developing 'maintenance capability' on the shop floor, and it was not until the 1980s that broader managerial processes (including TQC)—amounting to 'evolutionary capability'—were taken up seriously as a topic for supplier development. As described below, the history of Nissan's supplier development activity is marked by (a) significantly early starts in adopting new techniques, but also by (*b*) discontinuities in initiatives for Nissan's internal factories and those for its suppliers.

DISCONTINUOUS HISTORY OF DIFFUSING SYNCHRONIZED PRODUCTION AND TQC

Synchronized production (*doki seisan*) is Nissan's own philosophy and method for a demand-pull low-buffer production system, dating back to the early 1960s. As a management philosophy, it sought to exploit the existing imbalance between the firm and the environment as an opportunity for making continuous improvement. This philosophy was to be implemented in three stages: (*a*) through line balancing to improve the efficiency of machinery and manpower; (*b*) through balancing production processes with processes that precede and follow production; and (*c*) through synchronizing the production system with a future management vision (Takarakai 1994: 116). Juzo Wada, heading the purchasing department in the 1960s, is credited with devising the idea, and effected a 'synchronization experiment' in 1963 to spread this production system to core suppliers through the supplier association, Takarakai (Nissan Motor Co. 1965: 388; Takarakai 1994: 116). The experiment eventually faded way, and Nissan's purchasing function restarted supplier development with a focus on the Action Plate Method (APM) in the 1970s and 1980s, and on capability enhancement activity in the 1990s. The mid-1990s also saw Nissan establish a Synchronized Production Promotion Department in order to diffuse synchronized production—called Nissan Production Way (NPW) from 1994—internally to Nissan's factories. Thus, unlike at Toyota, the function responsible for diffusing synchronized production internally is separate from that for suppliers.

There is a similar delinking between Nissan's internal efforts and actions for suppliers in the area of TQC. Nissan was awarded the Deming Prize as early as in 1960, and used the supplier association, Takarakai, as an organ to provide education and training on TQC to member suppliers (Udagawa et al. 1995: 86). But Nissan tended to treat the Deming Award as an end in itself, and did not continue to nurture internal expertise or diffuse TQC to suppliers. In fact, it took Nissan twenty-two years before it established the Nissan QC Award for members of Takarakai in 1982. In the meantime, Nissan provided individual assistance to suppliers in quality control techniques, putting an emphasis on product quality. With the start of the teaching of company-wide TQC to suppliers, just over thirty suppliers obtained the Nissan QC Award, but only six years on in 1988, the award was suspended. In the 1990s, Nissan took a renewed interest in improving product quality, and newly established a TQM Promotion Department to revive TQC within Nissan.

FROM GROUP-BASED TO INDIVIDUAL SUPPLIER-BASED ASSISTANCE

Nissan, like other automakers, has classified its component suppliers using multiple gradations. Initially, the core group was Nissan's main supplier association, Takarakai, consisting of around 100 member companies throughout its history (1958–91). In 1966, a second supplier association, Shohokai, was formed as a looser gathering of bigger and more independent suppliers. In 1969, Takarakai introduced a distinction between activities for all members (e.g. lectures and QCC conferences) and 'autonomous activity' by six newly formed committees, each consisting of ten or less select member firms producing similar products (Takarakai 1994: 58; Udagawa et al. 1995: 88). These committees were very active in sharing information and ideas through mutual factory visits and study groups. Nissan's purchasing function was in charge of promoting supplier association activities by providing direction, advice, and expertise.

In 1983, Takarakai's organization was restructured again by creating (*a*) a joint committee to seek common themes across the six committees, and (*b*) five specialist functional committees (in TQC, education, logistics, health & safety, and the promotion of Nissan cars) (Takarakai 1994: 92). Thereafter, the locus of activity shifted from the six committees to the specialist functional committees. Takarakai activities were streamlined further, as members felt that Takarakai had run its course. The most active part of Takarakai that remained was a Specialist Committee for Capability Improvement (*taishitsu kaizen senmon iinkai*), whose origin lay in the TQC committee of the 1980s (Takarakai 1994: 111). When Takarakai disbanded itself in 1991, this committee was also disbanded, and the Capability Enhancement Promotion Committee was established under the auspices of Nissan's Engineering Support Department. In order to be member of this committee, suppliers had to be more than 20 per cent owned by Nissan, over 30 per cent of the supplier's sales turnover go to Nissan group companies, and the total annual sales to Nissan must exceed 20 billion yen. Although the twenty-five suppliers that met these criteria are expected to learn from each other, Nissan's assistance is largely on a one-to-one basis (see below).

BROADENING AND DEEPENING SUPPLIER DEVELOPMENT ACTIVITY

Nissan has two foci of supplier development activity, namely component-based assistance and factory-wide assistance. The former involves the teaching of various techniques to improve cost, quality, delivery, and development, and is captured most recently by Saimal Activity. The latter, factory-wide assistance, is known as Capability Enhancement Activity, and incorporates synchronized production, TPM, and Genba Kanri.[3] In the mid-1990s, it consisted of a three-year programme to implement synchronized production. The aim in the first year was to improve the use of direct labour, in the second year to improve indirect labour, and in the third year to cut overheads. Starting initially with three factories from three supplier firms, there were forty factories from twelve companies participating in this programme by 1997. Typically, a supplier specifies a model factory, which is diagnosed and improved with intensive help from Nissan engineers; three to four engineers visiting the factory four times a month is a guideline, and it is known for a Nissan engineer to be resident at the supplier for three months. Beyond this stage, the supplier receives a visit from a Nissan engineer twice a month. Not only is the supplier expected to expand the scope of his activity within the model factory (from direct to indirect labour, etc), it is also expected to apply what has been learnt at the model factory to another factory.

Nissan's Capability Enhancement Activity places great emphasis on evaluation and diagnosis. The thinking here is that without concrete evaluation measures, Nissan cannot provide effective assistance, nor would suppliers feel convinced of the need to make improvements. Since the mid-1990s, Nissan has developed a whole series of measures for suppliers concerning (*a*) their financial performance, (*b*) data on quality, cost, and delivery, and (*c*) evaluation of systems governing components, factories, and companies. For example, component-based evaluation involves benchmarking 90 component types of 200 Japanese companies, along six criteria, namely quality (e.g. in-process defect rate), reliability (e.g. equipment breakdown), flexibility (e.g. die change time), speed (e.g. cycle time), economy (e.g. output per time unit), and continuity (e.g. the proportion of processes that are continuous).

Since 1995, up-to-date performance measures of the twenty-five core supplier companies are displayed in a showroom located within the Engineering Support Department. Moreover, there are three meetings every year for the twenty-five companies, one at the company president level and the other two for manufacturing directors. The meetings have the purpose of sharing information about evaluation data and of creating a consensus about future directions. The sensitivity of the information and the presence of direct competitors within the group of twenty-five suppliers require much care and attention in the way it is handed out. But on balance, Nissan's Engineering Support Department believes that the disclosure of evaluation data has a beneficial effect of stimulating healthy rivalry for improvement. Besides the meetings of the twenty-five suppliers as a whole, there are other smaller group meetings of suppliers located in specific geographical areas, when suppliers make presentations of *kaizen* examples from their factories. These are fora for exchanging ideas about successful results, but not where joint studies and problem-solving (à la Toyota's Jishuken) are carried out by supplier groups.

Saimal Activity (Saimal standing for 'simultaneous' in simultaneous engineering) is a 1990s programme to help suppliers improve the component development process. The timing coincides with Nissan's drive to adopt simultaneous engineering as a major corporate vehicle to improve its performance (Okurasho 1997: 71). The component technology group of Nissan's Engineering Support Department is in charge of developing a number of tools (such as the Saimal Job Plan spelling out detailed steps in developing a part for a new model) and evaluation measures to assess suppliers' capability in managing the component development process. Saimal Activity has targeted specific components, particularly (*a*) components that tend to have unstable interface quality, such as lamps and weather strips; (*b*) components that suffer from many design changes before Job 1, such as harnesses, carpets, seats, and door trims; and (*c*) expensive components whose costs are difficult to reduce, such as metal pressings, air conditioners, door locks, air bags, steering wheels, and engine and transmission parts. The Engineering Support Department evaluates whether the Saimal Activity has taken root at the supplier companies, by monitoring and appraising not only outcomes (in terms of quality, cost, and delivery) but processes. The latter involve such things as whether the Saimal Job Plan has been adhered to or not, whether in-company education system is adequate at the supplier, and whether the supplier takes an initiative to make suggestions to Nissan. Only if a supplier scores highly on both outcomes and processes would it graduate from the stage of receiving regular visits by Nissan engineers.

To summarize, as at Toyota, Nissan's supplier development activity has broadened and deepened considerably over time, starting with teaching 'maintenance capability' in the 1960s to replicating higher-level capabilities in broader areas (e.g. component design and development). Nevertheless, significant differences exist between Nissan and Toyota. First, Nissan's supplier development is much more individual company-based than at Toyota, relying less on lateral inter-supplier learning. Second,

Nissan suppliers share ideas and achievements through presentation meetings, but not through the practice of joint problem-solving. Consequently, less tacit knowledge is shared between Nissan suppliers. Third, at Nissan, there is a decoupling of the function to diffuse capabilities within Nissan's own operations and the function to teach the same capabilities to key suppliers. This means that the replication of internal capabilities at suppliers may not be as smooth as at Toyota. But Nissan has strengthened its unified structure for providing supplier development programmes through its Engineering Support Department, doubling its size in the 1990s from around forty to over eighty engineers, and incorporating activities hitherto carried out by other functions such as quality and logistics. Nissan operates on the belief that a single point of contact for suppliers promotes a consistent set of development activity starting from the comparison of suppliers' technological standards, the setting of improvement targets, the implementation of programmes, and the reflection of improvements made in the next round of supplier selection.

6.2.3 Honda

HONDA'S PHILOSOPHY OF SUPPLIER RELATIONS

Honda espouses free competition, equal partnership, and suppliers' managerial self-reliance as three fundamental principles in purchasing. These principles arose out of necessity and the experience of being a motorcycle firm that entered the auto sector late in the 1960s. Free competition means that as a matter of policy, Honda is to buy products from anywhere in the world as long as they are good and cheap. Equal partnership means the avoidance of heavy-handed tutelage that has typified the relationship between Toyota and many of its long-standing loyal suppliers. Supplier's self-reliance implies balancing responsiveness to Honda's needs with a sufficiently diversified customer base.

Honda places its supplier development activity in the context of this purchasing philosophy. Its purchasing department sees its history of supplier development as reflecting a shifting balance between cooperation and competition, with equal weights in the 1970s, in favour of cooperation in the 1980s, and back towards competition in the 1990s. This seesaw began after 1973 when some of Honda's smaller suppliers found themselves at risk with a large reduction in Honda's orders. The recession since the 1990s poses a similar risk for some suppliers, but before Honda is able to throw them out to face global competition, it is devoting resources to bring them up to a world-class level of competitiveness.

MULTIPLE CHANNELS OF SUPPLIER DEVELOPMENT

Honda's supplier development activity may be traced back to the formation of study groups in the aftermath of the first oil shock in 1973. By this time, Honda had nurtured a core group of suppliers with either shareholding or heavy trading linkages with Honda, in order to cope with a 16-fold increase in car production in its initial ten-year history. Suddenly, with no growth prospects for the auto industry, Honda realized the need to cut costs to survive. Since fifty to sixty per cent of Honda's purchased parts costs were in materials, attention naturally turned to cutting the costs of materials. This material-focused activity eventually extended to examining production processes and capital equipment. At first, a team of seven Honda engineers from the Purchasing Department identified a group of eight supplier companies, and started implementing changes, starting with cleaning the shop floor and changing the factory layout. This activity came to be known as the 'Soft Best Position' (SBP) as part of the Maru A Plan (1974–9).

Typically, a model line was chosen at a supplier. At first, the Honda team made essential changes and showed what could be done, so as to convince the supplier that making those changes were worthwhile. According to a leading member of this initial team, talking about a typical supplier's shop floor:

It was dirty, it was messy and there were so many problems. The starting point was what to do with all these problems. Honda realized that changes had to be made to compete globally, and that its affiliates were not keeping up with the competition. Once the main action points were listed, it became clear that suppliers would not be able to implement them if they were just told what to do. There was no choice but to work together. So we started by asking a supplier company to form a joint Kaizen team with Honda engineers.

Once such a joint team was formed, the Honda engineers were fully active in implementing shopfloor improvements, starting with 3S. Moreover:

We chose to work on the thing that would have the greatest impact on profits or quality. The issue was how to make suppliers' top management realize that the changes made would lead to greater profits or better quality, because once they realize this, things would run on an automatic pilot. We therefore had to work together to increase performance, and when that was achieved, Honda did not take away the fruit of the achievement. We entrusted this capital gain to the supplier management.

During the Maru A Plan period, a 50–50 sharing rule came into effect, and has been strictly adhered to ever since.

The shop floor *kaizen* activity on a chosen model line was followed by 'autonomous activities' by suppliers themselves. The activities focused on two extensions: applying what was achieved on the model line to other production lines in the supplier company, and forming a study group with other suppliers in the same sector to take turns to improve a model line at one of the suppliers. The Maru A Study Movement consisted of 68 suppliers, later rising to around 100. They were grouped into sectoral categories such as pressing, welding, plastic moulding, casting, forging, diecast, machining, and assembly. Honda's initial focus on materials, then on capital equipment in the form of HBP (see later), made the choice of this sectoral organizing principle seem natural. An alternative organizing principle of dispersing direct competitors in different groups, as for Toyota's Jishuken, has the advantage of minimizing barriers to sharing know-how amongst direct competitors. But Honda's group arrangement has the advantage of focusing on sector-specific technology. 'There is no point in talking to the machining group about plastic moulding. The machining group must discuss what has to be done to become No. 1 in the world of machining, while the plastic moulding group discusses what it takes to be No. 1 in that sector', explained Honda's purchasing manager.

FROM SOFT BP TO HARD BP AND SSP: BROADER AND DEEPER SUPPLIER
DEVELOPMENT INTERVENTION

The core supplier development activity at Honda has been BP. BP, when the term was devised in the mid-1970s, stood for Best Position, although later in the 1980s it came to be various things, including Best Practice, Best Process, Best Performance, Best Profit, and so on, particularly when applied to Honda of America Manufacturing (HAM) (MacDuffie and Helper 1997). Within BP, there is also a distinction between Soft BP (SBP) and Hard BP (HBP) which is very well known within Honda and the community of Honda suppliers. The two may be distinguished as follows.

(1) SBP is achieved through changes that can be made without spending money (e.g. 3S), while HBP is achieved by making new capital investment.

(2) SBP involves changes made after Job 1, while HBP starts from pre-production stage, around two years prior to Job 1.

(3) SBP results in *kaizen* (small improvements), while HBP results in *kaikaku* (larger jumps in performance improvement). For instance, a stamping press speed is made faster these days by relying on two speeds in a stroke, a fast speed until the press is close to the metal,

and a slower speed when the press actually touches the metal sheet. A large jump in performance was achieved when new investment was made to incorporate this two-speed stamping idea.

SBP originated in the post-1973 oil shock effort, while HBP became popular after the 1985 yen appreciation and the ensuing investment boom. HBP started towards the end of the Maru B Plan (1984–6), when Honda demanded a 15 per cent cost reduction from its suppliers over the three years. Since there were limits to how much change one could make after Job 1, attention turned to HBP before the start of production. The HBP Campaign in Japan was formalized by setting up study groups of suppliers and Honda factories. Capital investment, particularly in labour-saving automation using specialized transfer lines, was regarded as a solution to productivity bottlenecks. While rapid capital investment was a general trend in the late 1980s bubble economy, Honda's own philosophy concerning its production system—particularly the idea of increasing line speed and shortening the lines by relying on specialized functional robots (Amikura 1989, 1992)—also fuelled this tendency. With the benefit of hindsight, BP Campaign in Japan is therefore regarded as responsible for the expensive over-reliance on capital investment in Honda's supply chain.

During the 1990s recession, Honda shifted its emphasis away from HBP back to SBP, and sought less expensive improvements in work organization, process layout, and problems with second-tier suppliers. In this vein, Honda announced a new initiative called Slim and Solid Production (SSP) as part of its Fifth Medium-Term Plan. SSP marks a departure from previous supplier development programmes at Honda in extending the scope of development from a production line to the entire supplier company. A three-step development is envisaged, first efficiency improvements in the production line, second in the product development system, and third in the management system so that it can expand sales and invest overseas. One Honda supplier development engineer is in charge of three SSP suppliers, and spends full time in guiding these three firms. Each SSP supplier appoints a Large Project Leader (LPL) and a Project Leader (PL), who are involved in setting performance targets that become part of the supplier's management plan. Linking the supplier's improvement activities to a company-wide management plan at the supplier may be seen to be the replication of Honda' own practice of linking supplier development programmes to its medium-term (three-year) business plans.

Honda's expansion in the scope of supplier development has been facilitated by changes in internal organization structure. The year 1974, when Honda formally began its supplier development activity, also saw the establishment of a supplier development support team at the headquarter Purchasing Department, which later became the Purchasing Technical Centre. The headquarter Purchasing Department incorporates the Purchasing Quality Centre and the Purchasing Technical Centre, the two centres taking a lead in supplier development. The Purchasing Technical Centre (initially with seven engineers in 1974, increasing to fifty-eight engineers by 1997) corresponds to Toyota's OMCD and Nissan's Engineering Support Department. Since the early 1990s, these centres are located at Honda's Tochigi site, which also has the product development function, just like at Nissan Technical Centre, in order to intensify coordination between purchasing and the design and development function. Maru I Study Group, a supplier forum for promoting concurrent engineering and the use of online links as a tool for management decision-making, is predicated on such close cross-functional coordination.

To summarize, one may conjecture that little supplier development would follow from Honda's purchasing philosophy of open competition and equal partnership, if taken at face value. In reality, however, Honda's supplier development activity started after the 1973 oil shock, and looks similar to Nissan's and Toyota's in using both individual-based shop floor assistance and study groups. Moreover, the content of Honda's supplier development activity has broadened and deepened over time, ultimately addressing the supplier's company-wide capability. This is evident in the progression from SBP to HBP, and the setting of SSP performance improvement targets as part of suppliers' business plan.

6.3. Comparisons and Discussion

Figure 6.2 summarizes the main supplier development activities at the three Japanese automakers, by juxtaposing them along two axes identified in Section 6.1, namely the type of capability taught to suppliers and the scope of activity. This section discusses three things with reference to Section 6.1's framework: (*a*) similarities among the three companies' organizational capability in supplier development, (*b*) how the three companies differ in this respect, and (*c*) the issue of replication of such supplier development systems outside of Japan.

6.3.1 Common Features of the Three Companies

(1) *Multiple channels of supplier development are offered, in order to transfer both explicit and tacit knowledge.* Each automaker has an array of supplier development programmes, ranging from individual assistance to group-based assistance, from classroom teaching to joint problem-solving in concrete settings. Different programmes also have different aims, ranging from short-term fixes to instil 'maintenance capability' to the long-term development of 'evolutionary capability'. Multiple channels satisfy two aims. First, they ensure that both explicit and tacit knowledge are transferred to suppliers. All three companies expend a considerable amount of resources (fifty to eighty engineers) to teach suppliers in a hands-on manner, reflecting their belief that tacit knowledge can be replicated only through this mode of teaching. Second, multiple channels help to achieve a balance between self-learning (or mutual learning amongst suppliers) and more heavy-handed assistance for immediate tangible results. Toyota has achieved this by making the OMCD and the Purchasing Planning Department separately responsible for supplier development, and by complementing individual assistance with Jishuken groups. Nissan and Honda also give individual assistance and facilitate study groups for their suppliers.

(2) *The scope of supplier development activity has become broader and deeper over time.* Starting with the enterprise group diagnosis at Toyota and Nissan in the mid-1950s, the automakers were expected to nurture their suppliers in a holistic manner. This meant not just teaching a toolkit of shop floor *kaizen* techniques but teaching suppliers a modern management control system, most tangibly in the form of TQC. Even at Honda, which did not attempt to spread TQC to its suppliers, the linking of performance improvement targets to business plans (especially in HBP and SSP) has ensured a company-wide commitment at the recipient supplier companies. In practice, all three companies started with assistance in shop floor improvements. But the case studies show that over time, their activities extended to areas outside the shop floor, into product development processes and management systems (see Figure 6.2). This broadening of the scope of supplier development is due to the complementarity in the hierarchy of organizational processes, notably between TPS and TQC, or between pre-production and post-production processes in simultaneous engineering.

(3) *Corporate governance at supplier companies has been able to sustain the voice of customer companies as legitimate semi-insiders and the appropriation of*

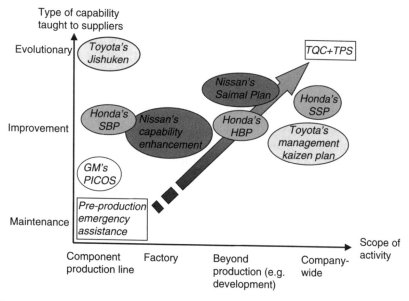

Figure 6.2 Typology of supplier development activity

gains from learning new capabilities. As Toyota, Nissan, and Honda broadened the scope of supplier development from shop floor improvements to addressing suppliers' company-wide business plans, they generally encountered no barriers to suppliers opening their books for advice. Suppliers' trust of customer companies lay in the latter's competence as teachers, but also in devising a clear set of rules for sharing specific gains from short-term intervention, and for letting suppliers appropriate wider gains from long-term capability enhancement.

6.3.2 How Firms Differ and Why Differences Matter

The three broad similarities listed above skate over some significant differences among the three automakers. These differences matter to the extent that they affect the nature and sustainability of the mechanism for transferring capabilities to suppliers. In particular, Toyota differs from Nissan and Honda in at least two ways.

(1) *Toyota has a distinctly different internal organizational structure for delivering supplier development from Nissan and Honda, relying on decoupling the teaching of TPS and TQC.* Toyota's OMCD is in charge of diffusing TPS, whilst the Purchasing Department is responsible for diffusing TQC to suppliers. This bifurcated structure proved to be advantageous in giving

175

suppliers the opportunity to learn about TPS as though they were extensions of Toyota's internal factories, shielded in part from the Purchasing Department's commercial negotiations. At the same time, TQC helped diffuse TPS within each supplier company, contributing to the self-sustainability of capability enhancement activity. By contrast, the establishment of Nissan's Engineering Support Department and Honda's Purchasing Technical Centre led to the incorporation of supplier assistance in various arenas (including quality, logistics, product development) within the purchasing function. The centralized unified structure has the advantage of making suppliers have a single point of contact for consistent guidance, but is accompanied by the potential danger of creating a barrier between learning within Nissan's or Honda's internal operations and learning by suppliers.

(2) *Toyota has the most systematic institution for inter-supplier sharing and learning of tacit knowledge, in the form of Jishuken (self-study) Groups.* Although all three companies created small groups of supplier companies to engage in joint study at different times, Jishuken Groups, each with several supplier participants, truly share the know-how in the practice of problem-solving, while those at Honda and Nissan tend to share successful solutions mainly through presentation meetings and factory visits. The focus on the latter assumes that much can be communicated through the representation, rather than the practice, of routines. At Toyota, Jishuken Groups contain no direct competitors, whereas Honda and Nissan group suppliers according to their component sector. Know-how sharing is more likely to take place among suppliers in the absence of direct rivalry in business.

These two differences between Toyota on the one hand and Nissan and Honda on the other are reinforced by differences in the companies' policies towards suppliers. Toyota and Honda lie at the two extremes in the spectrum of purchasing philosophy, from organizational commitment to market competition, with Nissan hovering in between. One of the manifestations of this difference in purchasing philosophy is that Honda does not have a supplier association, in the way Toyota and Nissan do. The supplier association constitutes a relatively stable group, and represents the entire population of recipients of supplier development assistance of some shape or form (Sako 1996). However, within this group of long-term suppliers, each automaker clearly distinguishes between the inner core of suppliers to which *processes* for 'capability enhancement' are taught in a hands-on manner, and the rest who are mainly given *incentives* to make improvements through long-term customer commitment. This distinction ensures that tacit knowledge is shared only with the inner core. This inner core ranges from twenty-five companies at Nissan and fifty-two at Toyota, up to sixty-three at Honda (see Table 6.1 for a summary).

The inner core group of suppliers may be regarded as within the boundary of the focal capability-based firm, in so far as common language and processes promote knowledge sharing within that boundary (Kogut and Zander 1992). At Toyota, OMCD ensures that Toyota factories transfer capability and learn from each other, and the inner core suppliers of Jishuken Groups learn from each other in the same fashion. Here, the long-term integration into Toyota's production network, rather than share ownership *per se*, is the key to establishing shared goals between the automaker and the suppliers. Toyota has been able to establish the most stable set of inner core suppliers to which the same teaching (of TPS) has been applied over three decades. Toyota's capability to sustain such cumulative efforts in supplier development, as compared to more discontinuous starts and stops in efforts at the other two automakers, must be in part a consequence of the greater organizational integration of inner core suppliers into Toyota than at Nissan or Honda.

6.3.3 Replication outside Japan?

The organizational capabilities perspective points to the root cause of the difficulty in replicating the Japanese automakers' supplier development capability outside of Japan. Apart from (*a*) differences in historical

Table 6.1 Categorizing suppliers at Toyota, Nissan, and Honda in the 1990s

	Toyota	Nissan	Honda
Number of key parts suppliers	Approximately 350	Approximately 350	Approximately 300
Supplier association	Kyohokai	Takarakai and Shoho kai (merged in 1991)	None
Member suppliers	229	174	
Recipients of core supplier development	52 (Jishuken Groups)	25 (Capability Enhancement)	63 (Slim and Solid Production)
Supplier development engineers	50 in Operations Management Consulting Division	80 in Engineering Support Department	58 in Purchasing Technical Centre

Source: Sako (1996) and author interviews.

trajectories and (b) tacit and difficult-to-codify knowledge contained in what is taught to suppliers, the enlarged scope of supplier development activity renders the replication of the whole system more difficult and unlikely. This is a serious point, indicating a deeper current that goes against an appearance of convergence towards 'partnership'-based supplier relations in North America and Europe (Helper and Sako 1995; Sako, Helper, and Lamming 1995).

The IMVP supplier survey,[4] conducted by the author in collaboration with Helper, asked suppliers how their customer company would react if a competitor offered a lower price for a product of equal quality. An increasing proportion of suppliers said their customers would 'help them to match a competitor's effort' (from 39 per cent in 1990 to 81 per cent in 1994 in the UK, 33 per cent in 1990 to 53 per cent in 1994 in the rest of Europe, and from 34 per cent in 1989 to 53 per cent in 1993 in North America). Japanese suppliers that expected their customers to offer help, by contrast, declined from 45 per cent to 40 per cent of the total. But 18.7 per cent of Japanese suppliers continued to receive long-term supplier development assistance ('customer company provided personnel who worked two weeks or more on suppliers' shop floor to improve its processes'), while the proportions were 9.6 per cent in North America and 6 per cent in Europe. This is one indication that when suppliers answer 'customers help match a competitor's effort', they mean different types of help. Some help is for the long-term development of a supplier's capabilities. Others are more of a quick fix. An example of the latter is General Motor's PICOS programme, a one-week shop floor *kaizen* workshop that is rarely repeated for the same supplier. Thus, even with the diffusion of stable supplier relationships, supplier development in North America and Europe may continue to have a less ambitious aim to improve suppliers' maintenance capability and perhaps their improvement capability, but rarely their evolutionary capability.

This less ambitious aim in supplier development is intricately related to differences in corporate governance between Japan, North America, and Europe. In particular, key customer companies in North America and Europe do not have the same degree of legitimacy as in Japan to act as semi-insiders that have a voice in how their suppliers might invest their resources. Moreover, suppliers in North America and Europe may distrust their customer companies' intention, to appropriate gains from short-term assistance through immediate price renegotiations. By contrast, in Japan, to a varying degree, suppliers are governed by mechanisms for customer-induced learning that are separated from shorter-term pressures for commercial negotiations. Honda's distinction between SBP and HBP provides a concise illustration of this point. In Japan, Honda initially targeted SBP, then moved on to HBP, which required Honda to be intimately acquainted with its suppliers' investment and management plans. In the United States, Honda of America Manufacturing (HAM) began to implement SBP in earnest in 1987, but faced suppliers' reluctance to disclose financial and other information to HAM particularly when it came to HBP (e.g. involving capital investment in new plants) (MacDuffie and Helper 1997). In the UK, also, HBP was said to be difficult because it was considered too intrusive for supplier companies' managerial autonomy. Some supplier company managers told Honda UK that they needed shareholders' approval for the capital investment Honda recommended, an assertion that underlay their belief that shareholders were more legitimate than Honda as insiders to the supplier company concerned. A senior Japanese purchasing manager at Honda UK asserted: 'Various activities have started here, and UK managers have begun to understand the need for HBP in form, but not many have really felt the need under their skin as they continue to pay attention to shareholders.' Thus, corporate governance influences the breadth and depth of supplier development activity, through the customer company's status as 'insider' or 'outsider', and through the presence or absence of understanding about the appropriation of gains from learning by suppliers.

In conclusion, the contrast made in the current study is not so much just between short-term adversarial versus long-term cooperative supplier relationships, or between buying from a lean supplier versus creating one. Even with an apparent shift towards longer-term committed relationships, there remains an essential difference between a relationship in which the automaker is just a good source of information on 'best practice' and a situation in which the automaker actually teaches the know-how to enhance the supplier's organizational capabilities.

6.4. Conclusions

Social scientific research on supplier relations has been intricately linked to attempts at developing a valid theory of the firm that addresses both its internal governance and the boundary decision. From the supplier relations perspective, the theorizing was very much taken in two steps; first, firms decide over whether or not to make or buy (the boundary decision), and second, they decide over what sort of relations they wish to have with suppliers (arm's length or relational). Transaction Cost Economics (TCE) was used for the first decision (Williamson 1985), whilst TCE has been increasingly supplanted by other theories (e.g. on trust) to account for hybrid modes that lay between market and hierarchy (Adler 2001). This marriage of TCE with other theories has been uncomfortable, not least because TCE is primarily a static theory that has little to say about innovation and the internal governance of firms.

As a better alternative, the organizational capabilities perspective adopted in this chapter focuses on how firms can best draw their boundaries so as to enhance their capacity to accumulate their competence or capabilities. Accordingly, the boundary of the 'firm' is defined, not by law (and the share ownership patterns) or by exchange (i.e. calculations of transaction costs), but by considerations over the production of capabilities. As shown empirically, within the capability-based organization boundary, 'routines' exist for tacit knowledge to develop and replicate easily. This boundary, however, may go well beyond legally defined corporate entities if a buyer firm providing supplier development is allowed to take part in suppliers' investment decisions. Thus, the replication of organizational capabilities is not just a matter of collective cooperative learning, by shielding actors from 'high powered' market pressures, but a matter of corporate governance.

Notes

1. In making a conceptual distinction between maintenance and improvement capabilities, we assume that the daily management of production requires a conscientious application of the standard work methods. However, as Nemoto (1985: 63) points out, there are two meanings of standardization, one referring to absolute standards for safety or compatibility, such as British Standard or JIS, and the other to the process of improving any points that are found to be deficient by following the standard work methods. In the latter meaning, standardization is not an end but the beginning of making improvements (see also Adler and Cole 1993; MacDuffie 1997). In this sense, maintenance capability is intricately linked to improvement capability.

   One common 'routine' for 'improvement capability' (but not for maintenance capability) is policy deployment (Hoshin Kanri) in TQC, which involves the setting of objectives for improvement to be achieved within a specified period of time. The term, Hoshin Kanri, was coined in 1965 by the tyre maker, Bridgestone, when it was preparing for the Deming Award in 1968. The company felt the need to coin a new term that focused on processes, because the known technique of management by objective (MBO) tended to become too results-oriented (Kogure 1988: 162).

2. This subsection describes the situation at Nissan prior to Renault's equity participation in 1999, to benchmark subtle differences among the three companies within a broad Japanese pattern. Thereafter, Nissan's supplier relations became quite turbulent. Carlos Ghosn, the COO of Nissan, made it his top priority in the Nissan Revival Plan to return Nissan to profitable growth and to reduce its net consolidated debt of 2.1 trillion yen in 1998. Sales of assets tied in securities, real estate, and affiliates (including suppliers) helped reduce this debt to 8.6 billion yen in 2003, whilst the establishment of Renault-Nissan Purchasing Organization (RNPO) in 2001 to manage 40 per cent or more of the combined global annual purchasing spending contributed to reducing Nissan's purchasing costs by 20 per cent during 2000 and 2002. Thus, Nissan responded to a pressure to switch to a more market-based approach to supplier selection, within the context of sharing a global supplier base with Renault. In response, some smaller suppliers lost business within Nissan, and amongst those that continued to trade, some suppliers merged with each other (as in the case of Calsonic Kansei) or were sold (e.g. to Hitachi in the case of UNISIA JECS). Nevertheless, activities to spread Nissan Production Way (NPW) to suppliers continue.

3. Nissan has put much emphasis on educating both its own employees and suppliers about Genba Kanri. The internal education is the responsibility of the Personnel Department, while the responsibility for spreading it to suppliers resides with two experts in the Engineering Support Department. The Genba Kanri course for suppliers consists of the teaching of NTWI (Nissan's version of Training-within-Industry), and a five-day practice course involving a competition among three teams of seven participants each over solutions to building a plastic car model. Each team contains participants from several different supplier companies, and is potentially a forum for suppliers to learn from each other.

4. Questionnaire surveys were sent to first-tier suppliers in North America, Japan, and Europe in 1993 and 1994. Response rates were 55, 30, and 16 per cent, with valid samples of 675, 472, and 262 in North America, Japan, and Europe, respectively. See Sako, Lamming, and Helper (1995) for details.

7

Intra-Industry Differences II: Why Unions Differ

Why do unions differ, and how does it matter? This chapter turns to the labour side of the within-sector differences, having examined the corporate side of the story in Chapter 6. Chapter 5 identified key differences in the structure of *roren* between automobile and electrical machinery sectors, but there are also considerable variations within each sector. These within-sector differences in organizational structure and boundary, a central theme of this book, result from the interaction between labour and management with their respective strategies, and from the accumulated capabilities that result from the pursuit of specific goals. This chapter compares two union networks within the automobile sector. In particular, the experience of Nissan Roren is contrasted with that of Toyota Roren, already described in Chapter 4.

Much has been written about the corporate histories of Toyota and Nissan, tracing the rise and fall and the recent revival of Nissan Motor Corporation, in contrast to the more resilient success of Toyota Motor Corporation (Cusumano 1985; Fujimoto 1999; Ghosn 2002; Wada and Yui 2002). The labour side of the story, however, is highly incomplete. This is in part because of academic focus, and in part due to organizational discontinuity. Much academic interest has been on lean production (Monden 1983; Womack et al. 1990) and its implications for work organization (Ishida et al. 1996; Locke et al. 1997). Consequently, enterprise unions' compliant presence on the shop floor is noted, but without setting it in the context of the collective union representation structures in the Japanese automobile industry. This criticism applies even to the excellent study by Totsuka and Hyodo (1991), which contrasts the difference in the nature of union regulation and control on the shop floor at Nissan and Toyota.

Discontinuity in organizations has also made documenting union histories challenging, and this applies to accounts at all levels from the enterprise up to the industry. Toyota Union and its *roren* have written brief histories of their own organizations (Toyota Union 1956, 1966, 1976, 1996; Zen Toyota Roren 1983, 2003). By contrast, Nissan Union and its *roren* have no official histories beyond the 1953 strike. Both Cusumano (1985) and Nissan Roren (1992) give insightful accounts of the human drama of labour–management interaction in the late 1940s and 1950s and the early death of industrial unionism in the Japanese auto industry.

But beyond this, there has not been a study of how union strategies and structures at the company and industry levels became articulated through the corporate group structure. The auto sector provides perhaps the strongest case history of clashes in union strategies within a sector, with disagreements over how enterprise unions and their *roren* federations should relate to an industry-level union organization. The purpose of this chapter, therefore, is to trace this explicit debate on the pros and cons of *roren* structures within the auto sector.

Superficially, union structures at Nissan and Toyota are not dissimilar. Nissan Union leads Nissan Roren with 150,000 members at parts suppliers and dealers, just as Toyota Union leads Toyota Roren with 260,000 members at parts suppliers and dealers (MHLW 2003). But this structural similarity emerged only gradually and formally only since 1972 with the formation of the industry-wide union confederation. In order to understand the circuitous path that led to this resolution in 1972 and its consequences, this chapter traces the debates that took place at the time of the formation of a series of union organizations. In particular, it covers (*a*) the formation and dissolution of an industrial union, Zenji, between 1947 and 1954, (*b*) the establishment of the new Nissan Union and its *roren*, Jidosha Roren, since 1955, (*c*) the establishment of Zenkoku Jidosha led by Toyota in 1962, (*d*) the establishment of the industry confederation, Jidosha Soren, in 1972 and the accompanying debate on the pros and cons of *roren* as a unit of affiliation to the confederation, and (*e*) constitutional changes to weaken the role of *roren* when Jidosha Roren was renamed Nissan Roren in 1989. To conclude this chapter, comparisons are made of the strategic and structural differences between Nissan Roren and Toyota Roren. Figure 7.1 summarizes the chronology of these developments from 1945 to 2003.

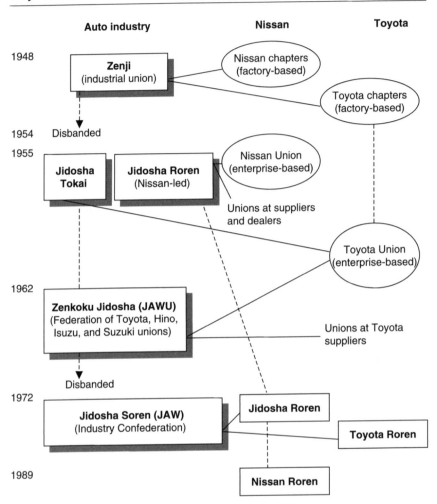

Figure 7.1 Chronology of union organizations in the Japanese automobile industry

Note: Solid line indicates affiliation. Dotted line indicates continuity of organizational entity.

7.1. Zenji during 1947–54: A 'True' Industrial Union?

The immediate post-war years saw the rapid establishment of union organizations at the factory level in the Japanese automobile industry. Diesel Motors (later Isuzu) saw factory unions spring up in all key locations, beginning with the Tsurumi factory union in November 1945. As we saw in Chapter 4, Toyota Kariya South factory formed an all-employees union in December 1945, followed by Toyota Komoro factory in January 1946. Similarly at Nissan, labour leaders were actively engaged in forming a union at its largest factory in Yokohama in February 1946, and at its factories in Yoshiwara, Tsurumi, and Atsugi in the ensuing months (Nissan Roren 1992: vol. I, 138).[1] The pace of factory-level organizing drive was spectacular, in line with GHQ's encouragement of unionization as part of its democratization programme for Japanese industry.

During 1946 and 1947, automotive factory unions began to form regional committees, as a precursor to the formation of an industrial union. This was Zenjidosha (the All Japan Automobile Workers Union) (or Zenji for short), founded with 108 chapters (*bunkai*) and 44,817 members in April 1947. At an early stage of the discussion, automotive union leaders felt optimistic that Sanbetsu (All Japan Congress of Industrial Unions) would develop into a broad labour federation joining workers in several key industries. But when its executive committee was captured by Communist Party members, the auto union leaders felt the need to withdraw from Sanbetsu and to form their own industrial union for the automobile industry.

Zenji union leaders aimed to establish an industry-wide front, which went beyond the framework of political alignments into Sanbetsu and Sodomei at the time. A united front was considered imperative in order to 'mount a struggle for industrial reconstruction, by destroying the hold that financial monopoly capital has over the Japanese economy' (*Zenji-dosha News* special issue, March 1948). Given this objective, Zenji gave top priority to organizing the unorganized, arranging organized workers into industrial unions, and further strengthening the power of the workers by joining forces with other metalworkers' unions. To this end, Zenji was reorganized in March 1948 as an industrial union in its 'true' form, i.e. a union to which automotive workers affiliated as individuals, whose conditions were negotiated and determined at the industry level, and for whom a dispute at a particular workplace became the concern of Zenji as a whole. Zenji's aim was to organize the whole of the auto industry and only the auto industry.

However, this ambition to create an industrial union was never realized in full. An immediate obstacle was the management practice of determining wages and conditions at the firm level (Koyama 1985: 225). Although Jikeiren (the automotive employers association) was established in reaction to the formation of Zenji, this never developed into a powerful organization that had much say over collective bargaining issues. The problem of uniting labour at the industry level was compounded by the financial difficulties suffered by all firms. As discussed in Chapter 2, after 1945 the Japanese economy suffered initially from inflation, then deflation created by the Dodge Line policies, forcing managers to fire thousands of workers, often through factory closures. In this climate, unions struggled to counter the reassertion of managerial prerogative, which in turn was backed up by labour law changes in the late 1940s.

The organization structure of Zenji was three-tiered, with headquarters overseeing nine regional branches (*shibu*) to which individual factory-based union chapters (*bunkai*) belonged. The term 'chapter' is used here for such a factory-based union organization unit, to distinguish it from a regional 'branch'. Table 7.1 outlines the regional distribution of union chapters in 1948 and 1953. The Tokyo and Kanagawa branches, which were later merged into the Keihan branch, contained some large Nissan factory unions (notably Nissan Yokohama) and Isuzu factory unions (notably Isuzu Kawasaki and Isuzu Tsurumi), whereas the Tokai branch contained union chapters at Toyota and its suppliers. Thus formally, Zenji's unit of affiliation was a factory-based union chapter, so that large automaker unions, for example, Toyota Komoro Factory Union (with over 5,000 union members), Nissan Yokohama Factory Union (with around 4,000 union members), and Isuzu Kawasaki Factory Union (with nearly 2,000 workers), affiliated to Zenji on the same basis as union chapters at smaller supplier and dealer companies.

The union rules and regulations made clear that Zenji was to encompass all types of workers in auto assembly, auto body, parts manufacturing, auto

Table 7.1 Organizational structure of Zenji, 1948 and 1953

Regional branch	1948		1953	
	Union chapters[a]	Union members	Union chapters	Union members
Tokyo	32	6,569	53[b]	15,847
Kanagawa	22	11,742		
Shizuoka	4	2,184	4	1,710
Tokai	20	13,980	25	9,940
Hokuriku	8	584	1	70
Kinki	8	3,090	7	1,189
Okayama	1	1,860	2	1,223
Hiroshima	1	2,170	3	152
Kyushu	—	—	4	256
Total	96	42,179	99	30,387

[a] Union chapter is organized at a factory location.
[b] Tokyo and Kanagawa regions merged to become Keihan region.

Source: Nissan Roren (1992: vol. I, 312) for 1948. Zenji internal documents at Tokyo University Institute of Social Science Library for 1953.

repair, and auto sales. But there existed a clear tension within the Zenji organization between the interests of large assembly workers and those of smaller company employees. This tension manifested itself in a number of ways. In March 1948, at Zenji's second annual conference, the executive committee, mostly manned by union officials from the three largest automakers, bowed to the wishes of the smaller union chapters to present a unified demand for a minimum wage and a higher base pay (Cusumano 1985: 145). This demand fell on deaf ears initially, as the automakers were preoccupied with mass redundancies and wage cuts. A few years later, in 1952, by the time Zenji was able to formulate its three principles on minimum wage, equal pay for equal work, and a solidaristic wage, Nikkeiren (the employers association) dismissed any demands based on such principles as Sohyo-dominated left-wing nonsense.

Another way in which this small union–large union tension manifested itself was the discussion over the so-called small and medium enterprise problems. Small firms, particularly component suppliers, were suffering from shortage of materials and pressures to reduce prices. Zenji took up the problem of defending jobs at supplier companies. For example, a meeting was held to which union representatives from suppliers and dealers were invited. Where there were no unions, owner-managers attended instead. Subsequently, the Toyota union chapter, for example, was entrusted with the task of discussing the problems supplier companies were facing with Toyota management at the bargaining table. However, at a time when the Toyota union chapter was preoccupied with defending its own members' jobs, suppliers' problems became of secondary concern.

Given the all-encompassing nature of Zenji's ultimate organizational boundary, it is not surprising that the unionization rate was low. The 44,818 members in 108 chapters in 1947 when Zenji was founded whittled down to 28,183 in 87 chapters by 1951 in the aftermath of the Dodge Line-induced firings. The Japanese automotive industry as a whole (including parts suppliers, repair shops, and dealers) was thought to be employing 120,000 workers, so this amounted to a unionization rate of less than 25 per cent in 1951 (at a time when the economy-wide union density rate was down from a peak of 56 per cent in 1949 to 43 per cent in 1951 (Shirai 1983: 140).

The domination of large union interest in Zenji manifested itself also in the concerted coordination by Isuzu, Nissan, and Toyota union chapters. Although factory-based union chapters were formally arranged into regional branches, the mobilization for wage bargaining took the form of a three-company joint struggle (*sansha kyoto*). In autumn 1949, Isuzu proposed 1,279 lay-offs and 10 per cent pay cut, and Nissan proposed 1,200 lay-offs and 10 per cent pay cut, whilst Toyota put to the union the need to reduce pay by 10 per cent. Under the leadership of Tetsuo Masuda from Nissan, the three-company joint struggle committee orchestrated a simultaneous strike over two months. But it ended in union acceptance of management terms at Nissan and Isuzu. At Toyota, a 10 per cent pay cut was accepted on the condition of no lay-offs in the future, but management reneged on this promise by laying off 1,600 in 1950.

In theory, the three focal union chapters leading the three-company joint struggle—in effect at the largest factories of Nissan, Isuzu, and Toyota—were meant to extend their help to bargain on behalf of smaller union chapters. Zenji classified union chapters into corporate groupings during their negotiation seasons. In 1952, for example, the autumn joint struggle for pay bargaining took place with fifteen chapters in Isuzu group, twenty-one chapters in Toyota Group, and fourteen chapters in Nissan Group (*Zenjidosha News*, 15 December 1952). Thus, Zenji instituted a *roren*-like coordination mechanism. But in practice, small union chapters at suppliers and dealers were left to fend for themselves (Zenkoku Jidosha 1972: 53).

By 1951, despite GHQ's Red Purge and its ban on a general strike, the economic climate was improving due to the Korean War-induced demand for trucks. Unions at Isuzu, Toyota, and Nissan all demanded significant pay increases, which, after striking, were accepted by management. Whilst some union leaders were content with moderate achievements in economic bargaining, others became increasingly politicized over the fear of US-led remilitarization of Japan. This led to the blurring of the boundary between economic and political struggles. By October 1952, Zenji joined Sohyo, the left-leaning national union centre that was formed in the aftermath of the Red Purge, reneging on its original intention not to join forces with any political party. Under Sohyo's direction, Zenji began a series of strikes, with a slogan 'even if the company were destroyed, the worker organization would remain' (*kaisha ga tsuburetemo soshiki wa nokoru*). Zenji, now under the leadership of Nissan's Tetsuo Masuda, grew into one of the most powerful class struggle-oriented unions within Sohyo.

The culmination of Zenji's activities, which proved to be fatal, was the prolonged four-month strike at Nissan in 1953. The summer round of pay bargaining was coordinated amongst the three large factory-based union chapters at Isuzu, Nissan, and Toyota, as before. But whilst the Toyota chapter and Isuzu chapter settled in early August for no pay increase and some bonus increase, the Nissan chapters found themselves in a deadlock. The company responded by closing the Yokohama, Yoshiwara, and Tsurumi factories, locking out workers and ultimately sacking Masuda and other union executive committee members.

The ultimate reason for the deadlock at Nissan was not wage demand—although this brought forth plenty of ire from Nikkeiren—but Nissan management's intent to break the union's hold over the shop floor. The Zenji chapter responded with a fierce will to fight to the end even if it meant the destruction of Nissan. Nissan, at the time of the strike, had seven factories, with Yokohama (3,600 workers), Yoshiwara (1,600 workers), and Tsurumi (800 workers) being the biggest three. At Yokohama, the centre of strike action, and at other factories to an extent, there existed powerful union shop leaders (*shokubacho*) whose sole task was to control the line speed, refuse job rotation and overtime, and call union meetings during work time (Miyake 1954: 12–15). In response to this practice, Nissan management declared that there would be 'no pay for no work', if time was taken off for union activity without the company's permission. Throughout the strike, middle managers who refused to go along with the union and tried to dock part of their subordinates' pay were humiliated in public. Zenji supported the strike with a strike fund set up with contributions from Sohyo and union members at other companies.

The dispute ended with the formation of a second union at Nissan and its acceptance of management terms in September 1953. A number of young activists, including the new union's first leader, Masaru Miyake, and his successor, Ichiro Shioji, formed a study group associated with anti-communist education. At Yokohama factory, they were able to gather as a group of 506 unionists to establish the Nissan Union. Many of them were employees in their early thirties, in staff functions such as design and development, cost management, purchasing, inspection, and general affairs. The new union criticized the first union for being communist and anti-democratic, for being akin to a dictatorship, for rushing to political struggles when workers' genuine need lay in economic improvements, and for alienating supervisors and middle managers. Its stated mission was to democratize the union and to reconstruct the basis for productivity improvement at Nissan. By December 1953, most workers had left the Zenji chapter and joined this new union, induced by a combination of management's financial incentive and the hope of a new start. The Nissan Union, with nine branches, came to organize 6,500 workers in a matter of half a year.

By December 1954, Zenji was disbanded after rank and file criticisms of the leadership, financial hardship (with the Nissan Union showing no intention of paying back the loan advanced during the strike), and internal factional splits.

In summary, Zenji, the first and the last industrial union in the Japanese auto industry, was destroyed by the Nissan strike. Nissan management was intent on undermining Zenji's Nissan chapter, and the deal that was struck between Nissan's management and its second union sounded the death knell for the Nissan chapter. But why should a powerful industry-wide union of 30,000 workers be brought down as a result of a dispute with just one company? This was because Zenji's agenda were captured by Masuda, the Zenji president, who was responsible for the collapse of a united front amongst unions at Nissan, Toyota, and Isuzu. Ultimately, not only did Masuda face opposition from within his own Nissan chapter; he was unable to carry the other companies' union leaders to agree to his view that the destruction of Nissan was a price worth paying for the joint struggle.

Within a year of the end of Zenji, in December 1955, the three major enterprise unions of Toyota, Nissan, and Isuzu met to agree on what came to be known as the 'two principles and four conditions' for re-establishing a united front (Zenkoku Jidosha 1972: 80). The two principles were: (*a*) that a new national organization should be truly free and democratic; and (*b*) that this national organization should lead to the improvement of auto workers' living standards. The four conditions were: (*a*) the resolution of the Nissan strike fund problem, (*b*) a reflective self-criticism on the joint struggle of Nissan, Toyota, and Isuzu unions under Zenji, (*c*) the elimination of 'excessive competition' in the car industry, and (*d*) non-affiliation to higher-level union organizations controlled by political parties.

Despite an attempt to agree on these principles and conditions, Nissan and Toyota unions went their separate ways, taking another seventeen years before the two could finally come together to form a single union confederation for the auto industry. Most visibly, differences in the opinion over the political alignment of auto unions led to a split, with the Nissan Union favouring affiliation to Zenro (which later became absorbed in Domei) and the Toyota Union favouring non-affiliation.

At the same time, union leaders who remained at Nissan struck a very different bargain with management than those at Toyota. At Toyota, as discussed in Chapter 4, the reassertion of management prerogative with the abolition of the management council in 1950 led to a union whose say was limited in matters other than operational issues. However, with continuity of leadership, some Toyota union leaders remained wedded to the idea of an industrial union of workers at automakers, and saw the interests of automaker workers as being apart from those of suppliers and dealers. At

Nissan, by contrast, any trace of Zenji thinking disappeared with the 'all change' of union leadership in 1953. This enabled the new Nissan union leaders, such as Miyake and Shioji, to wield considerable influence on management through the re-establishment of the management council and their promotion up the managerial career ladder. At the same time, Nissan union leaders believed in the importance of uniting with supplier and dealer unions in order to enhance their overall bargaining power.

Thus, when it came to a fight for the leadership of the industry-level union confederation, Jidosha Soren, in 1972, this took the form, not only of a personal contest between those in favour of Nissan's powerful union leader, Ichiro Shioji, and those against, but also of debating about organizing principles, between those in favour of the Nissan way (with a formally constituted *roren*) and those in favour of the Toyota way (with automaker unions organized separately from unions at suppliers and dealers). Sections 7.2 and 7.3 demonstrate how the differences in these organizing principles manifested themselves in the Nissan and Toyota unions. Between 1955 and 1971, Nissan Union organized suppliers and dealers more thoroughly and quickly than the Toyota Union, through its trade linkage-based *roren*, Jidosha Roren (see Section 7.2). By contrast, Toyota Union was instrumental in organizing a competing federation, Zenkoku Jidosha, whose Tokai region branch contained unions at Toyota's key supplier companies (see Section 7.3). This split between a Nissan Union-led federation and a Toyota Union-led federation is represented in Figure 7.1.

7.2. Nissan-Led Jidosha Roren: Trade Linkage-Based *Roren*

The new Nissan Union and Toyota Union were different in at least two respects by the time they came out of the Zenji-inflicted ordeal in the mid-1950s. First, the new Nissan Union promptly convinced management of the importance of a labour–management consultation council (*keiei kyogikai*), which has been held regularly since October 1953. The union argued that it was all in favour of Nissan management capturing the right to manage, but that it would comment on and make suggestions on management issues along the lines of the German joint consultation system. President Katsuji Kawamata, leading the management team, acquiesced to the arrangement on the basis of a clearly laid out set of rules and an understanding that the union would observe strict confidentiality of management information. Top management (including the president

and managing directors) all attended the meetings of this central consultation council and the subcommittees in production, technology, management control, and welfare. A wide range of issues were discussed at these
meetings, including long-term production plans, whether or not auto
bodies should be made in-house to improve engineering and quality
levels, problems associated with purchasing, and relations with dealers
(Miyake 1954: 153). By contrast, after management abolished the management council (*keiei kyogikai*) in 1950, Toyota ended up with a much less
powerful discussion meeting (*roshi kondankai*) and a labour–management
consultation forum (*roshi kyogikai*) (see Chapter 4). This difference between Nissan and Toyota in the extent of joint consultation persisted
well into the 1980s (Totsuka 1991; Totsuka and Hyodo 1991).

Second, from the start, the new Nissan Union was intent on expanding
its influence beyond Nissan by working towards a federation of affiliates,
suppliers, and dealers (Miyake 1954: 173). This federation was Jidosha
Roren (Federation of Labour Unions in the Japanese Automobile Industry), established in January 1955. As the name indicates, the federation's
ambition was to organize workers beyond the Nissan Group to incorporate
general workers at even non-automotive companies. The name of this
Nissan-based federation, which sounded like an industry federation,
proved to be convenient when it decided, in 1956, to affiliate to Zenro
Kaigi (later part of Domei). Zenro Kaigi was a national union centre that
insisted on industrial federations as units of affiliation. Through this
affiliation, Jidosha Roren and Nissan Union broke an earlier promise of
political neutrality. Their refusal to change this stance created a deadlock,
resulting in the formation of an alternative Toyota-led industry federation, Zenkoku Jidosha, in 1962 (see Section 7.3).

Jidosha Roren was, however, primarily a trade linkage-based *roren* for
the Nissan group, created on the basis of pragmatic wisdom that arose
from the bitter experience of the 1953 Nissan strike. Ichiro Shioji, second
in command after Miyake in the Nissan union leadership at the time,
reflected:

When Nissan went on strike, its lines stopped, and dealers and parts suppliers could
not earn a living. We learnt then that there were parts makers that existed for the
sole purpose of producing for Nissan, the so-called *keiretsu* suppliers, and dealers
that existed to sell Nissan cars only. When Nissan Union was established, I thought
that we had to take account of fellow workers at these operations. So soon after-
wards, this led to our establishing an extended union federation for the purpose of
protecting employment and working conditions of fellow workers at Nissan dealers
and parts suppliers.[2]

Of course, such feelings were based neither on the notion of class solidarity nor on a sense of duty towards the weak and the disadvantaged but on a pragmatic reason. In order for the Japanese car industry to become internationally competitive, suppliers and dealers also had to become internationally competitive. This could be achieved only through the reduction of the dualistic structure in the Japanese economy. Dualism meant that car manufacturers benefited at the expense of squeezing cheap prices out of suppliers, undermining the latter's ability to improve their technical and managerial capabilities. By bringing supplier and dealer workers into the same labour movement, Nissan Union believed that it could exert the necessary influence on management, not only to equalize wages through bargaining, but also to improve the competitiveness of the Japanese car industry vis-à-vis foreign competition.

The *keiretsu*-based union federation anchored its bargaining power in its ability to influence management policies through the system of management–labour consultation, for example over relations with suppliers and dealers. The union presence in sales, purchasing, inspection, and other departments also helped towards enhancing the *roren*'s bargaining power (Miyake 1954: 187). Ishiro Shioji explained thus:

What we realized then was that the management policy of *keiretsu* parts suppliers and dealers is controlled by Nissan. So, unless we, as Nissan union, were to exercise our influence over Nissan management, we would not be able to protect workers at these suppliers and dealerships. So, the union had to have an ability to make effective proposals on managerial and industrial issues. At the same time, it had to have power as a union. I thought that if we got together with suppliers and dealers, then we would be second to none in bargaining power. In order to threaten Nissan management, there's no need to stop a Nissan line of 8,000 workers; all we had to do was to stop the line of a *keiretsu* supplier of 100 workers. Once we realized this, not that we actually had to go ahead with such a tactic, we knew we had bargaining power on our side by insinuating from time to time that we could take such action if compelled to do so.[3]

When it was founded in 1955, Jidosha Roren was a federation of twenty-two enterprise unions, representing just over 9,000 workers (of whom 7,000 were at Nissan Motors). Thereafter, this *roren* grew rapidly, increasing its membership more than eight-fold to 77,300 workers in 1963 (Nissan Motor Co. 1970: 481). By 1958, three councils (*kyogikai*) were formed by key unions in three sectors, namely automotive assembly, parts manufacturing, and sales. The fifth annual conference of Jidosha Roren in 1960 also decided to organize non-automotive workers who were sympathetic to the cause of Jidosha Roren, into another committee known as Minro.

In the same year, it was also decided that each of these sectoral councils should become a unified union so as to create a bigger and stronger organization. Economies of scale that arose from sharing unions' financial and human resources were considered beneficial to modernize management–labour relations and to promote productivity. Table 7.2 lists the key differences between such a unified union and a federation of enterprise unions. The former is more centralized with respect to the collection of union dues, the level of collective bargaining, and the right to call a strike.

The first council to go forward was in automobile assembly, with the unions at Nissan Auto Body, Nissan Diesel, and Atsugi Auto Parts in effect merging with Nissan's focal union in 1961 (Nissan Motor Co. 1965: 481–2). Whereas there had been four separate unions each with its own rules, personnel, and the right to collect dues and to call a strike, after the merger, a single union rule governed the newly formed All Nissan Motor Workers' Union with branches at these four separate companies. The right to collect union dues and the right to call a strike were both centralized, taken away from the previously autonomous enterprise unions. Each enterprise-based branch retained the right to bargain collectively, but the president of All Nissan Motor Workers' Union was present at the branch-level bargaining and consultation sessions. A collective agreement at Nissan Diesel, for instance, was signed by the Diesel management and by two levels of the union, the Diesel branch president and the All Nissan Union president.

Table 7.2 A typology comparing a unified union to a federation of enterprise unions

	Federation of enterprise unions	Unified union
Unit of affiliation	Enterprise unions	Individual members
Union dues collected by	Enterprise unions	Unified union HQ
Union rules set by	Each enterprise union	Unified union
Collective bargaining level	At each enterprise union	At each enterprise union, but in the presence of officials from the unified union
Collective agreement signed by	Each enterprise union and enterprise management	Three parties (enterprise management, enterprise union branch leader, and the unified union president)
Right to call a strike by	Each enterprise union	The unified union on behalf of enterprise-based branch

Note: This comparison assumes that the unified union maintains the same organizational boundary as the federation of enterprise unions.

The same logic was applied to other parts of Jidosha Roren, as the other sectoral councils followed suit to become unified unions. Minro, the council of non-automotive unions, became unified in October 1963, and Hanro, the council of dealers, became unified in November 1964. After the unification, Hanro (or Minro) came to be known as the 'union' (*roso*), whereas the union organization at each enterprise, be it a dealership or a non-automotive firm, came to be known as a union branch (*shibu*).

The last to become unified was Buro, the council of parts supply unions, in 1965. The long period allowed to prepare for a unified Buro was in contrast to the great haste made towards a unified structure in the case of Zenji. In 1959, the council contained only sixteen parts supply unions. In preparation for unification, the council set out to recruit new members and to educate them.

First, they targeted Nissan *keiretsu* suppliers, typically belonging to the supplier association, Takarakai, in their organizing drive. By 1965, Buro established union branches at sixty-eight supplier companies, fifty-four of which were members of Takarakai (see Figure 7.2). Second, union members had to be educated as to the benefits of a unified union structure. The union journal, *Buro*, ran numerous issues that put forward arguments

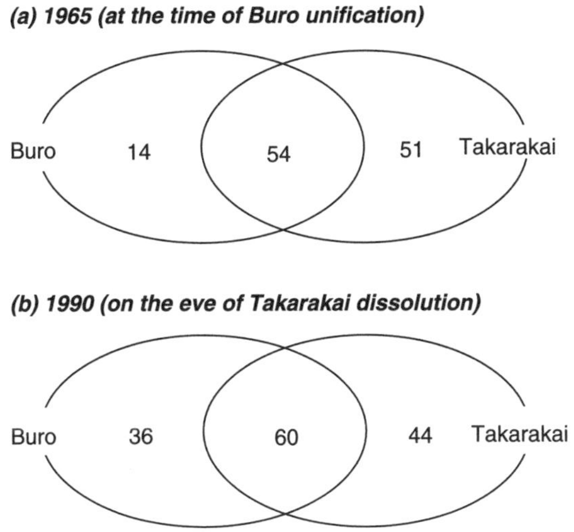

(a) 1965 (at the time of Buro unification)

Buro   14   54   51   Takarakai

(b) 1990 (on the eve of Takarakai dissolution)

Buro   36   60   44   Takarakai

Figure 7.2 Overlap in Buro and Takarakai membership: 1965 and 1990

Note: Buro is the parts supplier union of Nissan Roren (previously Jidosha Roren until 1989); Takarakai is Nissan's supplier association, formed in 1958 but dissolved in 1991.

Source: Buro (1995); Takarakai (1994); author's interviews with Nissan Roren.

in favour of having a single set of union rules and a unified financial structure, without undermining the autonomy of the workplace. The key benefits were believed to come from the narrowing of wage differentials through productivity improvements, as Buro would work towards modernizing labour–management relations (*Buro*, Special Issue No. 12, 26 October 1961). Moreover, Buro espoused the importance of labour–management consultation meetings in order to pre-empt any redundancies or bankruptcies (*Buro*, Issue No. 24, 5 February 1962). This notion harks back to one of Jidosha Roren's aims to relieve *roren* union members of the fear of unemployment, by intervening to facilitate job reallocation between firms (Miyake 1954: 175).[4] Successful instances of intervention raised the reputation of Buro in the eyes of supplier company managers as a capable partner in 'modern' industrial relations based on mutual trust.

In 1965, the motion to make Buro into a 'unified single union' was put to a vote by 20,000 members, and was passed. Ichiro Shioji gave a keynote speech, in which he noted:

It is often said that we must have an industrial union because enterprise unions are too weak. But arguments in favour of industrial unionism tend to be in abstract terms. ... Our union unification is not based on such superficial theory of organization. We realized, in the process of putting things into practice, why it was better for workers to organize by industry, and what were the demerits of such form of organization. We achieved unification by adopting only those aspects of industrial unionism that were deemed beneficial, and these emerged as a result of much trial and error (*Buro*, Issue No. 60, 25 March 1965).

This appears to be an implicit criticism of Zenji's notion of industrial unionism that put political struggle before economic bargaining. At the same time, the creation of a centralized union structure whose boundary goes beyond a single firm is associated with the beneficial aspects of industrial unionism.

This unified union status is characterized by having a single set of union rules and regulations, a unified financial resource, and a single president. A single framework collective agreement is also signed at the Buro level, between the Buro union president and each company management. Wages and hours are collectively bargained at the union branch and enterprise level. Not only is there coordination over what to bargain during the Shunto rounds, but also Buro officials from outside the enterprise concerned are typically present and participate in enterprise-level negotiations. This mechanism facilitates Jidosha Roren's effective intervention to avoid job losses resulting from corporate restructuring. As an example, when Nissan acquired Prince in 1966, Prince's subcontractor, Takada Kogyo, was to be terminated, according to Nissan's purchasing plan. Shioji, the All Nissan Union President, was contacted by Takada Kogyo, at which both management and union relied on him to lean on Nissan purchasing department to revise its plan. Nissan reconsidered its position, and Takada Kogyo subsequently grew into a 3,000 worker-strong subcontractor undertaking final assembly of speciality models in the 1980s.

To summarize, Jidosha Roren consisted of four unions, the All Nissan Motor Workers' Union, Hanro (for dealerships), Buro (for the auto component sector), and Minro (for non-automotive firms) (see Figure 7.3). Each of these unions was centralized, in the sense that its headquarters had the rights to collect union dues, to appoint union officials, to be present at branch-level (i.e. enterprise-level) bargaining and consultation sessions, and to call strikes. Thus, the employees of Nissan's parts supplier companies came to be organized into a union that clearly crossed the boundary of a single firm. The Nissan Buro Union is a far cry from the standard image of enterprise unionism. Members within this unified union worked at nearly 100 different companies that were not necessarily related by shareholding links (as in the case of the Matsushita Union), but by trading links with Nissan. As we shall see in Chapter 8, these trading linkages were used by the Buro Union to coordinate closely during the rounds of collective bargaining over wage and bonus negotiations.

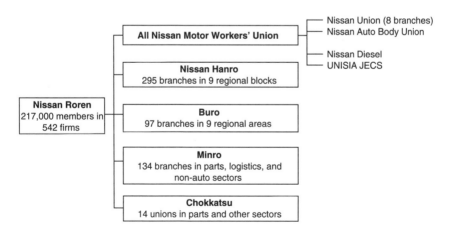

Figure 7.3 Organizational structure of Nissan Roren, 1995

7.3. Formation of Toyota-Led Zenkoku Jidosha

We now turn to developments after the dissolution of Zenji in 1954 for unions other than those at Nissan. In 1955, Nissan-led Jidosha Roren was the only formal union association that professed to be (or become) an industrial federation. In the same year, unions in central Japan formed an interim federation, called Jidosha Tokai, with 23 unions and 19,000 members (Zenkoku Jidosha 1972: 81). This was a regionally based federation, consisting of Toyota Union, Suzuki Union, and unions at large parts suppliers. Jidosha Tokai's activities focused on pay bargaining, with coordination within each geographical area such as Kariya, Mikawa, and Owari. Thus, when Jidosha Tokai was absorbed into Zenkoku Jidosha in 1962, wages were determined with much coordination area by area, but with little notion of coordination with the focal union. For example, in Kariya, unions at Nippondenso, Toyoda Koki, and Aichi Kogyo coordinated their wage demand, but had little exchange of information with Toyota Union.

In the second half of the 1950s, Toyota Union was party to a series of discussion to attempt to form a unified union movement in the car industry. Initially, unions at Toyota, Nissan, and Suzuki met, joined later by other automaker unions, to discuss two key issues, namely union finance and organizational form. On finance, Toyota Union was vocal in insisting that the money owed by Nissan Union to fund the 1953 strike should be paid back. Nissan Union insisted, however, that the union had no obligation to pay back what was owed by the defunct Zenji union. This issue therefore remained unresolved.

In the late 1950s, the discussion moved on to organizational matters, and in particular, to political affiliation and the internal structure of union federations. Nissan's Jidosha Roren, led by Ichiro Shioji, maintained that its affiliation with Zenro, a national centre with more moderate political views than Sohyo, must be followed suit by any industry-wide federation to be created. They argued that unless political affiliation was made explicit, no new initiative for an industry-wide union movement would succeed. Toyota Union, by contrast, considered political neutrality important, insisting that affiliation should be decided once an industry-wide body was created, and thinking that with Zenji's failure, affiliation to Sohyo had been ruled out.

In reality, the issue of political affiliation disguised a more fundamental difference in the organizational strategy of Nissan Union on the one hand and that of Toyota Union on the other. Nissan Union already had Jidosha Roren, which appeared like an industry-wide union federation. Toyota

Union insisted that unless Nissan Union took down the 'shop sign' (kan-ban), other unions would feel as though they were to be absorbed into this Nissan-led federation. Hisashi Sawada, a Toyota Union leader at the time, told Nissan's Shioji that 'after taking down the shop sign, we can then create a new federation to which automaker unions affiliate as automaker unions, parts supplier unions as parts supplier unions, and dealership unions as dealership unions; you must dissolve Nissan's *keiretsu*-like union federation'.[5]

Nissan Union continued to insist on the corporate grouping-based *roren* federation as a unit of affiliation to the industry-level organization. In 1961, a final meeting of the union leaders from major automakers was held to pan out political differences. Nissan's Ichiro Shioji did not budge from his stance, had a verbal fight with Toyota's Hisashi Sawada, and left the meeting. Toyota Union made all the remaining unions promise that they would go back to their respective union members to obtain support to establish a federation without Nissan. But these union leaders failed to obtain backing from the rank and file for a national federation without Nissan. In the end, when Zenkoku Jidosha (JAWU) was inaugurated in 1962 as a rival industry federation to Nissan's Jidosha Roren, only unions at Toyota, Hino, Isuzu, and Suzuki joined.[6]

With this chequered history in its inception, the aim of Zenkoku Jidosha was nevertheless to join forces to improve working conditions in the Japanese automobile industry. There were thirty-six founding unions in 1962, of which twenty were in the Tokai branch led by the Toyota Union. Of these, thirteen were at parts suppliers that belonged to the Toyota supplier association, Kyohokai. The other branches were the Kanto branch consisting of twenty enterprise unions including those at Hino and Isuzu, and later the Shizuoka branch led by Suzuki Motor Union. In the same year, Nissan's equivalent, the Buro federation, consisted of seventy-six union branches (i.e. seventy-six component suppliers were already organized by Nissan union, as compared to only nineteen at Toyota).

By 1971, on the eve of the disbanding of Zenkoku Jidosha (JAWU) to give way to JAW confederation, the Tokai branch had sixty-eight unions (Zenkoku Jidosha 1972: 368). By this time, Nissan's Jidosha Roren Buro organized eighty-eight supplier companies. Thus, it is evident that Toyota Union started organizing its supplier companies later than Nissan Union, and the Tokai branch of Zenkoku Jidosha had unions at larger supplier companies than those at Nissan group. The average size of unions was eight times as big for Toyota as for Nissan in 1962, and twice as large in 1971 (see Table 7.3 for comparisons).

Table 7.3 Comparison of union presence at Nissan and Toyota parts suppliers

	Jidosha Roren Buro (Nissan-led)			Zenkoku Jidosha Tokai branch (Toyota-led)		
	Union branches	Total membership	Members per branch	Unions	Total membership	Members per union
1962	64	12,474	195	19 [a]	30,992	1,631
1971	88	30,981	352	68 [b]	52,518	772
1981	92	42,878	466	—	—	—
1991	96	51,168	533	—	—	—

[a] Excluding Toyota Union.

Source: Author's calculations based on Buro (1995) for Nissan, and Zenkoku Jidosha (1972) for Toyota.

Unions affiliated to Zenkoku Jidosha (JAWU) were enterprise unions of the textbook type, organizing workers from one enterprise. There was no notion within the JAWU movement to extend the boundary of the union beyond one enterprise, as was the case for Nissan Union. Although Toyota's suppliers were locationally concentrated in central Japan, and therefore their unions belonged to the Tokai regional branch of Zenkoku Jidosha, supplier unions continued to regard area-based coordination over wage and bonus negotiations of greater importance than coordination within trading linkage-based corporate groupings. In fact, as a retired Nippondenso union official remembered, 'it was only when Toyota Roren was formed that a nuanced change was felt towards the notion that we could not decide until Toyota Union settled, that we should do things like wage bargaining as a corporate group-based entity as we do today'.[7]

7.4. From Jidosha Rokyo to Jidosha Soren

Throughout the 1960s, auto union leaders never forgot the need for a forum for united action at the industry level. As early as in 1962, Toyota-led Zenkoku Jidosha was talking with Nissan-led Jidosha Roren and unions at other major automakers to discuss the possibility of 'creating a forum for unified action in order to defend the common interest of workers in the face of adverse circumstances likely to be brought about by trade liberalization' (Zenkoku Jidosha 1972: 179).

External threat and comparison came not only from impending capital and trade liberalization, but also from the International Metalworkers Federation–Japan Council (IMF-JC), which was created in 1964 to unite workers in all metalworking sectors. Through international comparisons, it became evident that Japanese autoworkers enjoyed relatively low wages compared with their German counterparts, and this was attributed to the absence of a united workers' voice in industrial policy and collective bargaining. During these years, several auto union leaders also spent time in the United States at the Harvard Trade Union Institute, and saw first-hand both the strength of United Auto Workers (UAW) and the prosperity of the US car industry. This stimulated a debate within the Japanese union movement on how to emulate UAW's strong organization and its practice of pattern bargaining.

Against this backdrop, Jidosha Rokyo was founded in 1965 as a forum for the main automaker enterprise unions (including at both Nissan and Toyota) to discuss how to maintain employment and improve living standards for all workers in the car industry. However, it took a further seven years before Jidosha Soren (JAW) was finally formed in 1972.

The debate amongst the auto union leaders was ostensibly about organization structure. Nissan Union continued to insist that Nissan-style trade linkage *roren* must be the unit of affiliation for an industry-wide union organization. An alternative principle of organization, advocated by Toyota Union, was to let automaker unions, parts supplier unions, and dealership unions affiliate on the same basis. This difference reflected a gap in organizing principles between Domei (supported by Nissan Union) that considered corporate grouping-based *roren* as beneficial to the union movement, and others that regarded such *roren* with suspicion. The basis of suspicion lay in vulnerability of unions to the vagaries of management, which could best be minimized by organizing along industry or other lines that cut across, and do not extend, the logic of corporate capital ownership.

In other words, Nissan Union, with its powerful leader, Ichiro Shioji, considered *roren* the only effective defence against corporate management, given the reality of the Japanese industrial structure. 'For instance, Nissan Union leaders cannot intervene in Toyota *keiretsu* companies. It would be better for an automaker union that can intervene to take responsibility and exercise influence in order to protect workers' (Jidosha Soren 1993: 9). Nissan Union also claimed that the *roren* was more encompassing in solving the problem of dualistic wage structure by protecting workers at smaller parts suppliers. In implicitly criticizing Toyota Union's stance at the time, Haruki Shimizu, a retired Nissan union leader, reminisced that there was an old-style boss-follower (*oyabun-kobun*) mentality between assembly workers on the one hand and parts supplier and dealership workers on the other. The latter 'had no confidence that the automaker union would intervene and put forward demands on their behalf, so there was no trust between these different types of workers'.[8]

By contrast, Toyota Union leaders such as Hisashi Sawada (who was president of Zenkoku Jidosha Tokai branch at the time) joined other automaker union leaders in opposing the *roren* as an organizational form. 'We were opposed to *roren* as a unit of affiliation. This was because we worried that if unions organized along *keiretsu* corporate groupings, then we would give further momentum to fierce competition between automakers' (Jidosha Soren 1993: 9–10). If one automaker lost against another, it was argued, the *roren* at the losing company would be hit immediately by reductions in parts prices and wages. Apart from such genuine fear of the adverse consequences of this organizational form, Toyota and other unions also remained deeply suspicious of the leadership at Nissan Union. The resistance to the idea of *roren* as an organizational form could not be separated rationally in their eyes from the fear that every *roren* might turn into a highly centralized and powerful machinery led by Nissan Union's leadership.

Nevertheless, by 1970, Toyota union leaders slowly came to adjust their stance, eventually laying the foundation for the decision to make *roren* the unit of affiliation to the confederation, Jidosha Soren (JAW). According to official accounts, Toyota union leaders came to see a number of benefits from forming a *roren*, such as organizational manageability (an alternative would be direct affiliation of thousands of enterprise unions) and concerted efforts to improve working conditions of employees from upstream (in parts manufacturing) to downstream (in dealerships) (Zen Toyota Roren 1983: 58). Behind the scenes, Shiro Umemura (who subsequently became Toyota Union president) was at work persuading Toyota union leaders and rank and file of the utility of the *roren* form of union organization at Toyota. He recalled: 'it was one of the strongest arguments we had to persuade members, that we cannot remain fragmented and effectively counter the management side when the company was strengthening its control over its suppliers to diffuse its Kanban system.'[9] For those who still opposed, Umemura used the argument that *roren* was a first step towards forming a true industrial union (Jidosha Soren 1993: 10).

Thus, a *roren* led by Toyota Union was born in 1972, incorporating enterprise unions at Toyota affiliates, suppliers, and dealers. Zenkoku Jidosha (JAWU) was dissolved at the same time. Unions at other automakers also followed suit to form *roren* federations. Reflecting the triumph of Nissan Union's principle of affiliation by *roren* federations over Toyota Union's preferred principle of affiliation by individual enterprise unions, Nissan Union president, Ichiro Shioji, became the first president of the newly formed industry confederation. As we noted in Chapter 5, however, the JAW confederation was from the start relatively resource-poor in relation to the *roren*.

But even after the formation of the confederation, significant differences continued to exist in the substantive mode of operation at Nissan's *roren* and Toyota Roren. In particular, Toyota Roren was essentially a coordination and communication forum, a federation of enterprise unions each with their autonomous bargaining rights. By contrast, as described in Section 7.2, Nissan's Jidosha Roren affiliated to the confederation, but remained a powerful body, consisting of unified unions that crossed the boundary of an enterprise.

7.5. From Jidosha Roren to Nissan Roren

By the mid-1980s, Nissan's Jidosha Roren had a powerful presence in the industry confederation, having won the battle to retain the *roren* as the unit of affiliation. Compared with other *roren* in the industry, however, Jidosha Roren was highly centralized in its structure, with essentially four large unified unions, each with centralized control over union funds and bargaining (see Figure 7.3). Interestingly, just as Matsushita Union was moving towards decentralizing responsibilities to union branches (see Chapters 3 and 8), the Nissan Roren Buro union also formally approved in 1987 a change in its rules and regulations to promote more autonomous operations. The decentralization was put into effect a year after Jidosha Roren changed its name to Nissan Roren (Federation of All Nissan and General Workers' Union) in 1989, when a union branch (*shibu*), typically organizing employees at a supplier company, came to be known as a union (*roso*).

In practice, *de facto* decentralization took place gradually in the late 1980s in certain aspects of union governance. Two out of the three dimensions in the typology of enterprise unions, namely union resources (money and people) and strike action, remained untouched and centralized. Thus, the Buro union (*kumiai*), organizing workers at nearly 100 parts supplier companies, remains a legal entity that collects union subscriptions, appoints union officials, and retains the right to call a strike.

However, collective bargaining and consultation have become decentralized. They have always taken place at the level of the enterprise-level union (*roso*), and collective agreements continue to be signed at the level of the enterprise by three parties, namely the enterprise management, the union branch president at the enterprise, and the Buro union president. But whereas in the past, union officials from higher levels of Buro's union hierarchy were present, they were now excluded from attending

negotiation and consultation meetings. At Unipres, a metalworking supplier that was created by merging Yamato Kogyo and Yamakawa Kogyo in
1998, the 2001 collective agreement specifies that worker representatives
for joint consultation and bargaining must be chosen from amongst Unipres employees. By contrast, an earlier agreement of 1980 at Yamakawa
Kogyo states that the union can appoint members of the negotiating
committee from amongst union officials from higher levels of the union
organization (i.e. non-employees of Yamakawa Kogyo) (Section 6, clause
38). Thus, Nissan Roren, and Buro in particular, has delegated greater
power to bargain at the level of individual supplier companies.

Reasons why Nissan Roren has become decentralized are multiple and
complex. One key reason for the timing of the rule change was the
expulsion of Ichiro Shioji from the Nissan Union leadership who begot
hostility from both Nissan management and within the union for maintaining a very high concentration of power over such matters as the
appointment of union officials. Decentralization was seen as a way of
rectifying the ossification of centralized control within Nissan's union
network, and of reviving grass-root initiatives.

Another important factor in pushing for decentralization related to the
trouble that Nissan management faced in the late 1980s and 1990s, leading to Renault taking an equity stake in 1999. Thereafter, Nissan's supplier
relations have gone through a turbulent period. Carlos Ghosn, as the
Chief Operating Officer of Nissan, made it his top priority in the Nissan
Revival Plan to return Nissan to profitable growth and to reduce its net
consolidated debt of 2.1 trillion yen in 1998. Sales of assets tied in securities, real estate, and affiliates (including suppliers) helped reduce this debt
to 8.6 billion yen in 2003. The establishment of Renault Nissan Purchasing
Organization (RNPO) in 2001 also contributed to reducing Nissan's purchasing costs by 20 per cent during 2000 and 2002. Thus, Nissan
responded to a pressure to switch to a more market-based approach to
supplier selection, within the context of sharing a global supplier base
with Renault. In the process, some smaller suppliers lost business with
Nissan, and amongst those that continued to trade, some suppliers
merged with each other (as in the case of Calsonic Kansei) or were sold
(to Hitachi in the case of UNISIA JECS).

One consequence of Nissan's corporate restructuring was a huge decline
in membership. Nissan Roren's 230,000 members in 1994 dwindled to
150,000 in 2002. This compared with the decline at Toyota Roren from
283,000 members in 1994 to 260,000 members in 2002. Nissan Roren
evidently argued for employment stability, but was not in a situation to

claim, as Jidosha Roren did in the 1960s and 1970s, that there should be no job losses from within its boundary.

Apart from Nissan's own troubles, there was also a general mood in the industry that the days were over when unions could demand a uniform pay increase regardless of the company's ability to pay. This is a subject that is explored in greater depth in Chapter 8. Thus, to summarize, pressures to decentralize Nissan Roren came from three directions, from within the union movement with the end of Shioji's leadership, from management that engaged in drastic corporate restructuring that also involved reducing *keiretsu* suppliers, and the general climate in the Japanese economy at large.

7.6. Conclusions: Why Do Nissan Roren and Toyota Roren Differ?

By way of a summary, the debate on organizing principles that took place within the automobile unions in the run-up to the formation of Jidosha Soren confederation in 1972 captures the essence of the wider debate on how best to organize workers in Japan. Going back to the immediate postwar period, Sanbetsu under Communist leadership believed in organizing workers at large firms by industry, whilst treating small companies and their workers somewhat differently (they were regarded as representing traditional indigenous capital (*minzoku shihon*)). After the Red Purge, Sohyo emerged as the largest national centre and engaged in both political class struggle and economic struggle. As we saw, Zenji, the auto industrial union, was formed when Sanbetsu held sway, then came to take a leading role within Sohyo.

Sohyo was no different from Sanbetsu in attempting to mobilize individual workers at the shop level into industrial unions. But it differed significantly in its policy towards wanting proactively to organize peripheral workers, be they temporaries, semi-unemployed, or workers at small- and medium-sized subcontracting firms. By making a broad appeal to workers and their families in their communities, Sohyo thought that they had a winning formula to mobilize all workers. But by the mid-1950s, the defeat of the Zenji union chapter at Nissan led Sohyo to question its own approach to union organizing. In particular, Sohyo came to realize that their two key organizing principles, namely industrial unions for large company workers and regional unions for peripheral workers, were not making much headway in undermining the basis of enterprise unionism. The 1958 Draft Principles of Organizing (*soshiki koryo soan*) (Rodo Kenkyu 1979) arose out of debate on this issue, and in particular, to seek answers to the question of how unions can survive if management or the public authority seriously engaged in union bashing.

The lack of confidence in answering this question in the affirmative was due to the distance between Sohyo's ideal of 'one industry, one union' and the Japanese reality of enterprise unionism. In 1958, Sohyo's diagnosis and policy recommendation were along the following lines (Rodo Kenkyu 1979: 93–6). Ideally, all unions should be industrial unions, but many industry-based labour organizations remained federations of enterprise unions. But there is no point in losing membership by making a hasty transition from a federation to a unified union. In thinking about this transition, one of the greatest obstacles was seen to be the existence of enterprise-based federation (*kigyo rengo*, the capital ownership-based *roren* in the terminology of this book). Some might argue that the unification of enterprise-based federations was a step towards the creation of an industrial union. But this was difficult if the enterprise was diversified into several sectors. Also, it was not clear whether or not the enterprise-based federations were meant to wither away—as they should—or remain as subsidiary units when industrial unions were established. Thus, Sohyo leadership was deeply suspicious of attempts at organizing unions along the lines of corporate capital affiliation, as it introduced the logic of capital in the centre of the labour movement.

The 1958 Draft Principles of Organizing were discussed at Sohyo's annual conference, but no formal decisions were made, an indication of how difficult it was to define a clear path from enterprise unionism towards industrial unionism. By the time they came to be revised and approved for the 1964 conference, Sohyo stuck to the same diagnosis: the fundamental reason why enterprise unions could not evolve into industrial unions was the enterprise consciousness of workers. Also at the bottom of why workers could not cast off such mentality was the existence of dualism. Dualistic structure enabled firms to undermine workers' bargaining power by threatening to replace them by using peripheral workers. Core workers who suffered from low pay and long hours might become complacent that their lot was not as bad as peripheral workers, and would not bargain hard. Interestingly, despite this consistency in the diagnosis, the 1964 Principles of Organizing took a softer stance on the utility of enterprise-based federations. Sohyo now recognized that actual tactics for engaging in industry-level struggle could be varied and that coordination by unions at corporate groups (which it called a Konzern joint struggle) or by unions among *keiretsu* subcontractors would be worthwhile (Rodo Kenkyu 1979: 268–9).

Although automotive unions were distanced from Sohyo by the 1960s, this change in stance by Sohyo provided a backdrop for the contest between Nissan Union and Toyota Union over what should be the predominant organizing principle for the Japanese automotive union movement. As this chapter demonstrates, Nissan Union had a *roren* structure since 1955, whilst Toyota Union resisted having one until 1972. Nissan Union considered *roren* as an essential defence against management power, and created a structure of centralized control. Toyota Union, by contrast, continued to believe that corporate group-based *roren* would weaken unions' position vis-à-vis management, and wished to think of it as a stepping stone to creating a more genuine industrial union to which unions at automakers, parts suppliers, and dealerships would have equal status as affiliates. Thus, when Toyota Roren was formed, it did not create a structure beyond a coordinative federation of enterprise unions. Thus, although both came to be called *roren*, Toyota Roren has been more decentralized than Nissan Roren. Moreover, centralization *per se* is neither a necessary nor a sufficient feature for the well-functioning of *roren* federations.

The greater degree of centralization at Nissan Roren than at Toyota Roren manifests itself in many ways. First, because a Nissan Roren union, such as Buro, incorporates workers at several dozen parts supplier companies, there are fewer multiple branch union (MBU) organizations in Nissan Roren than in Toyota Roren, only 21 as compared to 264 in 2002 (see Table 7.4).

Table 7.4 Number of unions and membership at Toyota Roren and Nissan Roren in 2002

	Single branch unions (SBUs)			Multiple branch unions (MBUs)	
	Number of unions	Total members	Average members per union	Number of unions	Total members
Jidosha Soren	1,505	688,802	458	789	698,936
Nissan Roren	513	142,018	277	21	151,729
Toyota Roren	312	264,217	847	264	264,217

Note: The number of MBUs is the number of unions with more than one branch, plus the number of unions without any branch structure. The number of SBUs is the sum of the number of unions without any branch structure and the number of branches in MBUs.

Source: MHLW (2003), 76.

Second, MBU organizations at Nissan are governed by tall organizational hierarchies. Toyota Roren has a unified structure with one headquarter office in Toyota City. By contrast, at Nissan Roren, each union (*kumiai*), such as Buro for the parts supply sector, has its own administrative structure, with the union president, a general secretary, and a set of regional offices that oversee the affiliated company-based union units (*roso*). The elongated hierarchy consists of company-level union branch (*roso*) affiliating to Buro union (*kumiai*), which in turn affiliates to Nissan Roren, creating a distance between rank and file and the union leadership.

Third, another indicator of centralization, and the consequent lack of resources at the lower levels, is the proportion of union representatives who are posted away from their immediate workplaces to a higher level of the *roren* organization as full-time officials (e.g. at the regional offices or at the head office).[10] This proportion, which may be regarded as a centralization index, declined from 22.5 per cent in 1983 to 19.3 per cent in 1994 at Toyota Roren (Jidosha Soren 1983, 1994). But it continued to increase from 28.0 per cent to 38.5 per cent during the same period at Nissan Roren when bargaining and consultation were becoming gradually decentralized.

The detailed comparison of Nissan Roren and Toyota Roren undertaken in this chapter demonstrates a wide within-industry contrast in union strategy and the resulting organizational structure. Even after the adoption of the *roren* federation by all automotive unions since 1972, differences between Nissan Roren and Toyota Roren have remained starker than have similarities. Nissan Roren is both formally and substantively more centralized than Toyota Roren in the levels at which union resources (money and people) are held. Until recently, also, bargaining and consultation were more centralized at Nissan Roren than at Toyota Roren. These differences emerged as a result of a fundamental difference in organizing principles and strategy towards management. Chapter 8 evaluates the consequences of these structural differences on union members' working conditions.

Notes

1. The Nissan Heavy Industries Employees Union was initially formed at Yokohama factory, which also had a corporate headquarters function. This union was therefore a factory union at the time of formation, but became an enterprise union as Nissan's other factories were organized one by one subsequently. Unlike at Toyota or Isuzu where independent factory-based unions came to

form a federation and then a unified enterprise union at a later date, Nissan's other factories were organized as branches of the enterprise union from the start. The centralizing tendency of Nissan's organizing drive is evident from this early stage, but factory-based sentiments were not automatically in favour of centralized control. Yoshiwara factory came to be led by Tetsuo Masuda who moved from other parts of Nissan explicitly to start a union. Tsurumi factory considered the pros and cons of forming an independent factory union and resolved that joining forces with Yokohama would be better to strengthen its bargaining power. Atsugi employees felt more strongly about preserving the autonomy of its factory, and agreed to become a union branch only after the union explicitly incorporated 'respect for branch autonomy' in its rules (Nissan Roren 1992: 138).

2. Interview with Ichiro Shioji on 11 September 2003.
3. Interview with Ichiro Shioji on 11 September 2003.
4. As a concrete example, a family-owned company, Sato Ltd., was in near bankruptcy. Buro's negotiations led to two group companies (organized by Buro unions) offering help, in the form of capital participation, to restructure Sato Ltd. into a new company, Kyoei Parts Industries (*Buro* Issue No. 45, 25 May 1964).
5. Interview with Hisashi Sawada on 8 April 1997.
6. This left the unions at Toyo Kogyo (later Mazda), Mitsubishi, Daihatsu, and Fuji Heavy Industries outside the frame of the two competing industry federations.
7. Interviews with Minoru Yamada, an ex-Nippondenso union official on 8 April 1997.
8. Interview with Haruki Shimizu on 31 July 1996.
9. Interview with Shiro Umemura on 8 April 1997.
10. It is a peculiarity of the Japanese system that the vast majority of union officials are on leave from their workplace, and have the option to return after their term is over.

8

Harmonization versus Differentiation, Employment Security versus Labour Flexibility

What has been the impact of union and *roren* strategies on human resource outcomes? And how has the interaction between corporate and union strategies affected the degree of homogeneity or diversity of human resource systems within the firm and the corporate group? We are interested in pay (wage and bonus) as an easily quantifiable outcome, but also in other outcomes such as working hours, pensions, benefits, and employee representation systems to effect employment adjustment. This chapter examines this part of the SSI framework that links strategic interactions to performance outcomes.

Since the late 1990s, labour markets in Japan have become decisively more diverse and flexible, due in part to a number of changes in the law as well as in corporate strategy. Non-regular employees increased from 20.2 per cent of the Japanese workforce in 1990 to 29.8 per cent in 2002, and to 32.3 per cent in 2005 (JILPT 2004: 18). In 2002, 12.6 million were part-time workers, whilst 2.13 million were temporary workers (Sato 2005). Of the latter, 1.79 million were 'dispatched workers', dispatched from labour placement agencies (Morishima and Shimanuki 2005: 80).[1] How has employment diversity been introduced where in the past a more homogeneous system prevailed? And how much numerical flexibility has been introduced in workplaces that had been characterized by a high degree of employment security? What is the impact of employment diversity on work organization and labour–management relations?

This chapter addresses these questions not just from the perspective of corporate strategy (in labour management) or union strategy, but by giving regard to the interaction between the two. As explained in Chapter 1, both the firm and the union may be equally centralized and favour uniform human resource practices, or equally decentralized and favour more diverse human resource practices. But the structures of the human resource system pursued by corporate strategy and labour strategy may not necessarily coincide. In such a situation, the boundaries of organizational structures are likely to be contested. Ultimately, the resulting structures and human resource systems are those preferred by the party that can mobilize greater power resources in the bargaining process. Applying this framework leads us to a view that the process of introducing greater diversity and flexibility in Japanese workplaces has been highly managed and contested to a varying degree. The pace of introduction has been slow, though accelerating since the late 1990s. Moreover, it is not always the case that management has preferred a drastic move toward decentralization, whilst unions are hanging on to old ideas of centralized bargaining.

Section 8.1 begins by comparing trends in collective bargaining outcomes in wage and bonuses at Nissan Roren, Toyota Roren, and Matsushita Roren. As noted in Chapter 5, *roren* federations have had an explicit policy to standardize conditions in workplaces belonging to the same federation. However, there has been a gradual increase in the degree of variation in wage and bonus settlements within a *roren* in the last decade. We explore reasons why settlements became more dispersed over time.

Section 8.2 examines how and why diverse working conditions came to be introduced at Matsushita Group and at NTT Group. In both cases, the first step towards introducing a looser rein on standardized conditions is to allow diverse levels of provision whilst keeping the human resource system the same for operating companies within a corporate group. This is in part to enable the movement of employees between group companies, through job transfers in the internal labour market.

Section 8.3 focuses on specific instruments that Japanese companies have used to preserve the lifetime employment norm in the 1990s and 2000s. As compared to the 1970s, these instruments are much sharper, eroding at the margin the implicit guarantee of secure jobs and stable income. Particularly since the late 1990s, employers have increased the use of contingent workers, not just to weather cyclical downturns, but also to reduce labour costs by delegating responsibility to those not directly on their payroll. Such outsourcing activity is beginning to spread to workplaces in which the core regular workforce is ever diminishing. As regular workers become a smaller and smaller proportion of the total workforce, a representation gap, i.e. a level of worker representation and participation below that which workers desire, is likely to grow. Unless enterprise unions reconsider their workforce boundary, this would have adverse implications for industrial democracy and may further undermine the influence of unions.

8.1. Shunto Bargaining Outcomes: Greater Dispersion since the late 1990s

Shunto—the Spring Offensive—is a highly coordinated annual wage bargaining round, and is regarded as a functional equivalent of an incomes policy that contributed to the competitiveness of the Japanese economy. As the name indicates, Shunto started in 1955 when radical union leaders sought greater solidarity in bargaining, in order to overcome the shortcomings of enterprise unions (see Sako 1997*b* for details). Nevertheless, formal negotiations and settlements over pay and bonus take place at the decentralized level of the enterprise, leading some writers such as Calmfors and Driffil (1988) to classify the Japanese bargaining structure as one of the most decentralized in the world.

Such characterization, however, missed the key mechanisms of information sharing and coordination that ensured that Shunto settlements were compatible with good macroeconomic performance and superior international competitiveness. First, at the national level, the two peak organizations, Rengo (Japanese Trade Union Confederation) and Nikkeiren (Japan Federation of Employers Association, now merged with Keidanren (Japan Federation of Economic Organizations) to become Nippon Keidanren), engage the government and the public in a debate on what pay increases Japan can afford. The resulting white papers that Rengo and Nikkeiren separately issue lay down 'guidelines' for the percentage increase in wage demand and offer what they respectively perceive to be compatible with macroeconomic forecasts for growth and inflation.

Second, private-sector unions and leading companies in export-oriented manufacturing sectors take a lead in Shunto discussion. Unions and companies in an exposed export-oriented sector have greater incentives than those in a protected sector to be concerned about international competitiveness. Oligopolistic employers in key sectors, such as steel, shipbuilding, electrical machinery, and automobiles, meet frequently not only to exchange information about their respective bargaining situation but also to agree on a specific settlement offer. At the same time, unions in the same key sectors, formally part of IMF-JC, are pattern setters. The union leaders met to determine a specific settlement figure and generally succeeded in sticking to the agreed rate. Deviation from the agreed rate was considered impossible and a treacherous act if such deviation occurred without formal approval of the industry federation's Shunto committee.

Third, pay settlements are highly synchronized, thus eliminating the possibility of wage leapfrogging. Spring became the timing of pay settlements because new recruits start on 1 April in Japan after the academic year comes to an end in March. Over the decades, synchronization in settlement dates became more and more marked. Particularly after 1975, all key IMF-JC unions have settled on the same date, which was 24 March in 1994 for example. Other sectors settle soon thereafter, so that most settlements are completed before the summer.

Fourth, and perhaps most pertinent to the subsequent analysis in this chapter, wage settlement norms diffuse in an orderly fashion from the private sector to the public sector, from leading pattern-setting sectors to follower sectors, from large to small firms, and from corporate headquarters to subsidiaries and affiliates. The social order roughly corresponding to all these dimensions is clearly not just a ranking according to the company's ability to pay, but the ranking according to the prestige of companies. Consequently, through employer coordination within corporate groups, mirrored by union coordination within *roren* federations, the focal union and the focal firm always settle first before any of the affiliates and suppliers can settle by taking account of the focal settlement.

Such diffusion mechanism is important to the extent that Shunto acts as a functional equivalent of encompassing organizations (in Olson's sense (Olson 1982)) in an age of declining union density from 34 per cent in the mid-1970s to less than 20 per cent by 2005. Encompassing organizations police free riders and provide members with incentives to internalize externalities (here in the form of wage-push inflation). The Olsonian logic of collective action works along three channels: first, through the organized business interests at the national and industry levels; second, through organized labour articulated from national, industry, down to enterprise levels; and third, through the institutional nexus between labour and product markets in bargaining within the corporate group. Employer coordination within corporate groups is mirrored by union coordination within *roren* federations. Specifically, labour costs are reflected in the prices of intermediate goods. Thus, affiliated suppliers' wage settlements affect the price competitiveness of the focal firm.

It is in this institutional context with a prevailing social norm of 'equal pay increases for companies of equal prestige' that we turn to an examination of Shunto bargaining outcomes at Nissan Roren and Toyota Roren in the 1990s and the early 2000s.

8.1.1 Nissan Roren versus Toyota Roren

Chapter 7 showed that despite being in the same industrial sector, Nissan Roren and Toyota Roren had different histories and philosophies, and these differences were reflected in their respective strategies and structures. In particular, we found that Nissan Roren was more centralized in its governance than Toyota Roren. Compared with Toyota Roren, Nissan Roren incorporated multiple enterprises into unified unions, organized more small suppliers earlier, and was explicit in its policy to narrow the wage gap between Nissan and smaller companies.

After 1972, with the formation of Jidosha Soren, the industry confederation, the formal policies of the newly constituted Toyota Roren and Jidosha Roren (as Nissan Roren was still known at the time) became more similar. But it was not until the 1976 Shunto that the dates of settlement were synchronized for all affiliated unions of the *roren* (Zen Toyota Roren 1983: 89). Until then, settlement dates were varied, as were the agreed pay increases. Particularly in 1975, in the aftermath of the 1973 oil shock, despite a demand for 27 per cent increase, the negotiations were tough and resulted in a wide variety of settlements ranging from 14.9 per cent to 3.8 per cent (Zen Toyota Roren 1983: 81). In the late 1970s and into the 1980s, however, the practice of synchronizing not only the settlement dates but also the levels of wage settlement themselves became institutionalized. By the mid-1980s, the settlements, in terms of percentage wage increase, were virtually identical for all Toyota Roren-affiliated unions, with a difference of 0.1 to 0.2 percentage points between them (Ueda 1992, Table 7). Moreover, there is some evidence that during 1982–92, dispersion among affiliated unions' wage *levels* (as distinct from wage increase rates) narrowed at both Toyota Roren and Nissan Roren (Nakata 1994: 239).[2]

What has happened in more recent years since the 1990s? The data for this analysis were obtained from respective *roren* offices on the agreement that no individual union name would be disclosed. The *roren* federations have had a mission to standardize conditions. The data are understandably sensitive to the extent that dispersion in settlements might be interpreted as indicative of failure to satisfy this mission. It is therefore quite a rare opportunity to be able to track wage dispersion over time at the disaggregated level of individual *roren*. The period covered is 1990–2002 in the case of Nissan Roren, and 1993–2002 in the case of Toyota Roren. Nissan Roren's sample is the 96 parts supplier unions that belong to the Buro section of the Roren. Toyota Roren's sample is the 102 parts supplier unions, excluding therefore the unions at dealerships. The sample of 96 and 102 makes it a good comparison, as the similarity in size implies that similar amounts of resources would be required for coordination and information exchange, and that the risk of a breakdown in coordination is also similar, other things being equal.

Figures 8.1 and 8.2 show time trends in wage and bonus settlements at Nissan Roren and Toyota Roren, respectively. Wage settlements are shown in terms of agreed pay increases per month in Japanese yen, as the practice of negotiating percentage increases has given way to negotiating increases in absolute sums by the 1990s.[3] Bonus settlements are shown in terms of an amount equivalent to the number of months' worth of basic salary. So if the monthly basic salary is 400,000 yen, 'five-months' bonus means 2,000,000 yen, normally paid out in two lumps, in the summer and in the winter. In each diagram, the maximum and the minimum settlements are shown, as are the average and the standard deviation.

One measure of dispersion—how widely values are dispersed around the mean—that enables us to compare Nissan Roren and Toyota Roren is the coefficient of variation (which is standard deviation divided by the mean). Two points of similarity and two points of difference are of note when comparing the extent and timing of dispersion in wage and bonus settlements at Nissan Roren and Toyota Roren. First, it is evident that the coefficients of variation for wage and bonus settlements all increased over time, particularly since the mid-1990s (see Figure 8.3). Greater dispersion is also caused mainly by some below-average unions not able to keep up, rather than above-average unions breaking the ranks. From 1999, the minimum settlements in all cases have been widely different from the average, indicating that the unions with these settlements were unable to follow any guidelines set by the *roren* head office.

Second, at both Nissan and Toyota federations, bonus settlements began to disperse earlier than wages (see Figures 8.1 and 8.2). It is not surprising that Shunto coordination started to break down first in bonus, as it became more acceptable for bonuses to reflect company-level performance. Thus, in 1995, Nissan settled for a rather low 4 months bonus payment, whereas a number of better-performing large suppliers were able to offer 4.9 months, closer to the 5 months minimum, which had been a sacred benchmark up to that point. By contrast, the basic wage remained more truly part of guaranteed income.

Apart from these similarities, Nissan Roren and Toyota Roren have had a different experience with respect to the timing and degree of dispersion. First, Nissan Roren's Shunto coordination started collapsing earlier than at

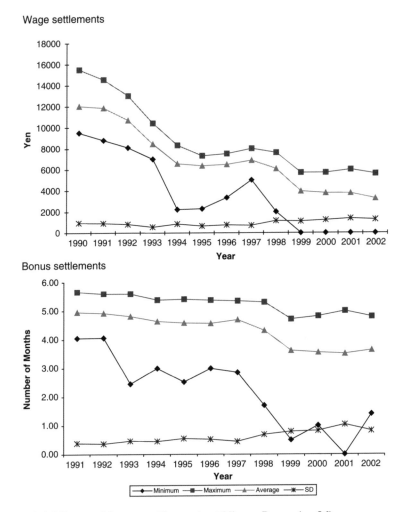

Figure 8.1 **Wage and bonus settlements at Nissan Roren** (n=96)

Toyota Roren, in 1993 for bonuses (with a minimum of 2.5 months as against an average of nearly 5 months) and in 1994 for wages (with a minimum of 2,000 yen compared with an average of just over 6,000 yen). This initial wave in the early 1990s was followed by a deeper breakdown in coordination in 1998 and 1999 (see Figure 8.1). These outcomes reflect Nissan's bad corporate performance with worsening losses and accumulated debts during this period, with a large negative net income and a return on assets ratio of − 9.6 during the 1999/2000 financial year. At Toyota Roren, the turning points came in 1996 when the minimum bonus

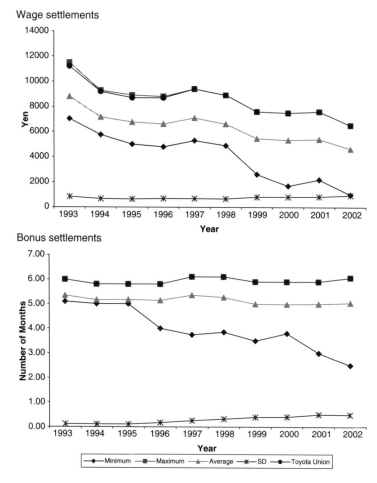

Figure 8.2 Wage and bonus settlements at Toyota Roren (n=102)

settlement collapsed, and in 1999 when pay settlement dispersion increased suddenly (see Figure 8.2).

Second, in absolute terms, Nissan Roren's dispersion is significantly greater around a lower mean than Toyota Roren's during most of the decade (see Figure 8.3). The result is clear-cut for bonus settlements, the variance for which was statistically significantly larger at Nissan Roren than at Toyota Roren for all years between 1993 and 2002. For wages, Nissan Roren's variance was significantly smaller than Toyota Roren's in earlier years (namely 1993 and 1995), but became significantly larger in 1996 and then from 1998 to 2002.

Wage settlements

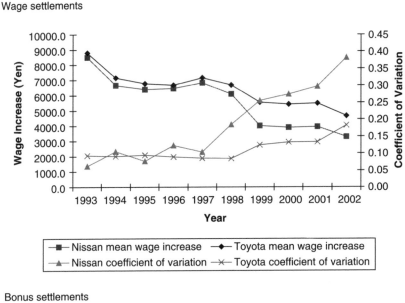

Bonus settlements

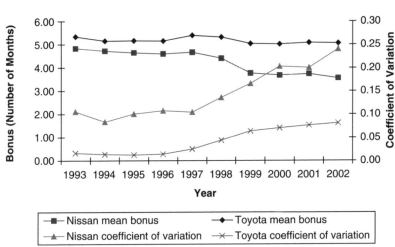

Figure 8.3 Comparing within-*roren* dispersion at Nissan Roren and Toyota Roren

8.1.2 Matsushita Roren

Now, we turn to Matsushita Roren. As noted in earlier chapters, Matsushita Roren is a much smaller *roren* than at Nissan or Toyota, consisting of only thirty-six unions whose enterprises are related to the focal firm more by shareholding than by trading. The focal union, Matsushita Union, dominates the *roren*, accounting for half of the total *roren* membership of around 60,000. The rest consists of half a dozen unions at large Matsushita affiliates (such as Matsushita Denko) and much smaller unions with no more than a few hundred members.

As explained in Chapter 3, Matsushita Roren only came into existence in 1989, so the period of analysis here is 1989–2003. Before 1989, there was no formal Shunto coordination as such. But after 1989, despite the fact that some unions, such as at Victor Company of Japan and Miyata Kogyo, continued to affiliate to Zenkin Rengo (the metalworkers federation) for a historical reason, Matsushita Roren became the sole coordinating body for all affiliated unions during Shunto. The nature of coordination over pay and bonus is somewhat different at Matsushita Roren, as compared to at Nissan or Toyota, in part because of the recent establishment date, and in part because of the diversity in size and sector of unions within the *roren*.

Figure 8.4 shows that the time trends in settlements at Matsushita Roren are quite erratic, as compared to those at Nissan Roren or Toyota Roren. Similar to the automotive trends is the fact that dispersion, as measured by standard deviation, increased in the 1990s, but it went up and down during the decade. This fluctuation may, in part, reflect the fact that although Matsushita Roren has a relatively small number of affiliated unions, it contains unions that organize a more diverse set of sectors, including not just electrical appliances and electronic components, but also financial services, engineering, logistics, and bicycle manufacturing. Different sectors face different market pressures, reflected in differential corporate performance.

Perhaps most notable is the collapse in wage and bonus settlements at Matsushita Union in 1998, reflecting a drastic decline in Matsushita Electric's profitability. Interestingly, this had a different impact on wages as compared to bonuses within the *roren*. As for wages, Matsushita Union's inability to secure no more than 2,000 yen (less than a quarter of the amount in the previous year) did not have a marked effect of pulling down the other *roren* union settlements, although it led to a slight increase in standard deviation. By contrast, Matsushita Union's bonus settlement—2.5 months as compared to over 5 months in the previous year—pulled down the other *roren* settlements, to the extent that the standard deviation for 1998 actually declined.

The tighter coordination over bonus settlements than over wages is counter to the norm we saw in the automotive industry. But as the union president at Shinto Union, a leader amongst small unions affiliated to

Wage settlements

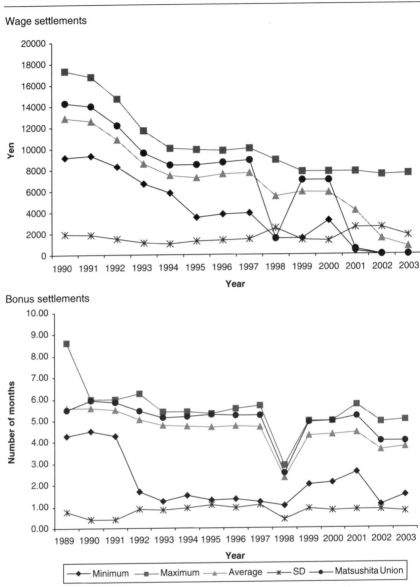

Bonus settlements

Figure 8.4 **Wage and bonus settlements at Matsushita Roren** (n=30)

Matsushita Roren, explained, 'bonuses are important because there is a long tradition of regarding bonus as a deferred wage to supplement what in effect is a low monthly salary'. By contrast, coordination over wages has become increasingly difficult for smaller unions, as Matsushita Roren gave guidance to its affiliated unions to bargain not simply for a percentage wage increase, but also over the distribution of the wage bill by specifying a certain job-grade salary scale (*kobetsu chingin seido*). Some smaller unions found no time to discuss the adoption of such a new wage system. However, since 1998, the focal firm, MEI, experienced declining profits, reaching a consolidated operating loss of 211.8 billion yen in 2001/2 (and a return on assets ratio of − 5.1), the largest in Matsushita's history. Consequently, Matsushita Roren has been in an odd situation in which the focal union could settle only for the minimum of the range of wage settlements.

What is invisible in Figure 8.4 is the greater diversity being introduced within the focal union, Matsushita Union, which, as we saw in Chapter 3, organizes twenty-eight separate group companies. Section 8.2 examines this intra-union diversity more in detail.

8.1.3 What Explains Increased Dispersion in Settlements?

Before we do so, however, what factors are responsible for bringing about greater dispersion in Shunto settlements? The economy-wide evidence from the Ministry of Health, Labour and Welfare (MHLW) (previously the Ministry of Labour) and the *roren* survey results for automotive and electrical machinery sectors (analysed in Chapter 5) are used here to interpret the key reasons. The annual MHLW survey of just over 3,000 firms employing 100 or more shows a gradual increase in dispersion of wage settlements in the 1990s, with a marked jump in the dispersion index since 1998 (see Figure 8.5). This is consistent with the trends noted for the three *roren* studied above, although it is not possible to distinguish, in this economy-wide picture, as between dispersion across industries and dispersion within industries.

The same MHLW survey clarifies the reason behind greater dispersion. This shows the increasing importance of 'company performance' (i.e. the ability to pay) as a determinant in Shunto wage settlements from the employers' perspective (see Figure 8.6). Price inflation, which was once a significant determinant after the 1973 oil shock, declined in importance to the extent that it is not an issue for most employers since the deflationary 1990s. 'Social norm', i.e. setting wages according to the going rate that is seen to be socially acceptable, has risen in importance in the late 1980s and early 1990s, but is declining ever since.

Labour's perspective is not too dissimilar from employers' perspective, although our data on unions are not economy-wide and are not longitu-

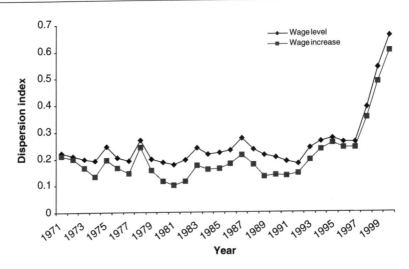

Figure 8.5 Dispersion in Shunto wage settlements in Japan

Note: Dispersion index = (3rd quartile − 1st quartile)/ (2 × average)
Source: Ministry of Labour (various years), *Chinage no Jittai* (Report on Wage Increases), Tokyo: Okurasho Insatsukyoku.

dinal. The *roren* survey conducted for this study asked union respondents what were the key reasons for wage differentials within the *roren* to which they belonged (see Appendix). According to them, by far the most important reason is 'differences in company performance (and the ability to pay)' (see Table 8.1). The second most important factor is 'differences in industry, corporate form, or products', followed by 'differences in firm's social prestige ranking', although the former is more important for electrical unions whilst the latter is more important for automotive unions. Evidently, electrical unions cover a broader set of industries, as some of them are affiliated to electrical *roren* by virtue of capital affiliation without any trading links to the focal firm.

Is there also evidence from labour's perspective of a declining importance of 'social norm' for wage setting? Some critics of Shunto point to the adverse effect of over-standardization of wages. But if 'differences in company performance' constitute an important reason for inter-union variations in pay, does this mean that if corporate performance worsens, the rate of wage increase (or its value) actually drops? Conversely, would an improvement in corporate performance lead to better wages? Let us examine this issue, specifically by considering what constraints unions perceive they face vis-à-vis the focal firm. The survey first asked respondents whether they were able to settle with a higher level than the focal firm over the past five years

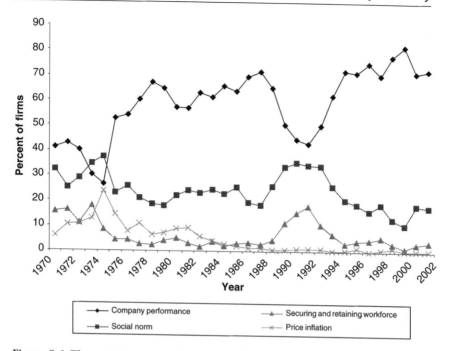

Figure 8.6 The most important factor in settling pay during Shunto negotiations

Source: Ministry of Labour (various years), *Chinage no Jittai* (Report on Wage Increases), Tokyo: Okurasho Insatsukyoku.

when their firm performed better than the focal firm. The survey then asked whether they think they would be able to do the same over the coming five years if the same favourable condition were to prevail. To the first question, as many as 40 per cent of unions said their firm's performance was better

Table 8.1   Factors that explain wage differentials within *roren* federations

Differences in:	Auto sector	Electrical sector	Both sectors
Corporate performance	56.5	57.6	57.1
Industry, corporate form, or products	28.0**	41.9**	35.0
Firm's social prestige ranking	31.5**	23.3**	27.4
Labour productivity	33.3**	20.3**	26.8
Production equipment	22.6**	8.7**	15.6
Unions' negotiating ability	11.3*	7.0*	9.1
Unionists' skill and education levels	11.3**	4.7**	7.9

** Sectoral difference is significant at 1 per cent level.
* Sectoral difference is significant at 5 per cent level.

Note: Per cent of union respondents who cited the factor as having 'a high degree of influence' in the *roren* survey.

Source: 1997/8 *roren* survey conducted by the author.

than the focal firm's. But the proportion of all unions that had ever settled their wages at a level higher than the focal firm was small at 12 per cent, consisting of only thirty-nine of the unions surveyed. In other words, even if the firm's performance exceeds the focal firm's performance, roughly only one in three or four unions manage to obtain a correspondingly better wage. The thirty-nine unions did better most in the rate of wage increase, followed by the number of months' worth of basic pay for bonus payment, and the amount of wage increase.

To a hypothetical question—whether the union would be able to settle at a level higher than the focal union in the next five years if the firm's performance is better than the focal firm's—32 per cent of the respondents answered yes. They break down into those who consider it 'possible for bonus payment' only (19 per cent), those who think it 'possible for both bonus and basic pay' (10 per cent), and those who think it 'possible with basic pay' only (3 per cent). Thus, introducing dispersion in bonus is considered easier than for basic wage. This survey took place in 1997/8, just before the degree of dispersion started increasing at a conspicuous rate. Thus, the 'next five years' projection is not so widely different from the experience in the past five years. It remains the case that the majority of the unions find it difficult to go beyond the settlements at the focal union, pointing to the continued importance of social prestige ranking of unions according to their size and position in the *roren* network.

In the survey, 61 per cent of unions considered exceeding the focal union's settlements inappropriate 'because of the difference in firms' social prestige ranking'. But there is an inter-industry difference in the other explanations for the difficulty. Sixty-two per cent of all unions agreed or strongly agreed with the reason 'because the focal firm as customer may demand tougher cost reduction'. Here, auto unions were twice as likely to cite this factor as electrical unions (83 per cent as compared to 41 per cent). This inter-industry difference might reflect the fact that auto unions are more likely to be affiliated to a *roren* on the basis of trading linkages with the focal firm than electrical unions. On further analysis, however, there is insignificant difference in citing this factor between unions with high trading linkage (50 per cent or more) and those with low trading linkage with the focal firm. Rather, it is the unions with both low capital affiliation linkage (less than 50 per cent of shares owned by the focal firm) and high trading linkage to the focal firm that cite this reason most. Thus, these unions in the most vulnerable position, concentrated in the auto sector, are quite sensitive to the adverse effect of a wage increase on business transactions.

Looking into the future, pay and bonus settlements may diversify further for a number of reasons. The first candidate factor is a greater dispersion in corporate performance within a sector, accompanied by the continued importance of 'company's ability to pay' as employers' criterion for granting pay settlements. The second factor is a further breakdown of social norm concerning the prestige ranking of firms, so that smaller companies, affiliates, and new start-ups become freer to pay their employees higher wages than the older established companies. The third and last factor is the possibility of a further erosion of the institutional nexus between labour markets and product markets. As suppliers diversify their customers, the nexus between wage increase and price negotiation becomes less visible. Pay may diversify, therefore, due to a compositional effect, with a reduction in the proportion of unions in the cell most vulnerable to this nexus, i.e. unions based at firms with a high trading linkage but low capital affiliation linkage.

8.2. Same System, Diverse Levels of Provision: What Are the Limits?

Section 8.1 demonstrated that firms and unions have come to rely more on the company's ability to pay and less on the notion of a socially determined going rate as a criterion for pay settlements. Accordingly, unions that belong to the same *roren* federations have come to settle for increasingly different rates of pay and bonus. Shunto coordination has been breaking down gradually, but more suddenly since the late 1990s. This section turns to the case of Matsushita Group and NTT Group to further our understanding of how greater diversity in broader working conditions including pay and bonus has been brought about.

In many ways, trends at Matsushita Group and NTT Group are very similar. Both are corporate groups engaged in related diversification, although the origin of NTT Group is more recent than that of Matsushita Group. Both have had powerful unions whose boundaries extend beyond the focal firm. Both groups have faced pressures to decentralize bargaining and consultation, with a view to introducing greater diversity in human resource systems. However, union strategy and reaction have been different. Matsushita's focal union has recognized the need to introduce diversified human resource systems, ultimately deciding to break up its own organizational boundary. By contrast, the NTT union has contested the move more fiercely, attempting to maintain a unified inter-firm union in

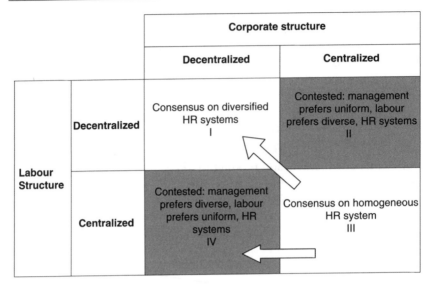

Figure 8.7 Human resource outcomes resulting from structural conditions at Matsushita and NTT Groups

Note: The trajectory for Matsushita Group is from III to I, and for NTT Group from III to IV.

the face of pressures to accept various modes of eroding a homogeneous human resource system. These different trajectories are summarized in Figure 8.7.

8.2.1 Matsushita Group

The process of decentralization in collective bargaining at Matsushita Group had been gradual, starting with the focal union's internal reorganization in 1990 (see Chapter 3). However, a decade later, two events signalled a step change in the degree of diversity allowed in the human resource system within the corporate group. First, the focal union decided in 2000 to decentralize bargaining over the adoption of two new schemes, namely the Sector-Specific Collective Agreement and the Location-Specific Employment Contract. These will be discussed in turn below. Second, in 2003, following the implementation of the corporate restructuring plan, the focal union announced its decision to break itself up into a federation of unions, one for each of the fourteen business 'domains'.

The Matsushita Electric Union remains the second largest enterprise union in Japan after the NTT Union, although its membership declined from a peak of nearly 95,000 in 1993 to 67,000 in 2003. The union has developed a multidivisional structure with as many as seventy union branches in order to cater for members based at twenty-eight separate affiliated companies. With each of these companies, the focal union insisted on signing a three-party agreement, between the Matsushita headquarters management, the subsidiary management, and the union. Consequently, collective bargaining became centralized in the sense that whatever was agreed between the focal union and the focal firm applied automatically to the three-party agreement companies. Not only were wages and bonuses identical across all these firms; an identical human resource system, the same labour–management consultation system, and the same welfare benefit schemes applied to all affiliated companies that signed the agreement. The focal union therefore maintained a high degree of centralization in its internal governance, saving union branches from the need to engage in local bargaining.

However, by 1990, the focal union was ready to devolve some responsibilities for negotiating over rest days and some aspects of work hours (e.g. shift patterns and flexitime) to union branch groups that were created by bundling union branches. In the 1980s, the addition of affiliated companies that were acquired rather than spun out to the list of three-party agreement companies was already creating a strain. Whilst Matsushita headquarters management acquired these firms in order to exploit locally based low-cost labour, the agreement required that they apply the same pay and conditions to these companies. Workers at Matsushita Kyushu in the southern island of Japan, for example, continued to enjoy a wage well above the going rate in the local labour market, identical to the level for MEI in metropolitan Osaka.

Some concessions were made by the union not to apply certain terms of the main collective agreement, but they were typically such things as welfare provisions and shift work patterns, not sufficient to make a significant difference to the cost of operations.

In the 1990s, around 45,000 union members of the focal union were hired directly by the MEI head office, and were assigned to internal divisions or to a handful of hived-off companies. There were, however, another 45,000 or so union members who worked at nineteen other companies that signed the three-party agreement. They benefited from the same pay and bonus levels and near-identical terms and conditions of employment, but were hired locally by operating companies. Thus, Matsushita Group's internal labour market was already segmented between 50 per cent of the focal union membership that was centrally hired and therefore expected to be mobile, and the other 50 per cent that was locally hired.

The 1990s recession, the threat of China as an alternative factory location, and the increasing diversification of Matsushita's operations put an enormous strain on the uniformity of labour conditions maintained by three-party agreements. MEI management hinted at abandoning these agreements, and wanted to incorporate regional factories as separate companies paying lower wages, as some of its competitors, notably NEC, had done for some decades. At the same time, Matsushita Union also recognized the need for 'multiple-track agreements' to allow for some degree of variation according to business sector, occupation, and location of work. Thus, labour–management contest at Matsushita was not over whether or not there should be greater diversity in human resource systems, but over how much diversity.

Consequently collective bargaining was partially devolved to the thirteen branch groups (*rengo shibu*) during the 2000 Shunto negotiations. Whilst basic wage and bonus continued to be negotiated centrally, the adoption of two specific schemes was subjected to local negotiations. The first scheme, known as the Sector-Specific Collective Agreement, gives local union branch groups the right to negotiate their own collective agreements in certain areas other than the core areas of basic pay and bonus. In particular, variations were introduced in the incentive component of bonus, work hours, shift patterns, and welfare benefits. A contentious issue was the shift premium, variations for which were enabled a year later in 2001. As the union documents indicate, these variations were justified not so much by differences in corporate performance but more by differential requirements arising from technology and demand patterns in different industrial sectors. For example, the union acquiesced to higher reward packages in software and finance than in consumer electronics.

The second scheme, the Location-Specific Employment Contract System (*chiiki gentei seido*), sought individual volunteers amongst regular employees to sign a new employment contract, in which the company guaranteed not to send them on assignments away from their home base in return for a cut in regular pay. For example, within Matsushita AVC Company, there are factories in Osaka, Okayama, Fukushima, Yamagata, and Sendai. Opting for this scheme implies not being transferred to any of the locations other than the home factory where one was initially hired.

This scheme was negotiated also in 2000 at the local—i.e. union branch group—level, and was a subject of much controversy. Matsushita management initiated the negotiation by pointing out that its domestic competitors are better able to meet the challenges from Taiwan and China by making factories into separate companies with cheaper labour costs. Matsushita Union countered management's wish to separate in-house factories by acquiescing to a pay cut. The union branch groups were given discretion to negotiate locally within the union headquarters guideline of 80 to 90 per cent pay cut. In practice, many (but not all) branch groups agreed to adopt the scheme, but some with larger pay cut than others and with a varying level of one-off bonus payment (*ichiji kin*) to entice volunteers. At the same time, since decisions were left to individual employees to opt in or out of this scheme, this introduced inter-personal diversity in employment contract within a location. No one likes taking a pay cut, and the union worked hard to convince members that the scheme was one way—if not the only way—to protect employment.

These two schemes therefore struck a death knell for the three-party agreements by introducing significant variation between the core Matsushita companies and between individuals in the same company. Conditions are likely to diverge further with the breakup of the focal union into fourteen separate unions in 2006. However, one consideration that might prevent too rapid an introduction of diversity is corporate management's wish to preserve a degree of homogeneity to enable inter-company and inter-locational labour mobility. Such mobility would become more difficult as sector-specific agreements lead to diversity of labour conditions, and as the option of location-specific employment contracts reduces the availability of workers who are contractually required to move from one location to another. The resulting rigidity in the internal labour market would make it even more difficult for Matsushita Group companies to offer an implicit guarantee of lifetime employment. In view of a relatively strong and centralized head office at Matsushita Group, it is possible that no such rigidity and fragmentation would occur for managerial employees. It is uncertain, however, as to how quickly shop floor workers and engineers, both on regular and contingent contracts, might face greater segmentation.

8.2.2 NTT Group

The challenges facing the focal union at NTT, the telecommunications company, are remarkably similar to those at Matsushita. Before the privatization of the NTT Public Corporation, Zendentsu (Japanese Telecommunication Workers Union) was the largest enterprise union in Japan. It wielded much power vis-à-vis management through negotiating a co-decision-based consultation system and vis-à-vis the government by mobilizing resources to influence the ruling Liberal Democratic Party as well as the Ministry of Post and Telecommunications (JIL 1996). Its successor, the NTT Union, is still the largest with a membership of 185,000 in 2003. The legacy of a powerful union contributed to its decision to remain centralized in the face of decentralizing pressures from management.

NTT in the 1990s faced a turbulent environment with technological change, privatization, deregulation, competition in global markets, and the growing importance of stock markets. In the midst of all this the company pursued a strategy to diversify from being primarily a fixed-line telephone carrier to a telecoms group incorporating various branches of the information services industry. Diversification led to transforming the corporate structure dominated by functional departments and regional offices into a weak holding company structure. In 1999, this organizational form emerged as a compromise between those that wanted a complete breakup, AT&T style, and those that wanted to keep the unitary structure. Since then, the NTT Group consists of eight core companies including the holding company. The seven core operating companies are NTT East and NTT West (both in fixed-line business, which is regulated by the government); NTT Communications (IP integration and networks), NTT Data (in data communication), NTT DoCoMo (in mobile communications), NTT Facilities (in design, construction, and maintenance services), and NTT Comware (in software). The first three were established in the 1999 restructuring, whilst the other companies had been created earlier in the late 1980s and the 1990s.

When NTT Corporation started hiving off divisions after privatization, starting with the creation of NTT Data in 1988, the Zendentsu union had a clear policy to defend the living standards of existing members who moved to the hived-off companies. The logic behind this was identical to that for Matsushita's three-party agreement: why change the working conditions of existing members at existing workplaces when the only thing that had changed was the corporate form? NTT management did not challenge this stance at the time. Nevertheless, this decision had two important consequences that subsequently became a bone of contention. First, the practice of extending an existing central collective agreement to group companies meant applying the agreements not only to existing employees but also to new recruits. In growth areas, such as in mobile telephone, as many as half of the workforce (e.g. half of DoCoMo's 11,000 employees) had never worked for NTT Corporation but were bound by its human resource system.[4] Second, the union strategy to extend the collective agreement coverage led to a highly centralized internal governance, with centralized collective bargaining and joint consultation structures for the NTT Group.

The union decided to retain a structure encompassing the whole NTT Group after explicit deliberation. In anticipation of the adoption of the holding company structure, Zendentsu renamed itself All NTT Workers Union of Japan (NWJ) (although we retain the label NTT Union in the current narrative), and restructured from being a regionally based to a company-based organization in December 1998 (NWJ 2002). Each of the eight core group companies became a union branch. The union considered an alternative structure, namely the federation of separate enterprise unions for each operating companies, but rejected it. Some members argued that the centralized union would pull down wages towards the weakest companies, but were swayed by the advantages in facilitating internal employment adjustment and pooling of union resources. In particular, union members at the shrinking core fixed-line businesses had little to gain from decentralization, which might undermine opportunities for job transfers to growing segments of the NTT Group. The 'logic of influence' overruled the 'logic of membership' (Schmitter and Streeck 1999).

A consequence of NTT Union's decision to remain unified is that the union is more centralized than corporate management (see quadrant IV in Figure 8.7). From the start in 1999, the NTT holding company management gave full autonomy for collective bargaining to the group companies. Meanwhile, the NTT Union headquarters initially conducted centralized bargaining, i.e. the union head office bargained with each of the eight group companies, with a view to arriving at an identical agreement for all. Company-level union branches did not have any authority to bargain and settle their own agreements with their respective company managements. So, an identical pay level and human resource system applied to all group companies, and an identical wage increase was applied to all employees of the NTT Group through the Shunto bargaining round. In effect, a DoCoMo engineer was paid an identical amount, and was granted an identical bonus, as an NTT East engineer, despite the fact that DoCoMo in mobile business was growing faster and more profitably than NTT East's fixed-line business.

Such internal disparity in corporate performance, and the subsequent need for deeper corporate restructuring, led to slow decentralization in bargaining. From spring 2001, NTT Union gave the company-level union branches the right to bargain over all issues except the core work conditions (especially the wage levels, although there is considerable disagreement among union branches as to what else constitute the core conditions). Consequently, management at each group company bargains at two levels, with the union headquarters over basic pay and with the company-level union branch over other issues, most notably bonus. As Table 8.2 demonstrates, DoCoMo's bonus was higher than at NTT East or West, to reflect corporate performance.

Thus, despite this slow and managed process of decentralization, the substantive outcomes and policies pursued by the union have thus far remained more or less uniform (Yoshihara 2000). In effect, the NTT Group retains a single human resource system for the whole group. When a performance-related pay system was centrally negotiated in 2001, the same system was introduced to all group companies at the same time. As shown in Figure 8.7, corporate and labour strategies had in the past coincided regarding the maintenance of a uniform human resource system, but the introduction of diversity is subject to much contention because the union has demonstrated a clear preference for a greater degree of centralization than management. To date, NTT Union has been more powerful than management, and has therefore been able to impose its preference for a relatively centralized bargaining structure to retain a homogeneous human resource system for the corporate group.

Negotiations that took place over the 2002 restructuring of the NTT Group, and the unusually harsh mood that prevailed, are testimony to a fundamental disagreement between management and labour. Management proposed to narrow the corporate boundaries, externalizing a significant proportion of the existing organization by establishing outsourcing companies. The union bargained for, and failed to attain, what had been the norm thus far, namely the maintenance of living standards for existing union members when corporate forms change.

The negotiated outcome involved a plan to reduce costs by 110 billion yen (of which 35 billion yen was to come from labour cost reduction) at NTT East and 155 billion yen (of which 65 billion due to labour cost reduction) at NTT West during the 2002/3 fiscal year. There were four instruments to reduce labour costs. First, various benefit systems (including retirement pension) were reviewed and some allowances (e.g. for cold climate) abolished with a view to introducing more performance-related elements. Second, 16,400 employees (6,400 from East, 10,000 from West) were to be made to take early retirement, in addition to 9,400 who had already retired by December 2001. Third, it was agreed that a total of 6,500 would be transferred from East and West to other group companies. Fourth, and this was the most contentious issue negotiated,

Table 8.2 Wage and bonus settlements at NTT Group companies, 1998–2003

Wage increase (yen)

Company name	1998			1999			2000			2001			2002			2003	
	Settled	% Increase	Demand	Settled	% Increase	Demand	% Increase	Demand	Settled	% Increase	Demand	Settled	% Increase	Demand	Settled	% Increase	Demand
NTT	2,306	0.66	8,800	921	0.26	3,200	0	1%	0	0	none	0	0	none	0	0	none
Holding company				921	0.26	3,200	0	1%	0	0	none	0	0	none	0	0	none
East				921	0.26	3,200	0	1%	0	0	none	0	0	none	0	0	none
West				921	0.26	3,200	0	1%	0	0	none	0	0	none	0	0	none
Communications				921	0.26	3,200	0	1%	0	0	none	0	0	none	0	0	none
Facilities	2,306	0.66	8,800	921	0.26	3,200	0	1%	0	0	none	0	0	none	0	0	none
Comware	2,306	0.66	8,800	921	0.26	3,200	0	1%	0	0	none	0	0	none	0	0	none
Data	2,306	0.66	8,800	921	0.26	3,200	0	1%	PAY-500	0	none	PAY-500	0	none	0	0	none
DoCoMo	2,306	0.66	8,800	921	0.26	3,200	0	1%	PAY-1000	0	none	PAY-300	0	none	0	0	none

Bonus (number of months)

Company name	1998	1999		2000		2001		2002		2003		
	Settled	Demand	Settled	Demand	Settled	Demand	Settled	Demand	Settled	Demand	Settled	Demand
NTT	5.48 + 0.42		5.48 + 0.42		5.1		4.8		4.4		4.3	4.6
Holding company			5.48 + 0.42		5.1		4.8		4.4		4.3	4.6
East			5.48 + 0.42		5.1		4.8		4.4		4.3	4.6
West			5.48 + 0.42		5.1		4.8		4.4		4.3	
Communications	5.48 + 0.42		5.48 + 0.42		5.1		4.8		4.4		4.15	
Facilities	5.48 + 0.42		5.48 + 0.42		5.1		4.8		4.4		4.3	
Comware	5.48 + 0.42		5.48 + 0.42		5.1		4.8		4.4		4.3	
Data	5.48 + 0.47 + 50,000 Yen		5.48 + 0.47 + 60,000 Yen		5.82 + 50,000 Yen		5.89 + 25,000 Yen		5.48 + 166,000 Yen		5.96	4.4
DoCoMo	5.48 + 0.52 + 280,000 Yen		5.48 + 0.57 + 220,000 Yen		5.98 + 218,000 Yen		5.98 + 233,000 Yen		5.48 + 386,000 Yen		5.48	

Note: PAY refers to performance – related pay.

100 outsourcing companies were to be established by NTT East and West, and nearly 60,000 employees were transferred to these companies in May 2002. Employees aged 50 or over were asked to take early retirement, and to be re-employed by the new companies at a wage up to 30 per cent lower than in their previous jobs. The union started by negotiating for no pay cut, but ended up agreeing to the 15–30 per cent wage reduction after management hinted at the ultimate horror of dismissals during negotiations. As at Matsushita, a lump sum payment at the point of transfer was negotiated to ease the pain of adjustment.

These 60,000 or so employees are doing the same job (in sales, maintenance, etc.) as before, but with pay reductions of up to 30 per cent. This is the cost of treating employment security as the top priority under all circumstances, as both management and labour shun the use of compulsory redundancy. Thus, the norm of income maintenance has been broken, but so as to defend the norm of lifetime employment. Employees at the outsourcing companies retain their NTT Union membership. So the outsourcing companies remain within the bounds of the focal union. But agreeing to wage reductions is the thin end of the wedge, providing an opener to differentiate amongst diverse workers within the same union.

To summarize, NTT Union has retained the unified union status, unlike Matsushita Union, and has retained a more centralized collective bargaining structure, thus leading to the retention of a more homogeneous human resource system for the entire corporate group than at Matsushita Group. The trajectories followed in introducing diversity in human resource practices thus encountered a greater degree of contention at NTT Group than at Matsushita Group (as illustrated in Figure 8.7). But diversity is creeping in through managed decentralization in bargaining, and more seriously via transferring employees to outsourcing companies.

8.3. Key Instruments to Retain Employment Security: Have Flexible Rigidities Turned into Rigid Flexibilities?

Dore (1986) characterized structural adjustment in the Japanese economy in the 1970s as 'flexible rigidities'. 'Rigidities'—such as oligopolistic industry structure, tenured job security, union monopolies, and state underwriting or provision of industrial capital—had been denounced as market imperfections responsible for deepening stagflation in Anglo-American economies. However, by using this oxymoron, Dore pointed out that such rigidities had been turned into a recipe for flexibility in Japan. For instance, adhering to commitment for lifetime employment engendered much internal flexibility in multi-skilling, teamwork, job transfers between factories, and more broadly internal employment adjustment within enterprises or corporate groups.

In the 1970s, Japanese industrial firms responded to demand downturns and cost rises due to the oil shocks by leveraging such flexible rigidities. First, they reduced the hours of work, before terminating contracts for temporary workers and part-timers. Second, they implemented reassignments and temporary transfers (*shukko*) within business groups, from the focal firm to affiliates and subsidiaries. Third, they sought volunteers for early retirement, before contemplating compulsory dismissals as the ultimate horror in the eyes of both management and labour. One condition for this recipe to work was a belief that the gains from trust and cooperation—by eliminating a lot of time wasting in bargaining situations—should more than compensate for the relative absence of market competition, in short a belief in 'the benevolence of the butcher, the brewer, or the baker' rather than the invisible hand (Dore 1986: 250).

Since then, the flexibly rigid institutions in Japanese labour markets, financial markets, and intermediate product markets proved to be at their best in responding to the strong yen in the mid-1980s. The late 1980s, with its bubble economy of high land prices and stock market speculation, also coincided with Japanese foreign direct investment, giving overseas managers and workers a direct insight into how some of these Japanese 'ways of doing things' worked. When the bubble burst in the early 1990s, however, the Japanese economy went into a prolonged recession from which it is yet to recover.

What is different in the 2000s from the 1970s in the instruments used for employment adjustment? In the 1970s, as noted above, companies resorted to shorter working time, cutbacks in recruitment and non-renewal of contracts for temporary and part-time workers, and voluntary early retirement. In the 2000s, the same instruments are being used as in the 1970s, and the same belief in making employment security a top priority continues to be upheld by both management and labour.

Nevertheless, a logical extension of the use of the 1970s instruments through slow incremental change is eroding the very basis of the institution of lifetime employment that they mean to preserve. Such transmutation is happening through at least two key channels, namely (*a*) the erosion of income guarantee that accompanied the notion of lifetime employment; and (*b*) extensive use of contingent labour not only to weather cyclical downturns but, permanently, in order to turn more components of the total costs into variable costs.

8.3.1 Erosion of Income Guarantee

Lifetime employment in the 1970s used to mean not only job security within the enterprise but also a guarantee of a seniority-based income level. Subsequently, it came to be redefined when job transfers (*shukko*) took place as income guarantee with career support within a corporate group. In the 2000s, however, it became further redefined as an eroded job security with no income level guarantee. Moreover, the age at which income and job guarantees end is becoming earlier and earlier.

Examples of the above were described in Section 8.2. At Matsushita, the Location-Specific Employment Contract System in 2000 led to a pay reduction of up to 20 per cent for employees who opted for the system, in return for a guarantee to remain at the same home base workplace until retirement. In this case, the identity of the employer as well as the location of work remained the same for these workers. At NTT, 'outsourcing' companies were created in 2002 in order to facilitate the early retirement of NTT employees and their re-employment at these 'new' companies at pay levels up to 30 per cent below their pre-retirement jobs. Here, the identity of the employer changed although the place of work did not. Other similar examples of retirement and redeployment via in-house labour placement agencies have existed, but typically for workers reaching the mandatory retirement age.

Thus, what is new in the 2000s is the pervasive use of early retirement schemes at an earlier age, combined with a sharp reduction in regular wage that workers are expected to accept in the name of a new employment contract. These features would eventually put an end to the essence of lifetime employment, be it job guarantee or income guarantee.

8.3.2 Continuous Use of Contingent Labour

The other significant difference between the 1970s and the 2000s is the greater use of different types of contingent workers, such as agency labour and fixed-term workers as well as part-timers. Whereas in the past, these non-regular workers were hired as a buffer to cope with cyclical fluctuations in demand, the prolonged recession of the 1990s has encouraged firms to use them on a continuous basis to reduce personnel costs and to turn fixed costs into variable costs (Chubu Sanseiken 2004; Denki Soken

1998). Competition from China has put extra pressure on Japanese firms to make greater efforts towards cost reduction. This also means that the recent wider use of contingent labour is prevalent on the manufacturing shop floor, whereas the services sector (especially retailing) has had a more long-standing practice of incorporating part-time and temporary workers in their operations. Even in manufacturing, however, there are as many workplaces where regular and non-regular workers are doing the same tasks as workplaces where the two are clearly separated (Sato et al. 2004: 81).

In Japan, workers who are not on a regular full-time contract are collectively known as atypical workers (*hi tenkei rodosha*). What is 'atypical' or 'non-standard' depends on country-specific notions of 'typical' or 'standard' employment (Ogura 2005). In Japan, 'atypical' refer to workers who are not in full-time employment with an indefinite contract length. However, implicit in the notion of 'lifetime employment' is the absence of restrictions placed on job scope and workplace location (Sato and Sano 2005: 44). In theory, therefore, 'typical' employees would have no restriction on either, whilst 'atypical' workers would have limited job scope and no expectation of relocation. In reality, however, increasingly, as we saw in the case of Matsushita, regular contracts have come to impose restrictions on workplace location or job scope, thus blurring at the margin the distinction between what is a typical and what is an atypical employment contract.

Despite the problem that this fact causes for data, the existing government statistics (Labour Force Survey) show clearly that the proportion of atypical workers in the total employee workforce increased from 20.2 per cent in 1990 to 32.3 per cent in 2005. A 1999 Survey on the Diversification of Employment Status, undertaken by the Japanese Ministry of Health, Labour and Welfare, found that 27.5 per cent of the Japanese employee workforce were atypical, and of those, three-quarters were part-time workers, 8.4 per cent were 'professional contract workers', 6.7 per cent were 'temporary workers', and 3.9 per cent were 'dispatched workers' (dispatched from labour placement agencies) (Sato et al. 2003; Iwata 2004).

In response to employer demand, changes in labour law are likely to lead to even greater use of specific types of contingent workers. First, the 2003 revision of the Labour Standards Law extended the maximum length of fixed-term contracts from one year to three years, and this is likely to increase the use of fixed-term employees (*kikanko*). At Toyota, for example, the number of fixed-term employees increased from 3,140 in 2000 to 9,520 in 2004, constituting 25 per cent of the total shop floor workforce (Chubu

Sanseiken 2004: 50). At the forty-four supplier companies surveyed by Chubu Sanseiken, the proportion of atypical workers to total workforce ranged from 9 per cent to 80 per cent. At one extreme, six out of the forty-four suppliers had 50 per cent or more of their workforce on atypical contracts (Chubu Sanseiken 2004: 1). Similarly at Nissan Oppama Factory, 20 per cent of a total of 2,560 shop floor workers were on fixed-term contracts in 2003; Calsonic Kansei's cockpit assembly line inside Oppama Factory was operated totally by a team of thirty-five temporary workers.[5]

Second, the 2004 revision of the Labour Dispatching Law (*haken ho*) lifted the prohibition of the use of agency labour in production areas. Before the prohibition was lifted, on-site contractors (*kounai ukeoi*)—who must provide machinery and equipment as well as supervision of labour—came to occupy manufacturing areas where employers would have preferred to hire agency labour. They are concentrated in electronic components manufacturing, automobile assembly and parts manufacturing, and telecommunications equipment (Sato et al. 2004: p 30). However, agency labour is replacing on-site contractors in production areas where employers prefer direct supervision. On-site contractors are therefore being forced to rethink their business strategy, by diversifying into labour placement agency business or by focusing on more specialist high skill tasks (Kimura et al. 2004; Fujimoto and Kimura 2005).

A wider use of contingent labour in the name of greater numerical flexibility and labour cost reduction has potentially adverse implications for work organization and industrial relations. At the level of work organization, there is a view that due to labour turnover, contingent workers cannot be expected to be as multi-skilled and problem-solving-oriented as regular workers, thus making it more difficult to accumulate and transfer know-how and capability on the shop floor. Perhaps a more immediate impact in the same direction is brought about by an increased burden on regular employees to train and supervise contingent workers (Sato et al. 2004: 100). At the level of labour-management relations, enterprise unions are 'hollowed out' in two senses (Chubu Sanseiken 2004: 84). First, unless enterprise unions change their policy to exclude contingent workers from membership, a group of workers with whom the union has no contact will grow. Second, if management ignores or simply informs unions on hiring contingent workers, unions' bargaining power and voice are undermined (Nakamura and Rengo Soken 2005).

To conclude, in the 2000s employment has become more diverse and more flexible with greater reliance on numerical rather than functional flexibility, but all in the name of paying utmost effort to making employment security for the core workforce a top priority. Nevertheless as the core of employees with secure employment and good pay diminishes over time, there would be at some stage a point at which a qualitative change would occur in the attitudes and motivation of workers as well as union leaders and managers. If income guarantee ends at the age of 50 or 45 or 40 in the future, what is left of the notion of seniority-plus-merit pay? If unions continue to exclude contingent workers from membership, how long before enterprise unions lose legitimacy as representative bodies that can negotiate effectively with management? And if more and more workers are not required to be functionally flexible beyond their immediate workplace, what will become of the geographically mobile internal labour markets for large corporations? Will Japan's flexible rigidities inevitably turn into rigid flexibilities as internal labour markets become more segmented and fragmented?

Notes

1. Original statistical sources are *Rodoryoku Tokubetsu Chosa* (Special Labour Force Survey) and *Shugo Keitai no Tayouka ni Kansuru Sogo Jittai Chosa* (General Survey on the Diversification of Employment Status), both conducted by the Japanese Ministry of Health, Labour and Welfare.
2. Unfortunately, this analysis is based on a subset of the population, nineteen unions at Toyota Roren and twenty-four unions at Nissan Roren that responded to the annual survey conducted by the industry confederation.
3. This move from coordinating over percentage increases to absolute increases was part of a move to narrow wage differentials between low-wage and high-wage companies. Given pre-existing wage levels, an across-the-board 2 per cent pay increase would maintain the pre-existing wage differentials, whereas a 5,000 yen increase would constitute a higher percentage increase on a lower wage, thus contributing to narrowing wage differentials.
4. Unlike at MEI that recruited employees centrally, NTT group companies recruited their own employees separately.
5. Factory visit by the author as part of the International Motor Vehicle Program (IMVP) plant tour, on 10 September 2003.

Conclusions
Taking Stock and Looking Ahead

Japanese corporations and labour unions are clearly at the crossroads. The purpose of this conclusion chapter is threefold: first, to summarize the key themes and findings in the book; second, to briefly capture the Japanese case in a broader comparative scene; and third, to speculate about the future of Japan's enterprises, unions, and the business system.

1. Summary of Key Themes in the Book

This book used a combination of the strategy–structure literature and institutional analysis to explain changes in corporate enterprises and labour unions in Japan. The Strategy–Structure–Institutions (SSI) framework, elaborated in Chapter 1, regards institutions not only as a set of opportunities for, and constraints on, strategy (as Hall and Soskice (2001) did), but also as the outcome of strategic interaction. Institutional explanations are often too focused on national macro-level factors and thereby overlook the dynamics of organizational strategy that may modify the nature of these institutions. Conversely, the SSI framework also recognizes that the stability of institutional structures might coexist with contention and power play in cases where corporate and labour strategies diverge.

The SSI framework may be distilled into four propositions, as follows.

Proposition 1 (P1): *Strategies of product diversification lead firms to adopt either M- or H-form structures. Diversified M- or H-form firms will adopt more diversified human resource systems within the boundaries of the organization in order to take account of different employment needs and skill patterns in different lines of business.*

Proposition 2: (P2a) *Strategies based on the logic of membership (e.g. diverse member demands) lead labour unions to adopt decentralized structures and smaller organizational boundaries in order to accommodate members' demand for diversified human resource systems within the boundary of their organizations.*

(P2b) *Strategies based on the logic of influence (e.g. influencing centralized external interlocutors) lead labour unions to adopt centralized structures and larger organizational boundaries. This results in promoting more homogeneous human resource systems within boundaries of the organization.*

Proposition 3 (P3): *Whenever the structures of the human resource system pursued by corporate strategy and labour strategy do not coincide, the organizational boundaries are likely to be contested. The resulting structures and human resource systems are those preferred by the party that can mobilize greater power resource in the implicit bargaining process or are the result of a compromise.*

Proposition 4 (P4): *National institutional patterns affect strategy through the nature of resources available to organizations. They also affect structure by providing legitimacy to specific structures of authority. Thus, differences in institutional patterns across national business systems give rise to differences in strategies and structures of organizations across countries.*

These propositions were applied in order to make sense of the developments of Japanese corporate and labour organizations in the second half of the twentieth century. Chapter 2 portrayed a general trend towards consolidation and the extension of organizational boundaries from factories to enterprises to business groups, with union structures mirroring corporate structures. Since the 1990s, however, the course has been reversed towards decentralization, fragmentation, and internal diversity. As demonstrated in Chapter 8, more diverse organizational forms and labour market outcomes have resulted from the interaction between corporate strategy and labour strategy, with varying degrees of consensus or contestation (P3).

The book documented and analysed these interactions at various levels. First, Matsushita (Chapter 3) and Toyota (Chapter 4) were chosen as case studies of enterprise-level interactions. Matsushita's corporate strategy of diversification led to an early adoption of the multidivisional structure, whilst Toyota's focused product strategy in automobiles resulted in sustaining a functional structure (P1). Matsushita Union's policy to participate in strategic management decisions led the union to adopt an extensive boundary containing over two dozen hived-off and affiliated firms. By contrast, Toyota Union's focus of activity on the shop floor (*genba*) led it to choose a relatively narrow boundary of the enterprise union for the focal firm only (P2). Until recently, corporate strategy and labour strategy in both companies have been broadly compatible with each other, with a consensus on the degree of homogeneity to be maintained in the human resource system within the organizational boundary.

Second, the ways in which labour strategy impacts upon its structural decisions, and vice versa, may differ from industry to industry (P2). Chapter 5 demonstrated this by analysing a survey of unions in *roren* federations from two export-oriented sectors in the Japanese economy, namely automotive and electrical machinery industries. Electrical *roren* federations draw their boundary around unions at firms with both high capital ownership affiliation and trade linkage with the focal firm, whilst automotive *roren* federations contained more unions at firms with trading linkages only. These differences derive in part from the nature of products, more complex and involving greater input from suppliers in cars than in electrical machinery. The different criteria used by automotive and electrical *roren* to draw their boundaries also led to differential emphases placed on *roren*'s functions. Compared with the automotive *roren*, the electrical *roren* were found to be more centralized in their coordination during Shunto wage bargaining, and more active in mediating movement of surplus workers between affiliated unions.

Third, and most important for illustrating the utility of the 'strategy meets institutions' framework, two chapters were devoted to analysing the causes and consequences of variations in strategy and structure within a sector. The automobile industry was chosen for this. Chapter 6 investigated why firms differ and how it matters, and Chapter 7 analysed why unions differ and how that matters. Intra-sectoral differences in corporate strategy or union strategy have led to differential structures, which in turn gave incentives to accumulate capabilities in different ways.

Thus, compared with Nissan and Honda, Toyota has a distinct organizational structure for delivering supplier development, maintaining a separate engineering consulting wing (in the form of OMCD) from the purchasing department. This structure gave Toyota and its suppliers a distinctive set of incentives and mechanisms to develop organizational capabilities over time. It is underpinned by a deep commitment to invest in diffusing its management methods (in TPS and TQC) to its internal factories and key suppliers.

On the union side, the key structural difference was found to be that Nissan Union had a *roren* structure since 1955, whilst Toyota Union resisted having one until 1972. Chapter 7 spelt out in detail the differential principles and strategies of Nissan Union and Toyota Union that account for these structural differences. In particular, compared with Toyota Union, Nissan Union considered *roren* as an essential defence against management power, and created a structure with unified unions whose boundary went beyond a single enterprise. Toyota Union, by contrast, continued to believe up to the early 1970s that corporate group-based *roren* would weaken unions' position vis-à-vis management, and preferred a more genuine industrial union federation to which unions at auto-makers, parts suppliers, and dealers would affiliate on an equal footing. Consequently, despite structural convergence since 1972, Nissan Roren remains a more centralized federation with greater coverage of members from smaller supplier companies than Toyota Roren.

2. Comparative Perspectives: What is Worldwide Universal, What Is Japan-Specific?

A focused account of specific sectors in the Japanese industrial economy contained in this book is good for addressing the first three propositions of the SSI framework. But it cannot fully address the fourth proposition, which is about the differential impact of different national institutions on strategy and structure. To fully examine whether or not differences in national institutional patterns give rise to differences in strategies and structures of organizations, we need an explicitly comparative study. Thus, the broader use to which the SSI framework may be put is best illustrated by cross-national comparisons.

The concluding chapter of a book is no place to begin a comparative exercise, however. So here, we merely sketch the findings of a study of NTT in Japan and DT in Germany (see Sako and Jackson 2006). Chapter 8 of this book gave a brief account of the NTT case.

Given the differences in institutional context, we expect the German system, with its dual system of industrial unions and works councils, to be able to resist pressures for decentralization better than the Japanese system. However, our findings in the telecommunications sector were the opposite. We found that DT Group had become more heterogeneous in its human resource systems than NTT Group. For example, the three parts of the DT Group—Deutsche Telekom AG, T-Mobile International, and T-Systems International—have considerable diversity in basic pay, the number of job categories and working hour arrangements, and the content of performance-related pay.

This result is explained with reference to the propositions in the SSI framework. First, DT's and NTT's corporate strategies were broadly similar, with diversification leading to the creation of a corporate group (P1). Second, unions and works councils at DT both had their own reasons to pursue a strategy that emphasized greater functional differentiation, whilst NTT Union pursued a centralizing strategy, maintaining full control over the extension of the existing collective agreement to the corporate group (P2).

Given these differences in labour strategies, the organizational boundaries were less contested at DT Group, with both management and labour preferring decentralization. By contrast, the prevailing boundaries at NTT Group were the outcome of greater contention. While labour preferred greater centralization than management, NTT Union proved powerful enough to maintain a centralized human resource system (P3). The differences in labour strategy between NTT and DT would not be expected based on the prevailing institutional patterns in their respective countries. The divergent outcomes show not only that human resource systems are shaped by the opportunities and constraints offered by existing institutions (P4), but also demonstrate that labour is a strategic actor that may modify these institutions, sometimes in unexpected ways. In particular, Germany's dual system of industrial relations has been modified as works councils increasingly engage in negotiating over wages in a decentralizing system.

The SSI framework is also useful in contextualizing comparisons (Locke and Thelen 1995). There is a general sense in all major industrialized countries that work is becoming more diverse, flexible, and externalized. In its heyday up to the early 1970s, the US corporation was a stable sovereign organization with well-understood boundaries, clearly defined internal roles, and predictable relationships with the external environment (Osterman et al. 2001: 7; Jacoby 2005). In many ways, large corporate hierarchies that offered developed systems of high job security and internal promotion were the dominant model in most OECD countries including Japan, Germany, and other European countries. Firms came to be relied upon as the institution that would provide, either on their own or through collective bargaining, secure long-term jobs and careers, private reserves for retirement, health insurance for workers and their families, and training and education to build human capital (Osterman et al. 2001: 61). But now, such corporate enterprise as a well-defined, stable, and enduring organization to which long-term employment rights could be attached is simply disappearing (Osterman et al. 2001: 9). The boundary of the firm is becoming blurred due to cross-company work teams, more project work, strategic alliances, and outsourcing.

According to the contextualized comparison framework, similar issues possess very different meanings in different national settings depending on differences in starting points and in the impact changes have on traditional arrangements (Locke and Thelen 1995). Thus, take the case of pay reduction in return for employment security. Agreements to take a substantial wage cut in return for keeping employment are being signed or negotiated also in Germany, at Siemens, DaimlerChrysler, General Motors, and Volkswagen to name a few. Serious though these cases are, they are led by works councils whose identity is not threatened by this security–flexibility trade-off. By contrast, wage cuts in return for employment security undermines the income guarantee part of lifetime employment as an institution. Consequently, wage reduction goes deep into the core of Japanese enterprise unions' foundational project. Thus, because a shift in the meaning of lifetime employment is bound up with redefining the identity of Japanese enterprise unions, this issue is likely to lead to either greater conflict or erosion in the *raison d'être* of enterprise unions.

Thus, what is worldwide universal and what is Japan-specific may best be understood by comparing across sticking points that threaten the very identity of specific actors in question. In this, it is important to bear in mind how the interests and motives on the part of Japanese managers and labour representatives continue to differ significantly from those in Germany or the United States. And their assumptions, attitudes, and practices continue to explain the organizing principles and the strategy they formulate. Thus, as Streeck (1993) points out, there is a two-way causal flow over time that links employee identities and interests, and also how institutions shape union structures and influence how employees see their interests.

3. Looking Ahead: Whither Japanese Business Groups and Enterprise Unionism? How much Diversity within the System?

What does the future hold for Japanese firms and unions? Japan is no longer a country of homogeneity with its convoy system for coordinating decisions in many arenas. Actually, it never was as homogeneous as thought in an ideal typical representation of Japan, particularly seen through the lens of the SSI framework. Moreover, the SSI framework projects a relatively high degree of variety that may be tolerated in the Japanese system as it highlights the importance of the interaction of strategy and structure on both sides of industry to bring about considerable variations within the economy.

For corporations, restructuring will continue with more M & A, alliances, holding companies, and the diversification of customer base. Many examples abound in Japan. For instance, Hitachi and NEC merged their DRAM business, whilst Toshiba and Mitsubishi Electric merged their electric power business. This signals continued fluidity in both share ownership structure and trading linkages. One main cause is capital market pressures, leading some Japanese firms to endorse the value of a more shareholder-oriented mode of corporate governance (Dore 2000; Jacoby 2005). Another significant cause is competition from low-cost countries, notably China, leading Japanese firms to relocate or to push for further cost reductions in domestic plants.

Turning to unions, it is belived that capital affiliation-based *roren* have a better chance of survival than trading linkage-based *roren*. Corporations are expected to pursue strategies for greater diversification of business fields and customers. The *roren* survey asked respondents to indicate the degree of likelihood in the next five years of each of the management strategies listed in the survey. The 'cultivation of new customers and diversification of customers' (75 per cent) and 'business expansion in fields other than in the focal firm's industry' (47 per cent) were the top two trends, followed by the 'implementation or strengthening of overseas production' (35 per cent), and the 'establishment of hive-offs, subsidiaries, and affiliated firms' (26 per cent).

In an environment where such management strategies are expected, *roren* union federations may be expected to revise their strategy and organizational boundaries. Two out of every three unions 'want to have the forum for union–management discussion and information exchange strengthened at the federation level'. Moreover, only a small minority of unions surveyed (14 per cent) agreed or agreed strongly with the statement that 'the *roren* should become a looser organization', while half of the respondents disagreed or strongly disagreed with this statement. However, as supplier relations become more diverse and fluid, trading linkage-based *roren* may have a difficult time stabilizing its membership. Indeed, as compared to 8.5 per cent of the electrical unions, about three times as many, or 25.0 per cent, of the auto unions agreed or strongly agreed with the expectation that 'customers will diversify, weakening the centripetal force to consolidate the unions under a federation'. This may signal a shift in emphasis, even within the automotive sector, towards drawing the *roren* boundary along the lines of capital ownership affiliation.

For enterprise unions in Japan, they continue to maintain a consensus with corporate management on the benefits of long-term employment outweighing its costs. Whilst this belief is not shaken in Japan, lifetime employment has been eroded from both within and without. Not only is the use of contingent workers becoming more widespread; the boundary between the core and the peripheral workers has also become more blurred, as some 'regular' workers face limitations in job scope and location. Moreover, lifetime employment has been redefined, from continuous employment within a firm to income guarantee with career support within a corporate group, and now to job security but with no income level guarantee. There has therefore been significant erosion in the essence of this institution through incremental processes in the name of defending the institution (Streeck and Thelen 2005).

Will the use of atypical workers rise and fall as the economy recovers, and can Japan go back to a 'normal' state once some atypical workers are co-opted into the core, as temporary workers (*rinjiko*) did in the 1960s? Or, are we moving towards a new state with more diverse practices, some with high degrees of contingent workers and others with low, within the Japanese economy? I rather think the latter might prevail. If so, in an age of greater internal diversity, certain challenges have to be faced by unions and management. Unions may re-examine their workforce boundary (e.g. should they organize more temporaries?) and corporate boundary (e.g. should they organize labour placement agencies?). Corporate managers are faced with the challenge of clarifying a new division of labour in responsibilities for training and integrating diverse sets of workers, in short in managing the so-called employment portfolio. If these challenges are not met, we are likely to see a faster erosion of the Japanese institutions—lifetime employment, enterprise unionism—as we know them.

The portrayal of Japan in this book is therefore of growing diversity within and between organizations, particularly since the late 1990s. But it is also a picture of the path-dependent accumulation of specific capabilities in strategy and structure that is distinctive to a particular enterprise or a particular union. This tempers much of the international comparisons that are at the level of countries or sectors, with much talk of converging divergences (Katz and Darbishire 2000) and directional convergence (Jacoby 2005). Instead, institutional analysis undertaken in this book emphasized embeddedness in national institutions, but this is tempered by the strategic choice of actors. Japan is undergoing slow institutional change, which is likely to bring about a system that tolerates a higher degree of organizational diversity than in the past.

APPENDIX

THE *ROREN* QUESTIONNAIRE SURVEY

In this survey, we would like to ask you about your union and (Hitachi)* Roren to which your union is affiliated. Please answer this questionnaire, in which the focal union refers to (Hitachi)* Union, and the focal firm refers to (Hitachi Ltd)*.
[* Change as appropriate, for one of the eleven *roren* federations surveyed.]

A. About the company that your union organizes

Q1. What is the main line of business at this company? Please indicate all that apply.

   1. Parts processing
   2. Parts assembly
   3. Manufacturing of tools and dies
   4. Manufacturing of machinery and equipment
   5. Transportation of products and parts
   6. Sales → please go onto Q4
   7. Other (Please specify _____)

Q2. We would like to ask about the ownership structure and directors of the company your union organizes.

   (1) Does the focal firm own this company's stocks and shares?
      (a) Yes, 50% or more of the capital
      (b) Yes, 49% or less of the capital
      (c) No

   (2) Does the focal firm send directors to this company?
      (a) Yes (if so, how many?)
      (b) No

   (3) Do the focal firm's affiliates:
      (a) Own this company's stocks and shares?
      (b) Send directors to this company?

Q3. What proportion of this company's sales turnover is attributable to trading with the focal firm and with other firms within its corporate group?

	0%	1–10%	11–33%	34–49%	50–66%	67–89%	90–100%	Don't know
With focal firm								
With focal firm's affiliates								

Q4. Please record the number of employees and union members at the company your union organizes.

(1) Number of regular employees

(2) Number of non-regular employees (include seasonal workers, part-timers, etc.)

(3) Number of union members

Q5. We would like to ask about management and industrial relations at the company your union organizes. Please choose all that apply, in relation to the past five years and their likelihood in the next five years.

(1) About management	Occurred in the last five years (select all that apply)	Likely to happen in the next five years (select all that apply)
More production overseas		
Development of own-brand products		
Establishment of hive-offs, subsidiaries, and affiliates		
Cultivation and diversification of new customers		
Expansion of business into sectors other than the focal firm's main line of business		
Loss making for two or more consecutive years		
Capacity utilization at 80% or less for over a year		

(2) About labour–management relations	Occurred in the last five years (select all that apply)	Likely to happen in the next five years (select all that apply)
Transfer of union members to other firms within *roren*		
Transfer of middle managers to other firms within *roren*		
Voluntary early retirement of union members		
Compulsory redundancies for union members		
Temporary transfer of union members to the focal firm or its affiliates		
Receiving transferees from the core firm or its affiliates		
Increase in non-regular employees		
Strike action by your union		

B. About your union organization

Q6. Are there full-time union officials at your union's headquarters and branches?

(a) Yes (if so, how many?)
(b) No

Q7. Among your union's representatives at headquarters and branches, are there those who spend 50% or more of their time on union activity?

(a) Yes (if so, how many?)
(b) No

Q8. How much is the subscription rate for your union? _____yen per month Of that sum, what proportion is paid to *roren*?_____%

Q9. When was your union established? 19_____

Q10. When did your union affiliate to the *roren*? 19_____

Q11. Is there any industry federation to which your union affiliates directly?

(a) Yes (if so, which?)
(b) No (if so, had there been an federation to which your union used to belong? Yes/No)

We would like to ask about your union's organizing activities.

Q12. Has your union organized affiliated companies in the last five years?
(a) There is no affiliates
(b) We unionized affiliates
(c) We did not unionize affiliates

Q13. Is there a *roren* or *rokyo* federation with your union as the focal union?

(a) No → please proceed to Q14
(b) Yes → What types of unions are part of the federation?

(1) Unions at affiliates of the company your union organizes
(2) Unions at suppliers and dealers of the company your union organizes

C. About the *roren*

Q14. Are there any full-time union officials at the *roren* headquarters who originated from your union?

(a) Yes (if so, how many?)
(b) No

Q15. Is there a union official at the *roren* headquarters or its regional organization who is in charge of 'looking after' your union?

    (a) No

    (b) Yes → if so, roughly how many times a year does this official visit your union?

Q16. How much *de facto* influence does the *roren* exercise in determining each of the following?

	No influence at all	Not much influence	Some influence	A lot of influence
Your union's subscription fee				
Your union's wage demand at Shunto				
Your union's wage settlement at Shunto				
Decision by your union to go on strike				
Signing of a collective agreement by your union				
Selection of your unions' officials to be assigned to *roren*				

Q17. We would like to ask you about the nature of information network between your union and other unions within the *roren*.

    (1) Which union(s) **influences your union**'s Shunto wage settlement?

        The most influential union _____

        The second most influential union _____

        The third most influential union _____

    (2) Which union(s) does **your union influence** to reach wage settlements during Shunto?

        The union you influence most _____

        The union you influence next _____

        The union you influence thirdly _____

    (3) With which union(s) does your union **exchange information** most closely during Shunto negotiations?

        The first union _____

        The second union _____

        The third union _____

    (4) Are there unions that provided **useful advice** concerning such matters as worker participation, management policies, and personnel management systems?

The most useful union _____
The second most useful union _____
The third most useful union _____

Q18. Please indicate the degree to which you agree or disagree with the following statements, on a 1–5 scale (1 = strongly disagree; 5 = strongly agree).

(a) Our union has been able to improve members' working conditions more by belonging to a *roren* federation than by negotiating on its own.

(b) Our union can obtain information concerning the focal firm's management trends more quickly by belonging to the *roren*.

(c) By belonging to the *roren*, it has become easier to exchange information and to engage in mutual learning with other unions in the same *roren*.

(d) Within the *roren*, unions at large- and medium-sized firms provide guidance and support for smaller unions.

(e) *Roren* performs an indispensable role in securing employment stability for union members in the face of corporate restructuring.

(f) We can engage in honest heart-to-heart information exchange with officials of other affiliated unions.

(g) *Roren*, by grouping unions at firms with shareholding and trading linkages, contributes to strengthening control by capital.

Q19. How much resource, such as money and people, does your union provide to the *roren*, relative to the amount of service that your union receives from the *roren*?

1. The contribution made by our union is much greater
2. The contribution made by our union is somewhat greater
3. About the same
4. The contribution made by the *roren* is somewhat greater
5. The contribution made by the *roren* is much greater.

D. Shunto wage bargaining

Q20. What was the date of 1997 Shunto wage settlement at your union? ____Month ____day
If the date is the same as for the focal union, please record the time of settlement also. _____a.m. / p.m.

Q21. From which of the following organizations did you receive direct advice or support during the process of Shunto negotiations between your union and the company your union organizes? Please choose all that apply.

1. *Roren* headquarter
2. Local organizations of *roren*

3. Focal union of *roren*
4. Other unions of *roren*
5. Retired officials of the union
6. Industry-level federation headquarters
7. Local organizations of industry-level federation
8. *Rengo* headquarters
9. Local organizations of *Rengo*
10. Other (Please specify _____)

Q22. During the 1997 Shunto, how frequently did your union meet with officials of *roren*?

	4 times a week or more	2–3 times a week	Once a week	Around once a fortnight	Less than once a fortnight
During the month preceding the submission of Shunto demand					
During the month preceding Shunto settlement					

Q23. In the last five years, has the performance of the firm your union organizes ever been better than the focal firm's performance? If so, was it possible for your union to settle wage increases at a higher rate than for the focal firm?

1. There was no period during which the firm's performance was better than the focal firm's performance.
2. The firm's performance was better than the focal firm's, but it was not possible to settle at a higher rate than at the focal firm.
3. The firm's performance was better than the focal firm's, and our union did settle at a higher rate than at the focal firm.

(In case of 3) Please choose which of the following was higher than at the focal firm.
1. Bonus payment
2. Bonus (in terms of the number of months of salary)
3. Wage increase
4. Per cent increase in wages

Q24. In the next five years, if the performance of the firm your union organizes is better than at the focal firm, would it be possible for your union to settle at a higher rate than at the focal firm?

1. No, it would be impossible for both wage and bonus
2. It would be possible to negotiate higher bonuses
3. It would be possible to negotiate higher basic pay increase

    4. It would be possible for both wage and bonus → go to Q26

    5. Don't know

Q25. (If you answered 1, 2, or 3 in Q24) Why do you think that it would be difficult to exceed the focal firm's settlement level? How much does each of the following reasons apply (1 = strongly disagree; 5 = strongly agree)?

    (a) Because pay settlements should reflect medium- to long-term performance rather than short-term performance

    (b) Because of the difference in firms' social prestige ranking

    (c) Because the focal firm as customer may demand tougher cost reduction if our union settles at a higher rate than at the focal firm

Q26. What are the key factors that explain wage differences among the unions that affiliate to the *roren* to which your union belongs?

	Not at all important	Not very important	Somewhat important	Very important
Difference in union's negotiating ability				
Difference in unionists' skill/education levels				
Difference in production equipment				
Difference in labour productivity				
Difference in industry, corporate form, or products				
Difference in firm's social prestige ranking				
Difference in corporate performance (ability to pay)				
Other (Please specify ____)				

Q27. Does the *roren* establish targets or guidelines for working conditions other than wages to be met by affiliated unions?

    1. No targets or guidelines are set

    2. Targets or guidelines are established → in the last five years, has it been possible to use these guidelines to improve working conditions for your union members?

        (1) No improvements were made

        (2) Improvements were made → please specify what was improved ____

E. Worker participation

Q28. We would like to ask about worker participation and labour–management consultation at the firm your union organizes.

    (1) In the last five years, has your union had occasions to discuss the following matters with company management? If so, what was the nature of the discussion?

(a) Discussion on annual management plans (investment, marketing, etc.)

    1. Yes, and the union modified the plan
    1. Yes, but the union's views put forward were not taken up by management
    2. Yes, but the union mainly listened to management explanation
    3. No

(b) Discussion on monthly production plans and manning levels

    4. Yes, and the union modified the plan
    5. Yes, but the union's views put forward were not taken up by management
    6. Yes, but the union mainly listened to management explanation
    7. No

(2) Are there non-regular, non-public meetings between your union leadership and the company's top management? Yes/No.

Q29. Is there a forum for labour–management consultation or discussion at the following levels? If not, does your union wish to establish such a forum?

(1) Meeting between *roren*-affiliated union leaders and the focal firm's top management
    1. Yes, it exists, and satisfied with the current state
    2. Yes, it exists, but it should be strengthened
    3. No, it does not exist, but we would like to establish it
    4. No, it does not exist, and we have no wish to establish it

(2) Meeting between *roren* officials and managers from firms in the focal firm's corporate grouping
    1. Yes, it exists, and satisfied with the current state
    2. Yes, it exists, but it should be strengthened
    3. No, it does not exist, but we would like to establish it
    4. No, it does not exist, and we have no wish to establish it

Q30. When the firm your union organizes experienced bad performance and the management proposed a reduction in the number of employees, how did your union react? Or, if such a proposal were made, how would your union react? Please choose all that apply.

1. Seek support and advice directly from *roren* headquarters
2. Exchange information with unions at affiliated companies
3. Find the reason for the firm's deteriorating performance through other unions in the same *roren*
4. Find firms that can employ surplus workers through discussion with other unions in the same *roren*

5. Ask *roren* headquarters to coordinate and mediate the process of finding the destination for excess workers
6. Other (please specify _____)
7. Don't know

F. About your union members

Q31. About your union members

1. Average age?
2. Proportion of female members?
3. Proportion of university graduates?

Q32. About pay and working hours for your union members in 1997

8. Monthly pay for 35-year-old male high school graduates
9. Bonus payments (the sum of winter and summer bonuses)
10. Annual working hours (exclude overtime)

G. The Future role of *roren*

Q33. What is your view on the following statements concerning the future of *roren*? Please indicate the degree to which you agree or disagree with each on a 1–5 scale (1 = strongly disagree; 5 = strongly agree).

(a) Customer companies' business will diversify, thus weakening the centripetal force to consolidate unions into a *roren* federation.
(b) Our union would be able to improve members' conditions more freely if it had not affiliated to a *roren*.
(c) There is an overlap in activity between the *roren* and the industry-level federation.
(d) There is no loss to our union's activity if we had not belonged to a *roren*, as long as we affiliate to an industry-level federation.
(e) The *roren* federation should facilitate greater autonomy of affiliated unions and become a looser organization.
(f) We would like to strengthen the forum for union–management discussion and information exchange at the *roren* level.
(g) The *roren* federation should be more involved in negotiations between our union and the company we organize.

Q34. Lastly, how many years of experience have you had as a union official, as member of the central executive committee or higher rank?
Approximately _____years

Lastly, please let us know of any further comments you have concerning your *roren* in the space below.

Thank you very much. Please return this questionnaire in the envelope provided, by 20 December.
If you would like a copy of the report of the survey results, please provide the postal details below.

References

Adler, P. S. (2001). 'Market, Hierarchy and Trust: The Knowledge Economy and the Future of Capitalism', *Organization Science*, 12 (2): 215–34.

—— and R. Cole (1993). 'Designed for Learning: A Tale of Two Auto Plants', *Sloan Management Review* 34 (3) 85–94.

Ahmadjian, C. L. and Lincoln, J. R. (2001). 'Keiretsu, Governance and Learning: Case Studies in Change from the Japanese Automotive Industry', *Organization Science*, 12 (6): 683–701.

Amikura, H. (1989). 'Seisan sisutemu no gakushu mekanizumu (Producing Knowledge and Product Simultaneously: Manufacturing Systems as Learning Mechanisms)', *Business Review*, 37 (1): 54–76.

—— (1992). 'Soshikikai shisutemukan no togo mekanizumu (Mechanisms for Integrating Organizational Sub-systems)', *Chiba Daigaku Keizai Kenkyu*, 6 (3): 109–46.

Armstrong, P., Marginson, P., Edward, P., and Purcell, J. (1998). 'Divisionalization in the UK: Diversity, Size and the Devolution of Bargaining', *Organization Studies*, 19 (1): 1–22.

Asanuma, B. (1989). 'Manufacturer–Supplier Relationships in Japan and the Concept of Relation-specific Skill', *Journal of Japanese and International Economies*, 3: 1–30.

AWU (1986). *Nijunen no Ayumi (Twenty Year History)*. Kariya: Aisin Workers Union.

Beaudet, A. (1998). 'Knowledge Diffusion in the Japanese Automotive Industry: The Role of Kyoryokukai and Jishuken', Mimeo, Graduate School of Economics, Hitotsubashi University.

Benson, J. and Gospel, H. (2005). *The Emergent Enterprise Union? A Conceptual and Comparative Analysis*. Mimeo, University of Melbourne.

Biggart, N. W. (1991). 'Explaining East Asian Economic Development: Towards a Weberian Institutional Perspective', *Theory and Society*, 20 (2): 199–232.

Blair, M. M. (1999). *Firm-Specific Human Capital and Theories of the Firm*. Washington, DC: The Brookings Institution.

Buro (1995). *Buro Sanju nen no Ayumi (Thirty Year History of Buro)*. Tokyo: Buhin Kanren Rodo Kumiai.

Calmfors, L. and Driffil, J. (1988). 'Bargaining Structure, Corporatism, and Macroeconomic Performance', *Economic Policy*, 6: 13–61.

Carlile, P. R. (2002). 'A Pragmatic View of Knowledge and Boundaries: Boundary Objects in New Product Development', *Organization Science*, 13 (4): 442–55.

Chandler, A. D. (1962). *Strategy and Structure: Chapters in the History of the Industrial Enterprise*. Cambridge, MA: MIT Press.

—— (1990). *Scale and Scope: The Dynamics of Industrial Capitalism*. Cambridge, MA.: Harvard University Press.

—— (1991). 'The Functions of the HQ Unit in the Multibusiness Firm', *Strategic Management Journal*, 12: 31–50.

—— (1992). 'What is a Firm? A Historical Perspective', *European Economic Review*, 36: 483–994.

Chubu Sanseiken (2004). *Rodoryoku Tayouka no nakade no Atarashii Hatarakikata* (*New Modes of Working in the Midst of Labour Force Diversification: Co-existence with Non-standard Workers*), Toyota City: Chubu Sanseiken.

Clark, K. B. and Fujimoto, T. (1991). *Product Development Performance: Strategy, Organization, and Management in the World Auto Industry*. Boston, MA: Harvard Business School Press.

Clegg, H. A. (1976). *Trade Unionism under Collective Bargaining*. Oxford: Blackwell.

Cole, R. E. (1971). *Japanese Blue Collar: The Changing Tradition*. Berkeley, CA: University of California Press.

Commons, J. R. (1909). 'American Shoemakers, 1648–1895: A Sketch of Industrial Evolution', *Quarterly Journal of Economics*, 24: 39–84.

Commons, J. R. (1934). *Institutional Economics: Its Place in Political Economy*. New York: The Macmillan Company.

Cusumano, M. (1985). *The Japanese Automobile Industry: Technology and Management at Nissan and Toyota*. Cambridge, MA: Harvard University Council on East Asia Studies.

Denki Rengo (1996). *Soshiki Ichiran* (*List of Affiliated Organizations*). Tokyo: JEIU.

Denki Soken (1998). *Denki Sangyo ni okeru Gyomu Ukeoi Tekiseika to Jaisei Hakenho eno Taio no Kadai: Denki Sangyo ni okeru Ukeoi Katsuyo no Jittai ni Kansuru Chosa Hokokusho* (*Standardization of On-Site Contracting in Electric Machinery Industry and Responding to the Revision of the Worker Dispatching Law: Report on the Survey on Utilization of Contract Workers in the Electric Machinery Industry*). Tokyo: Denki Soken.

Dore, R. P. (1973). *British Factory–Japanese Factory: The Origins of National Diversity in Industrial Relations*. Berkeley, CA: University of California Press.

—— (1983). 'Goodwill and the Spirit of Market Capitalism', *British Journal of Sociology*, 34 (3): 459–82.

—— (1986). *Flexible Rigidities: Industrial Policy and Structural Adjustment in the Japanese Economy 1970–80*. London: Athlone Press.

—— (1987). *Taking Japan Seriously*. London: Athlone Press.

—— (2000). *Stock Market Capitalism, Welfare Capitalism: Japan and Germany versus the Anglo-Saxons*. Oxford: Oxford University Press.

Dunlop, J. and Galenson, W. (eds.) (1978). *Labor in the Twentieth Century*. New York: Academic Press.

Dunlop, J. T. (1948). 'The Development of Labor Organizations: A Theoretical Framework', in R. A. Lester and J. Shister (eds.) *Insights into Labor Issues*. New York: Macmillan, 179–183.

References

Dyer, J. H. and Nobeoka, K. (2000). 'Creating and Managing a High-Performance Knowledge-sharing Network: The Toyota Case', *Strategic Management Journal*, 21: 345–67.

Eisenhardt, K. M. and Martin, J. A. (2000). 'Dynamic Capabilities: What are They?', *Strategic Management Journal*, 21 (10–11): 1105–22.

Fujimoto, T. (1997). *Seisan Shisutemu no Shinkaron* (*Evolutionary Theory of Production Systems*). Tokyo: Yuhikaku.

Fujimoto, T. (1999). *The Evolution of a Manufacturing System at Toyota*. New York: Oxford University Press.

—— (2000). 'Evolution of Manufacturing Systems and *Ex post* Dynamic Capabilities', in G. Dosi, R. R. Nelson, and S. G. Winter (eds.), *The Nature and Dynamics of Organizational Capabilities*. New York: Oxford University Press.

Fujimoto, M. and Kimura, T. (2005). 'Business Strategy and Human Resource Management at Contract Companies in the Manufacturing Sector', *Japan Labor Review*, 2 (2): 104–22.

Galenson, W. (1976). 'The Japanese Labor Market', in H. Patrick and H. Rosovsky (eds.), *The Japanese Labor Market*. Washington, DC: The Brookings Institution.

Gankoji, H. (2003). 'Kikan sangyo ni okeru roshikankei no kihonteki wakugumi to sono gendaiteki kadai (Basic Framework of Industrial Relations in Key Industries and its Contemporary Significance)', *Graduate School of Policy and Management, Doshisha University*, 4 (1): 163–82.

Gerlach, M. (1989). *Alliance Capitalism*. Berkeley, CA: University of California Press.

Ghosn, C. (2002) 'Saving the Business wlthout Losing the Company', *Haward Business Review*, 80 (1): 37–45.

Gordon, A. (1985). *The Evolution of Labor Relations in Japan: Heavy Industry 1853–1955*. Cambridge, MA: Harvard University Press.

—— (1998). *The Wages of Affluence: Labor and Management in Postwar Japan*. Cambridge, MA: Harvard University Press.

Gospel, H. (1992). *Markets, Firms and the Management of Labour in Modern Britain*. Cambridge: Cambridge University Press.

—— (1999). 'Institutional Approaches to the Nature of the Firm and the Management of Labor in Comparative Perspective', in D. Lewin and B. Kaufman (eds.), *Advances in Industrial and Labor Relations*. JAI Press, 95–124.

Granovetter, M. (1995). 'Coase Revisited: Business Groups in the Modern Economy', *Industrial and Corporate Change*, 4 (1): 93–130.

Hall, P. and Soskice, D. (eds.) (2001). *Varieties of Capitalism*. New York: Oxford University Press.

Hart, O. (1995). *Firms, Contracts and Financial Structure*. Oxford: Oxford University Press.

Hasegawa, H. (1984). *Senryoki no Rodo Undo* (*Labour Movement During the Occupation Period*). Tokyo: Aki Shobo.

Hazama, H. (1997). *The History of Labour Management in Japan*. Basingstoke: Macmillan.

Helper, S. (1990). 'Comparative Supplier Relations in the US and Japanese Auto Industries: An Exit/Voice Approach', *Business and Economic History*, Second Series 19: 153–62.

—— and Sako, M. (1995). 'Supplier Relations in Japan and the United States: Are They Converging?', *Sloan Management Review*, 36: 77–84.

Herrigel, G. (1993). 'Indentity and Institutions: The Social Construction of Trade Unions in Nineteenth-Century Germany and the United States', *Studies in American Political Development*, 7: 371–94.

Hitachi Factory Union (1964). *Hitachi Rodo Undoshi (Labour Movement at Hitachi)*. Hitachi City: Hitachi Factory Union.

Holmstrom, B. and Roberts, J. (1998). 'The Boundaries of the Firm Revisited', *Journal of Economic Perspectives*, 12 (4): 73–94.

Imai, W. (1985). 'Nippondenso ni okeru Toyota seisan hoshiki no hirogari (The Diffusion of Toyota Production System at Nippondenso)', *Kojo Kanri*, 31 (5): 69–77.

Inagami, T. (2003). *Kigyo Gurupu Keiei to Shukko Tenseki Kanko (Corporate Groups and Employment Transfer Practices)*. Tokyo: Tokyo University Press.

—— (ed.) (1995). *Seijuku Shakai no nakano Kigyobetsu Jumiai (Enterprise Unions in a Mature Society)*. Tokyo: Japan Institute of Labour.

—— and Whittaker, D. H. (2005). *The New Community Firm: Employment, Governance and Management Reform in Japan*. Cambridge: Cambridge University Press.

Ishida, M. et al. (1996). *Nihon no lean seisan hoshiki (Lean Production System in Japan)*. Tokyo: Chuo keizaisha.

Itoh, H. (2003). 'Corporate Restructuring in Japan Part I: Can M-Form Organization Manage Diverse Businesses?', *The Japanese Economic Review*, 54 (1): 49–73.

Iwasaki, K. (1994). 'Rodo Kumiai no Zaisei (Finance in Labour Unions)', *Nihon Rodo Kyokai Zasshi (Journal of the Japan Institute of Labour)*, 416: (October), 14–23.

Iwata, K. (2004). 'Diverse Working Conditions among Non-standard Employees: JIL Research Report and Policy Implications', *Japan Labor Review*, 1 (1): 77–91.

Jacoby, S. M. (2005). *The Embedded Corporation*. Princeton, NJ: Princeton University Press.

Japan Productivity Centre (1994). *1994 Nenban Roshi Kankei Hakusho: Nihonteki Koyokanko to Aratana Jinzai Katsuyo Senryaku (1994 White Paper on Industrial Relations: Japanese-style Employment Practices and a New Human Resource Utilization Strategy)*. Tokyo: Japan Productivity Centre for Socio-Economic Development.

Jidosha Soren (1983, 1994). *Soshiki Kihon Chosa (Basic Survey of Organizations)*. Tokyo: Confederation of Japan Automobile Workers Unions (JAW).

—— (1993). *Jidosha Soren Nijunen no Ayumi (20 Years of JAW)*. Tokyo: JAW.

JIL (1996). *Denki Tsushin Sangyo no Roshi Kankei: Rekishi to Genjo (Industrial Relations in the Telecommunications Industry: History and Current State)*. Tokyo: Japan Institute of Labour.

JILPT (2004). *Labor Situations in Japan and Analysis 2004/2005*. Tokyo: Japan Institute of Labour Policy and Training.

References

Kagono, T. (1993). 'Shokunobetsu Jigyobusei to Naibu Shijo (Functional Divisional System and Internal Markets)', *Kokumin Keizai Zasshi*, 167 (2): 35–52.

—— (1997). *Nihongata Keiei no Fukken (Restoration of Japanese-style Management)*. Tokyo: PHP.

——, et al. (1985). *Strategic vs Evolutionary Management: A US–Japan Comparison of Strategy and Organization*. Amsterdam: North-Holland.

Katz, H. (1993). 'The Decentralization of Collective Bargaining: A Literature Review and Comparative Analysis', *Industrial and Labor Relations Review*, 47 (1): 3–22.

—— and Darbishire, O. (2000). *Converging Divergences: Worldwide Changes in Employment Systems*. Ithaca, NY: Cornell University Press.

Kaufman, B. E. (2000). 'The Case for the Company Union', *Labor History*, 41 (3): 321–50.

Kawakita, T. et al. (1997). *Gurupu Keiei to Jinzai Senryaku (Management of Corporate Groups and Human Resource Strategy)*. Tokyo: Sogo Rodo Kenkyusho.

Kawanishi, H. (1992). *Enterprise Unionism in Japan*. London: Kegan Paul International.

Kerr, C., et al. (1960). *Industrialism and Industrial Man*. Cambridge, MA: Harvard University Press.

Kimura, T., Sano,Y., et al. (2004). 'Seizo Bunya ni okeru Ukeoi Kigyo no Jigyo Senryaku to Jinzai Kanri no Kadai (Business Strategy and Human Resource Management for Onsite Sub-contracting Service in Manufacturing Industry)', *Nihon Rodo Kenkyu Zasshi*, 46 (5): 16–30.

Klein, B., Crawford, R. and Alchian, A. (1978). 'Vertical Integration, Appropriable Rents and the Competitive Contracting Process', *Journal of Law and Economics*, 21: 297–326.

Kobayashi, Y. (2002). 'Ukeoi Rodosha no Kyuzo to Rodo Kumiai no Taio (Rapid Increase in Contract Workers and Trade Union Responses)', *Nihon Rodo Kenkyu Zasshi*, 44 (8): 49–55.

Kochan, T. et al. (1984). 'Strategic Choice and Industrial Relations Theory', *Industrial Relations*, 23 (1): 16–39.

Kogure, M. (1988) *Nihon no TQC (TQC in Japan)*. Tokyo: Nikka Giren.

Kogut, B. and Zander, U. (1992). 'Knowledge of the Firm, Combinative Capabilities, and the Replication of Technology', *Organization Science*, 3 (3): 383–97.

Koyama, Y. (ed.) (1985) *Kyodai Kigyotaisei to Rodosha: Toyota no Jirei (Giant Enterprises and Workers: The Case of Toyota)*. Tokyo: Ochanomizu Shobo.

Kyohokai (1967). *Kyohokai Nijugonen no Ayumi (Twenty-Five Years of Kyohokai)*. Nagoya, Japan: Kyohokai.

—— (1994). *Kyohokai Gojunen no Ayumi (Fifty Years of Kyohokai)*. Nagoya, Japan: Toppan Insatsu.

Lamont, M. and Molnar, V. (2002). 'The Study of Boundaries in the Social Sciences', *Annual Review of Sociology*, 28: 167–95.

Large, S. (1979). 'Perspectives on the Failure of the Labour Movement in Prewar Japan', *Labour History (Australia)*, 37: 15–27.

Lazonick, W. (1990). *Competitive Advantage on the Shop Floor*. Cambridge, MA: Harvard University Press.

Lea, D. (1971). 'MNCs and Trade Union Interests', in J. Dunning (ed.), *MNCs and Trade Union Interests*. London: George Allen.

Lincoln, J. R. and Gerlach, M. (2004). *The Evolution of Japan's Network Economy: A Structural Perspective on Industrial Change*. Cambridge: Cambridge University Press.

Locke, R. et al. (eds.) (1997). *Employment Relations in a Changing World*. Cambridge, MA: MIT Press.

—— and Thelen, K. (1995). 'Apples and Oranges Revisited: Contextualized Comparisons and the Study of Comparative Labor Politics', *Politics & Society*, 23 (3): 337–67.

McMillan, J. (1990). 'Managing Suppliers: Incentive Systems in Japanese and US Industry', *California Management Review*, 28: 38–55.

MacDuffie, J. P. and Helper, S. (1997). 'Creating Lean Suppliers: Diffusing Lean Production Through the Supply Chain', *California Management Review*, 39 (4): 118–51.

MacDuffie, J. P. (1997). 'The Road to "Root Cause": Shop Floor Problem-Solving at Three Auto Assembly Plants', *Management Science*, 43 (4): 479–502.

Macneil, I. R. (1985). 'Relational Contract: What We Do and Do Not Know', *Wisconsin Law Review*, 3: 483–525.

Marginson, P. (1985). 'The Multidivisional Firm and Control over the Work Process', *International Journal of Industrial Organization*, 3: 37–56.

Mass, W. and Robertson, A. (1996). 'From Textiles to Automobiles: Mechanical and Organizational Innovation in the Toyota Enterprises, 1895–1933', *Business and Economic History*, 25 (2): 1–37.

Matsushita Union (1957). *Matsushita Denki Rodo Jumiai Jusshunen Kiroku* (*A Record of the Tenth Anniversary of the Formation of Matsushita Electric Workers' Union*). Osaka: Matsushita Denki Rodo Kumiai.

—— (1966). *Tayuminaki Sozo: Matsushita Denki Sangyo Rodo Jumiai Kessei Nijusshunen Kinen Undoshi* (*MEI Workers Union Twentieth Anniversary History*). Osaka: Matsushita Denki Rodo Kumiai.

—— (1986). *Shin Tayuminaki Sozo* (*MEI Workers Union Fortieth Anniversary History*). Osaka: Matsushita Denki Rodo Kumiai.

Matsushita Union (1990). *Dai 45 Kai Teiki Taiki Giansho* (*Forty-Fifth Annual Conference Agenda*). Osaka; Matsushita Denki Rodo Kumiai.

—— (1997). *Tayuminaki Sozo IV: Matsushita Denki Sangyo Rodo Jumiai Kessei Gojusshunen Kinen Undoshi* (*MEI Workers Union Fiftieth Anniversary History*). Osaka: Matsushita Denki Rodo Kumiai.

MEI (2000). *Matsushita Denki Shashi Nenpyo* (*Chronological Table of Matsushita Company History*). Osaka: Matushita Electric Industrial.

MEI (1968). *Matsushita Denki Gojunen no Ryakushi* (*An Abridged History of the First Fifty Years of Matsushita Electric*). Osaka: Matsushita Electric Industrial.

References

MHLW (2001). *Roshi Kankei Sogo Chosa (Survey on Industrial Relations)*. Tokyo: Ministry of Health, Labour and Welfare.

—— (2003). *Nihon no Rodo Jumiai no Genjo I (The State of Labour Unions in Japan*, Vol. 1). Tokyo: Ministry of Health, Labour and Welfare.

—— (various years, *a) Rodo Kumiai Kiso Chosa Hokoku* (Report on the Basic Survey of Trade Unions). Tokyo: Ministry of Health, Labour and Welfare.

—— (various years, *b) Chinage no Jittai (Report on Wage Increases)*. Tokyo: Okurasho Insatsukyoku.

Milgrom, P. and Roberts, J. (1995). 'Complementarities and Fit: Strategy, Structure and Organizational Change in Manufacturing', *Journal of Accounting and Economics*, 19: 179–208.

Ministry of Finance (2003). *Nihon Kigyo no Tayouka to Kigyo Touchi (Diversification of Japanese Firms and Corporate Governance)*. Tokyo: Ministry of Finance Policy Research Institute.

Mintzberg, H. (1983). *Structure in Fives: Designing Effective Organizations*. Englewood Cliffs, NJ: Prentice-Hall.

Miyake, M. (1954) *Nissan Sogi Hakusho (White Paper on Nissan Dispute)*. Yokohama: Nissan Motors Labour Union.

Mizushima, I. (2004). 'Shokugyo Anteiho Rodosha Hakenho Kaisei no Igi to Houteki Kadai (Revision of the Employment Security Law and Worker Dispatching Law: A Legal Perspective)', *Nihon Rodo Kenkyu Zasshi*, 46 (1): 16–25.

Monden, Y. (1983). *Toyota Production System*. Atlanta, GA: Industrial Engineering and Management Press.

Morikawa, H. (1997). 'Japan: Increasing Organizational Capabilities of Large Industrial Enterprises, 1880s–1980s', in A. D. Chandler, F. Amatori and T. Hikino (eds.), *Big Business and the Wealth of Nations*. Cambridge: Cambridge University Press.

Morishima, M. and Shimanuki, T. (2005). 'Managing Temporary Workers in Japan', *Japan Labor Review*, 2 (2): 78–103.

Nakakubo, H. (2004). 'The 2003 Revision of the Labor Standards Law: Fixed-term Contracts, Dismissal and Discretionary Work Schemes', *Japan Labor Review*, 1 (2): 4–25.

Nakamura, K., Sato, H. et al. (1988). *Rodokumiai wa Honto ni Yakuni tatte iruka (Are Trade Unions Truly Useful?)*. Tokyo: Sogo Rodo Kenkyusho.

—— and Rengo, S. (eds.) (2005). *Suitai ka Saisei ka: Rodo Undo Kasseika e no Michi (Deterioration or Regeneration? Road to Reviving the Labour Movement)*. Tokyo: Keisou Shobo.

Nakamura, K. (2002). 'Matsushita Denki: Gurupuryoku no Genten (Matsushita Electric: The Origin of Corporate Group Power)', *Diamond Harvard Business Review* (August), 36–47.

Nakata, Y. (1994) 'Kigyo Chingin Kakusa no Kenkyu – Jidosha Sangyo ni okeru Sanbetsu Roren no Chingin Kiseiryoku ni Chumoku shite (Research on Inter-firm Wage Differentials: Focus on Industry Federations' and Roren's Control in

Auto Industry', in Koyo Sokushin Jigyodan (ed.), *Sutokku Choseika no Koyo to Rodoryoku Haibun (Employment and Distribution under Stock Adjustment)*, pp. 232–48.

Nelson, R. R. (1991). 'Why Do Firms Differ, and How Does it Matter?', *Strategic Management Journal*, 12: 61–74.

—— and Winter, S. G. (1982). *An Evolutionary Theory of Economic Change.* Cambridge, MA: Harvard University Press.

Nemoto, M. (1978). 'Toyota hinshitsu kanrisho no settei to unei ni tsuite (On the Establishment and the Operation of Toyota Quality Control Award)', *Hinshitsu Kanri*, 29(3): 42–6.

—— (1983). *TQC to toppu bukacho no yakuwari (TQC and the Role of Top and Middle Management)*. Tokyo: Nikka Giren.

—— (1995). 'Toyota seisan hoshiki to TQC no sojo koka: Toyota no seisan no kyosoryoku no kenzen (Synergy Between Toyota Production System and TQC: The Source of Competitiveness of Toyota Production', *Engineers*, (March).

Nikkei (1999). *Toyota: 'Okudaism' no Chosen (Toyota: Okuda's Challenge)*. Tokyo: Nihon Keizai Shinbunsha.

—— (2002). *Matsushita Fukkatsu eno Kake (Betting on Matsushita Revival)*. Tokyo: Nihon Keizai Shinbunsha.

Nippondenso Union (1996). *Mirai o Tsugumono—Nippondenso Rodo Kumiai Goju nenshi (Continuous Legend, Fifty Year History of Nippondenso Union)*. Kariya: Nippondenso Rodo Kumiai.

Nishiguchi, T. (1994). *Strategic Industrial Outsourcing: The Japanese Advantage*. New York: Oxford University Press.

Nissan Motor Co. (1965). *Nissan Jidosha Sanjunenshi (Thirty Years of Nissan Motor Company)*. Tokyo: Nissan Motor Co.

—— (1985). *Nissan Jidosha Shashi 1974–1983 (Company History of Nissan Motor Co.)*. Tokyo: Nissan Motor Co.

Nissan Roren (1992). *Zenji Nissan Bunkai—Jidosha Sangyo Rodo Undo Zenshi (Zenji Nissan Chapter: Pre-History of Labour Movement in the Automobile Industry)*, Vols. I, II and III. Tokyo: Nissan Roren Undoshi Henshu Iinkai.

NWJ (2002). *NTT Roso Hossoku Iko no Undo o Furikaette (Looking Back on the Movement After the Establishment of NTT Union)*. Tokyo: NTT Workers Union of Japan.

Odagiri, H. (1994). *Growth Through Competition, Competition Through Growth: Strategic Management and the Economy in Japan*. Oxford: Clarendon Press.

Ogura, K. (2005). 'International Comparison of Atypical Employment: Differing Concepts and Realities in Industrialized Countries', *Japan Labor Review*, 2 (2): 5–29.

Oh, H.-S. (2004). 'Paato Taimaa no Soshikika to Iken Hanei Sisutemu (Unionization of Part Time Workers and Systems that Reflect their Opinions)', *Nihon Rodo Kenkyu Zasshi*, 46 (6): 31–47.

Ohara (1952). *Nihon Rodo Nenkan 1952 nenban (Japan Labour Yearbook 1952)*. Tokyo: Ohara Shakai Mondai Kenkyusho.

Ohno, T. (1978). *Toyota Seisan Hoshiki (Toyota Production System)*. Tokyo: Daiyamondo sha.

References

Okazaki, T. (2001). 'The Role of Holding Companies in Pre-war Japanese Economic Development: Rethinking Zaibatsu in Perspectives of Corporate Governance', *Social Science Japan Journal*, 4 (2): 243–68.

—— (2002) *Senji Nihon no Rodo Soshiki: Sangyo Hokokukai no Yakuwari* (*Labour Organizations in Wartime Japan: The Role of Sanpo*). CIRJE *Discussion Paper Series J-73*, Faculty of Economics, University of Tokyo.

Okochi, K. (ed.) (1956). *Rodo Kumiai no Seisei to Soshiki* (*The Origin and Organization of Trade Unions*). Tokyo: Tokyo University Press.

Okurasho (1997). *Nissan Yuka Shoken Hokokusho*. Tokyo: Ministry of Finance, Japan.

Olson, M. (1982). *The Rise and Decline of Nations: Economic Growth, Stagflation and Social Rigidities*. New Haven, CT: Yale University Press.

Osterman, P. et al. (2001). *Working in America*. Cambridge, MA.: MIT Press.

O'Sullivan, M. (2000*a*). *Contests for Corporate Control*. Oxford: Oxford University Press.

—— (2000*b*). 'The Innovative Enterprise and Corporate Governance', *Cambridge Journal of Economics*, 24: 393–416.

Pascale, R. T. and Athos, A. G. (1981). *The Art of Japanese Management*. Harmondsworth: Penguin.

Polanyi, K. (1967). *The Tacit Dimension*. Garden City, NY: Doubleday/Anchor.

Pugh, D. S. et al. (1968). 'Dimensions of Organization Structure', *Administrative Science Quarterly*,13 (1): 65–105.

Rengo (2000). *Mochikabu Gaisha ni okeru Tekisei na Roshi Kankei no Kakuho* (*Securing Appropriate Labour–Management Relations in Holding Companies*). Tokyo: Rengo.

—— (2003). *Report on Survey on Union Dues*. Tokyo: Rengo.

Rodo Kenkyu (1979). *Sohyo Soshiki Koryo to Gendai Rodo Undo* (*Sohyo's General Principles of Organizing and Labour Movement Today*). Tokyo: Rodo Kenkyu Sentaa.

Sakamoto, K. and Shimotani, M. (eds.) (1987). *Gendai Nihon no Kigyo Gurupu* (*Corporate Groups in Modern Japan*). Tokyo: Toyo Keizai Shinpo-sha.

Sako, M. (1992). *Prices, Quality and Trust: Inter-firm Relations in Britain and Japan*. Cambridge: Cambridge University Press.

—— (1996). 'Suppliers' Association in the Japanese Automobile Industry: Collective Action for Technology Diffusion, *Cambridge Journal of Economics*, 20: 651–71.

—— (1997*a*). 'Introduction: Forces for Homogeneity and Diversity in the Japanese Industrial Relations System', in M. Sako and H. Sato (eds.), *Japanese Labour and Management in Transition*. London: Routledge.

—— (1997*b*). 'Shunto: The Role of Employer and Union Co-ordination', in M. Sako and H. Sato (eds.), *Japanese Labour and Management in Transition*. London: Routledge.

—— (2004). 'Supplier Development at Honda, Nissan and Toyota: Comparative Case Studies of Organizational Capability Enhancement', *Industrial and Corporate Change*, 13 (2): 281–308.

—— and Jackson, G. (2006) 'Strategy Meets Institutions: The Transformation of Management–Labour Relations at Deutsche Telekom and NTT', *Industrial and Labor Relations Review*.

—— and Sato, H. (1999). 'Roren wa ikanaru kinou o hatashite iruka (What is the Function of Roren Union Federations?)', *Kikan Rodoho (Journal of Labour Law)*, 188: 89–98.

Sako, M., Helper, S. and Lamming, R. (1995). 'Supplier Relations in the UK Car Industry: Good News, Bad News', *European Journal of Purchasing and Supply Management*, 13 (4): 237–48.

Sanken Sentaa (1995). *Rodo Kumiai no Zaisei (Union Finance)*. Tokyo: Sanken Sentaa.

Sato, A. (2005). 'Introduction: Diversification of Employment and Human Resource and Personnel Management Issues', *Japan Labor Review*, 2 (2): 2–4.

Sato, H., Sano, Y., et al. (2003) Dai ikkai Seisan Genba ni okeru Konai Ukeoi no Katsuyo ni kansuru Chosa (First Survey on the Use of Inside Contractors on the Production Shopfloor). *SSJ Data Archive Research Paper Series No. 24*. Tokyo: Institute of Social Science, University of Tokyo.

——, et al. (2004) Seisan Genba ni okeru Gaibu Jinzai no Katsuyou to Jinzai Bijinesu (Human Resource Management and the Staffing Business at Japanese Manufacturing Site). *RSI Research Paper Series No.1*. Tokyo: Institute of Social Science, University of Tokyo.

—— (2005). 'Employment Category Diversification and Personnel Management Problems', Japan Labor Review, 2 (2): 30–54.

Schmitter, P. C. and Streeck, W. (1999). *The Organization of Business Interests: Studying the Associative Action of Business in Advanced Industrial Societies. MPIfG Discussion Paper No 99/1*. Köln, Germany: Max-Planck-Instituet für Gesellschaftsforschung.

Shiba, T. (1997). 'A Path to the Corporate Group in Japan: Mitsubishi Heavy Industries and its Group Formation', in T. Shiba and M. Shimotani, (eds.), *Beyond the Firm: Business Groups in International and Historical Perspective*. New York: Oxford University Press.

Shimada, H. (1983). 'Introduction', in T. Shirai (ed.). *Contemporary Industrial Relations in Japan*. Madison, WI: University of Wisconsin Press.

Shimokawa, K. et al. (eds.), (1997) Toyota Jidosha ni okeru TQC to Toyota Seisan Hoshiki no Kanren ni tsuite–Nemoto Masao shi kojutsu kiroku (The Relation between TQC at Toyota Motor and Toyota Production System: A Record of Masao Nemoto's Speech). Faculty of Economics Discussion Paper Series 97-J-14. University of Tokyo.

Shimotani, M. (1987). 'Jigyobusei to Bunshasei: Matsushita Denki Sangyo no Keesu (The System of Product Divisions and Spin-offs: The Case of Matsushita Electric)', in K. Sakamoto and M. Shimotani (eds.), *Gendai Nihon no Kigyo Gurupu (Corporate Groups in Contemporary Japan)*. Tokyo: Toyo Keizai Shinposha.

—— (1997). 'The History and Structure of Business Groups in Japan', in T. Shiba and M. Shimotani (eds.), *Beyond the Firm: Business Groups in International and Historical Perspective*. Oxford: Oxford University Press.

—— (1998). *Matsushita Gurupu no Rekishi to Kozo (History and Structure of Matsushita Group)*. Tokyo: Yuhikaku.

References

Shimotani, M. (2001). 'Mochikabu Gaisha no Futatsu no Kino', *Kyoto Daigaku Keizai Gakkai Keizai Ronshu*, 167 (1): 1–18.

Shirai, T. (ed.) (1983). *Contemporary Industrial Relations in Japan*. Madison, WI: University of Wisconsin Press.

Smitka, M. (1989). *Competitive Ties: Subcontracting in the Japanese Automotive Industry*. New York: Columbia University Press.

Streeck, W. (1993). 'Klasse, Beruf, Unternehmen, Distrikt: Organizationsgrundlagen industrieller Beziehungen im Europaeischen Binnenmarkt', in B. Struempel and M. Dierkes (eds.), *Innovation und Beharrung in der Arbeitspolitik*. Stuttgart, Germany: Schaeffer-Poeschel Verlag, pp. 39–68.

—— and Visser, J. (1997). 'The Rise of the Conglomerate Union', *European Journal of Industrial Relations*, 3 (3): 305–32.

—— and Thelen, K. (eds.) (2005). *Beyond Continuity: Industrial Change in Advanced Political Economies*. Oxford: Oxford University Press.

Suzuki, A. (2000). 'The Transformation of the Vision of Labor Unionism: Internal Union Politics in the Japanese Steel Industry in the 1960s', *Social Science Japan Journal*, 3 (1): 77–93.

Suzuki, Y. (1991). *Japanese Management Structures, 1920–80: Studies in the Modern Japanese Economy*. Basingstoke: Macmillan.

Takarakai (1994). *Takarakai Kinenshi Sanjusannen no Ayumi (Thirty Three Years of Takarakai)*. Tokyo: Takarakai.

Teece, D. (2002). 'Dynamic Capabilities', in W. Lazonick (ed.), *The IEBM Handbook of Economics*. London: Thomson Learning.

—— and Pisano, G. (1994). 'The Dynamic Capabilities of Firms: An Introduction', *Industrial and Corporate Change*, 3 (3): 537–56.

Tekko Roren (1981). *Tekko Roren Undoshi: Sanjunen no Ayumi (Thirty Year History of Tekko Roren)*. Tokyo: Tekko Roren.

Tilly, C. (2004). 'Social Boundary Mechanisms', *Philosophy of the Social Sciences*, 34 (2): 211–36.

TJU (1996). *Jidai eno Koso: Toyoda Jidoshokki Rodo Kumiai Gojunen no Ayumi (Thinking for the Next Era: Fifty Years of Toyoda Automatic Loom Workers Union)*. Kariya: Toyoda Jidoshokki Union.

TMC (1967). *Toyota Jidosha Sanju nenshi (A 30 Year History of Toyota)*. Toyota City: Toyota Motor Corporation.

—— (1988). *Toyota: A History of the First 50 Years*. Toyota City: Toyota Motor Corporation.

Tokunaga, S. (1983). 'A Marxist Interpretation of Japanese Industrial Relations, with Special Reference to Large Private Enterprises', in T. Shirai (ed.), *Contemporary Industrial Relations in Japan*. Madison, WI: University of Wisconsin Press.

Toshiba Union (1981). *Sanjunen Kumiai Undoshi (Thirty Year History of Union Movement)*. Kawasaki City: Toshiba Labour Union.

Totsuka, H. (1991) *Transformation of Japanese Industrial Relations: A Case Study of the Automobile Industry*. Occasional Papers in Labour Problem and Social Policy, Tokyo: University of Tokyo Institute of Social Science.

Totsuka, H. and Hyodo, T. (eds.) (1991). *Roshi Kankei no Tenkan to Sentaku – Nihon no Jidosha Sangyo (Transformation and Choice in Industrial Relations: The Case of Japanese Auto Industry)*. Tokyo: Nihon Hyoronsha.

Toyoda Boshoku (1996). *Toyoda Boshoku Shijugo nenshi (A 45 Year History of Toyoda Boshoku)*. Toyota City: Toyoda Boshoku.

Toyota Union (1956). *Kumiai Soritsu Jusshunen Kinenshi (Ten Years of Toyota Union)*. Toyota City: Toyota Union.

—— (1966). *Nijunen no Ayumi (Twenty Years of Toyota Union)*. Toyota City: Toyota Union.

—— (1976). *Kagirinaki Zenshin: Sanjunen no Ayumi (Thirty Years of Toyota Union)*. Toyota City: Toyota Union.

—— (1996). *Shin Seiki ni Mukete – Gojunen no Ayumi (Fifty Year History of Toyota Union)*. Toyota City: Toyota Union.

Turner, A. H. (1962). *Trade Union Growth, Structure and Policy: A Comparative Study of the Cotton Unions*. London: George Allen & Unwin.

Udagawa, M. et al. (1995). *Nihon Kigyo no Hinshitsu Kanri (Quality Control at Japanese Firms)*. Tokyo: Yuhikaku.

Ueda, H. (1992). *Jidosha Buhin Maker ni okeru Flexibility no Kakuritsu to Roshikankei (Flexibility and Labour Relations at Auto Parts Suppliers)*. Mimeo, Osaka City University.

—— (1997). 'The Subcontracting System and Business Groups: The Case of the Japanese Automobile Industry', in T. Shiba and M. Shimotani (eds.), *Beyond The Firm: Business Groups in International and Historical Perspective*. Oxford: Oxford University Press.

Ujihara, S. (1989). *Nihon no Roshi Kankei to Rodo Seisaku (Industrial Relations and Labour Policy in Japan)*. Tokyo: Tokyo University Press.

Ulman, L. (1955). *The Rise of the National Trade Union: The Development and Significance of Its Structure, Governing Institutions and Economic Policies*. Cambridge, MA: Harvard University Press.

Undy, R. et al. (1981). *Change in Trade Unions*. Hutchinson.

—— et al. (1996). *Managing the Unions*. Oxford: Clarendon Press.

Wada, K. (1991a). 'The Development of Tiered Inter-firm Relationships in the Automobile Industry: A Case Study of the Toyota Motor Company', *Japanese Yearbook on Business History*, 8.

—— (1991b). 'Jidosha sangyo ni okeru kaisoteki kigyokan kankei no keisei: Toyota jidosha no jirei (The Evolution of Hierarchical Inter-firm Relations in the Car Industry: The Case of Toyota Motors)', *Keieishigaku (Business History)*, 26 (2): 1–27.

—— and Yui, T. (2002). *Courage and Change: The Life of Kiichiro Toyoda*. Toyota City: Toyota Motor Corporation.

Wakisaka, A. (1997). 'Women at Work', in M. Sako and H. Sato (eds.), *Japanese Labour and Management in Transition*. London: Routledge.

Whitley, R. (1999). *Divergent Capitalisms: The Social Structuring and Change of Business Systems*. Oxford: Oxford University Press.

Whittaker, D. H. (1998). 'Labour Unions and Industrial Relations in Japan: Crumbling Pillar or Forging a "Third Way"?', *Industrial Relations Journal*, 29 (4): 280–94.

Whittington, R. (2001). *What is Strategy—and Does it Matter?* London: Thomson Learning.

Williamson, O. E. (1985). *The Economic Institutions of Capitalism*. New York: Free Press.

Winter, S. G (1994). 'Organizing for Continuous Improvement: Evolutionary Theory Meets the Quality Revolution', in J. A. C. Baum and J. V. Singh (eds.), *Evolutionary Dynamics of Organizations*. New York: Oxford University Press, pp. 90–108.

—— (2000). 'The Satisficing Principle in Capability Learning', *Strategic Management Journal*, 21 (10–11): 981–96.

Womack, J. et al. (1990). *The Machine that Changed the World*. New York: Rawson Associates.

Yamamoto, K. (1982). 'Nihon-teki Koyokanko o Kizuita Hitotachi (Pioneers of Japanese-style Employment System)', *Nihon Rodo Kyokai Zasshi*, 24 (7, 8, 9): 38–55; 64–81; 25–41.

Yamamura, K. and Streeck, W. (2003). *The End of Diversity? The Prospects of German and Japanese Capitalism*. Ithaca, NY: Cornell University Press.

Yoshihara, Y. (2000). 'Kigyo no Gurupuka to Roshi Kankei: NTT Roso no Jirei wo Tsujita Kosatsu (Corporate Groupings and Labor-Management Relations: Thoughts Based on the NTT Union Case)', *Nihon Rodo Kenkyu Zasshi*, 484: 71–9.

Zen Hitachi Roren (1981). *Zen Hitachi Undo Shi (History of Zen Hitachi Labour Movement)*. Tokyo: Zen Hitachi Rodo Kumiai Rengokai.

Zen Matsushita Roren (1996). *Zen Matsushita Roren Kessei Sanjushunen Kinenshi (A Memorial for 30 Years Since the Founding of Zen Matsushita Roren Federation)*. Osaka: Zen Matsushita Roren.

Zen Toyota Roren (1983). *Junen no Ayumi (Ten Year History)*. Toyota City: Zen Toyota Roren.

—— (2003). *Toyota wa Hitotsu: Zen Toyota Rodo Jumiai Rengokai Sanjunenshi (30 Year History of Zen Toyota Roren)*. Toyota City: Zen Toyota Roren.

Zendentsu (1997). *NTT Keiei Keitai Mondai to Zendentsu no Torikumi: Bunri Bunkatsu Hantai Undo Shoushi (The Problem of NTT's Management Pattern and How Zendentsu Tackled It: A Short History of the Movement to Oppose Divestiture)*. Tokyo: Zendentsu.

Zenkoku Jidosha (1972). *Junenshi – Zenkoki Jidosha no Ayumi (10 Years of Zenkoku Jidosha)*. Tokyo: Zenkoku Jidosha Sangyo Rodokumiai Rengokai.

Index

brief histories 183
contribution to diffusion of
TPS 115–18
criterion for affiliation 129
established (1972) 107
focus of activity 130
focused on seeking steady
improvements in pay 93
Nissan Roren contrasted
with 182–209, 214–17
TPS (Toyota Production System) 92,
101, 105, 107, 115–18, 157, 174,
175, 177
OMCD diffusion of 159–62, 175, 176
simultaneous application of TQC
and 102, 164
TQC (Total Quality Control) 101,
102, 104, 105, 162–6
to suppliers 157, 159, 164, 174,
175, 176
trade liberalization 200
trade linkage 133–6, 137, 170,
191–7, 201
Trade Union Law (1946) 122
revision (1949) 41, 73, 76, 109
training:
education and 160, 165
in-company 15
multiskill 117
transportation tasks 52
trust:
gains from 235
mutual 112, 196
Tsurumi (Nissan factory) 43, 184, 186,
189
Tsutsumi (Toyota factory) 101
Tsuyama Matsushita Electric 80
Turner, A. H. 30, 31

U-form (unitary, centralized, and
functional structure) 11
UAW (United Auto Workers) 201
Udagawa, M. 165, 166

Ueda, H. 164
UI Zensen 50
Ujihara, S. 41, 43, 44
Ulman, L. 29–30, 32
Umemura, Shiro 116, 202
unemployment 196
Unified Coordination Committee
(Toyota) 109
unions 14–18, 19, 21
class struggle-oriented 188
closed 31
Communist leadership 33
continuity in leadership 33
differences 182–209
expansionist 31
extension of boundaries 46–50
leftist 82
legalized 34
manufacturing 84
membership increase 42
mergers and takeovers 31
national movement 34
non-manufacturing 84
open 31
smaller 220, 221
strategy and structure 72–86
strategy towards worker
participation 33
unitary 110
see also blue-collar unions;
company unions; conglomerate
unions; craft unions; enterprise
unions; factory unions; focal
unions; general unions; house
unions; industrial unions; inter-
firm unions; MBUs; occupational
unions; SBUs; white-collar unions
Unipres 204
Unisia JECS 204
United Kingdom 178, 179
United States 15, 29, 60, 96
divisionalized organization 58
prosperity of the car industry 201